NICA'S DREAM

ALSO BY DAVID KASTIN

I Hear America Singing: An Introduction to Popular Music

NICA'S DREAM

*The Life and Legend
of the
Jazz Baroness*

DAVID KASTIN

W.W. NORTON & COMPANY
NEW YORK · LONDON

Excerpt from "Little Butterfly," copyright © 1958 (renewed 1986),
1988 Thelonious Music Corp. and Boobar Publishing. Excerpt
from "Pull My Daisy," copyright © 1984 by Allen Ginsberg.
Reprinted by permission of HarperCollins Publishers. Copyright
1971 by the Estate of Jack Kerouac. Reprinted by permission of
City Lights Books. Excerpt from "Who Be Kind To" from *Collected
Poems 1947–1980* by Allen Ginsberg. Reprinted by permission
of HarperCollins Publishers. Excerpt from "The Day Lady Died"
by Frank O'Hara. Reprinted by permission of City Lights Books.
Excerpt from "Annus Mirabilis" by Philip Larkin from *Collected
Poems*. Reprinted by permission of Faber and Faber, Ltd.

Frontispiece: Courtesy of Bruce Ricker; p. xiv: William Gottlieb
Collection, Music Division, Library of Congress

For information about permission
to reproduce selections from this book,
write to Permissions, W. W. Norton & Company, Inc.,
500 Fifth Avenue, New York, NY 10110

For information about special discounts for bulk
purchases, please contact W. W. Norton Special Sales
at specialsales@wwnorton.com or 800-233-4830

Manufacturing by RR Donnelley, Harrisonburg
Book design by Judith Abbate
Production manager: Anna Oler

Library of Congress Cataloging-in-Publication Data
Kastin, David.
Nica's dream : the life and legend of the
jazz baroness / David Kastin. — 1st ed.
     p. cm.
Includes bibliographical references and index.
ISBN 978-0-393-06940-2 (hardcover)
1. Koenigswarter, Pannonica de.
2. Impresarios—United States—Biography.
3. Jazz—History and criticism. I. Title.
ML429.K72K37 2011
781.65092—dc22
[B]
                                        2011013213

W. W. Norton & Company, Inc.
500 Fifth Avenue, New York, N.Y. 10110
www.wwnorton.com

W. W. Norton & Company Ltd.
Castle House, 75/76 Wells Street, London W1T 3QT

1 2 3 4 5 6 7 8 9 0

For Laura and Alena, without whose love and inspiration . . .

CONTENTS

If you don't live it, it won't come out of your horn.
—CHARLIE PARKER

Interviewer: What is jazz?

Thelonious Monk: New York, man. You can feel it. It's around in the air.

NICA'S DREAM

Bird in the Baroness's Boudoir

Whether frozen in Weegee's tabloid flash or shrouded in the murky chiaroscuro of the era's low-budget movies, New York in the 1950s is a city in black and white. The familiar images seem to offer both the gritty texture of reality and the comforting illusion of a simpler time. But on 52nd Street, neon lights flicker from the brownstone façades, and within the basement jazz dens audiences gaze up through an azure scrim of cigarette smoke at musicians haloed in tinted stage lights.

For over a decade, "the Street," as it was known among the late-night set, had been New York's midtown jazz mecca. But by the mid-1940s, its swing-era stalwarts and Dixieland jazz veterans were being challenged by a vanguard of young modernists still in search of a label for their radical new style. Over the next few years, they would largely overcome the resistance of mainstream jazz fans (and fellow musicians), settle on a name (bebop) that none of them particularly liked, and anoint one of their own as the movement's reigning deity. Like the gods of old, Charlie Parker was both omnipotent and capricious.

But while his astonishing virtuosity and boundless creativity seemed to transcend the mortal realm, his fearsome destructiveness was directed only at himself.

Known to even the most casual jazz fan as Yardbird, or simply Bird, Parker not only helped forge the new style of jazz in Harlem's after-hours jam sessions, but beginning with the 1945 release of his groundbreaking bebop anthem, "Ko Ko," he produced a decade-long string of revolutionary recordings—of both his own engaging compositions and his transformative adaptations of popular songs—that were shot through with technical brilliance and blazing inventiveness. He also amassed a legion of devoted acolytes who sought to emulate his every attribute, document his every solo, and preserve his every bon mot—and tragic flaw—in well-honed anecdotes.

Among the tangible manifestations of Bird's status as the once and future King of Bop, was the establishment of his own musical Valhalla, a new four-hundred-seat jazz club at the intersection of 52nd Street and Broadway, appropriately dubbed Birdland. The club, which opened in late 1949, was owned by Irving and Moishe (Mo) Levy, Bronx-born brothers with organized crime connections; managed by the only slightly less notorious Oscar Goodstein; and hosted by Pee Wee Marquette, an ill-tempered three-foot nine-inch midget. From the beginning, the ambience of Birdland reflected the conflicted nature of the man for whom it was named—a volatile combination of transcendent artistry and drug-induced dysfunction.

Over time, the club would prove to be a microcosm of the dark side of New York's midcentury jazz scene, characterized by drug dealing, financial exploitation, prostitution, Mob-sponsored strong-arm tactics, police shakedowns, and random violence. Although celebrities (including Ava Gardner, Elizabeth Taylor, Marlon Brando, and Sammy Davis, Jr.) could often be found at front-row tables, late one night Irving Levy, the club's co-owner, was stabbed to death while tending bar (an unsolved crime the tabloids dubbed "the Bebop Killing"); another night, Miles Davis was assaulted by the police for "loitering" a few feet from the front door during one of his own gigs. In retrospect, it might have been an omen when, one morning not long after the club opened, the birds that had been placed in cages around the room were all found dead (probable cause: smoke inhalation).

Although Bird played on opening night and appeared there numerous times, by 1954 his unreliability and erratic behavior had made him persona non grata at the club that bore his name. During this period Parker also became ensnared in a series of personal tragedies. In fairly quick succession he had suffered the loss of his infant daughter, separated from his wife, attempted suicide (by swallowing iodine), was sued by his own band for breach of contract, and checked himself into Bellevue Hospital for acute depression. He had been off heroin for months, but he was typically drinking a quart of alcohol a day. Nevertheless, he was somehow able to line up a trial engagement at Birdland for the weekend of March 4 and 5, 1955, with an all-star band that included Art Blakey on drums, Charles Mingus on bass, and the brilliant but emotionally fragile Bud Powell on piano.

Opening night got off to a bad start when an obviously inebriated Powell greeted Parker with unprovoked hostility: "You know, Bird, you ain't shit. You don't kill me. Man, you ain't playing shit no more." The next night was even worse. When Parker showed up half an hour late, he was publicly chastised by Birdland's hard-nosed manager; and after joining the band onstage he was drawn into another verbal altercation with Powell, who was so drunk he could barely keep his fingers on the keyboard. Challenged by Parker to shape up, Powell unleashed a string of curses and abruptly walked off the stage, while Bird stood at the microphone in a kind of trance, calling out Powell's name over and over—"Bud Powell . . . Bud Powell . . . Bud Powell . . . Bud Powell . . ."—as the audience slowly filed out of the club. Later, after downing a string of double whiskeys, Bird ran into Charles Mingus. "I'm goin' someplace now pretty quick," he told the bass player, "where I won't be able to bother nobody."

Just a few nights later, however, Parker scheduled an engagement at the Boston jazz club Storyville in the hope that he could put his career back on track. He never made the gig. On March 12, 1955, a stormy

Saturday night in New York City, Charlie Parker died, at the age of thirty-four. While jazz insiders who had been following his precipitous decline could hardly have been shocked at his demise, even some of his most fervent admirers were startled at its rarefied setting.

For Bird aficionados, Parker's death was fraught with bizarre discrepancies and unanswered questions that immediately gave way to conspiracy theories. Why did his body lie unclaimed in the city morgue for three days? Why were there two divergent cause-of-death statements? Why was he initially identified as "John Parker, age fifty-three"? And why did rumors of a fatal blow suffered at the hands of a famous jazz drummer immediately circulate within bebop's inner circles? But when the news of Parker's death finally make it into the New York newspapers the following Tuesday morning, the headlines prompted a very different question: how did bebop's troubled genius come to meet his fate in a Fifth Avenue hotel suite overlooking Central Park that was the residence of an English baroness?

Of the various New York newspapers that reported on Parker's death, it was the *Daily Mirror*, a Hearst-owned tabloid, that provided the most colorful coverage, beginning with the classic hardboiled headline—"Bop King Dies in Heiress's Flat"—which appeared above its front-page masthead. Following the (mis)identification of Parker as a "53-year-old" saxophonist, and the race-conscious reference to his white wife, Chan, as a "lovely fair-skinned brunette," the page-three story presented a fairly straightforward account of how Parker had been taken ill shortly after arriving at the "swank Fifth Ave. apartment of the wealthy Baroness," a mother of "five children ranging in age from 5 to 18," who described herself as "an avid music lover and jazzophile." Although the paper reported that "Dr. Robert Freyman [sic], of 9 E. 79th Street [sic]," had been immediately called to treat him, Parker died a few days later "of an acute heart attack" while "watching a TV show."

A soberer account buried inside the *New York Times* added some context to the story by describing Parker's place in the jazz pantheon ("Mr. Parker was ranked with Duke Ellington and Count Basie and other outstanding Negro musicians"), but it too gave prominence to the lofty locale of Bird's death. After identifying the location as "the apartment of the Baroness de Koenigswarter in the Hotel Stanhope, 995 Fifth Avenue," the *Times* informed its readers that "the Baroness, who is 40 years old, is the former Kathleen Annie Pannonica Rothschild of the London branch of the international banking family of Rothschild."

So while initial reports of Charlie Parker's passing focused on what had led him to the Stanhope suite of a Rothschild heiress, before long the question became, what was *she* doing there? In the following weeks, gossip columns and scandal sheets launched a barrage of speculation about the answers to both.

The first to weigh in was Walter Winchell. On March 17, his syndicated column, "Walter Winchell of New York," carried a blind item about Bird's death that was charged with racial paranoia and sexual innuendo: "We colyumed about that still married Baroness and her old fashioned Rolls Royce weeks ago—parked in front of midtown places starring Negro stars. A married jazz star died in her hotel apt. . . . Figured." One of the era's celebrity pulps, exploiting the murky circumstances of Bird's death, punningly hinted at "fowl play," while an *Expose* magazine story, "Bird in the Baroness's Boudoir," drew on its deepest reserves of purple prose to depict the innocent jazzman as the victim of an exotic (and perhaps ethnically suspect) seductress: "Blinded and bedazzled by this luscious, slinky, black-haired, jet-eyed Circe of high society, the Yardbird was a fallen sparrow."

While the tabloid spotlight soon turned to other titillations, the short-lived attention of the media had already taken its toll. After hearing the news reports linking his estranged wife to the fallen Bop King, Baron Jules de Koenigswarter, who was then serving as the representative of the French government in New York, initiated divorce proceedings. Meanwhile, the management of the Stanhope Hotel, which had grudgingly tolerated its guest's "unsavory" visitors, made it clear she was no longer welcome. After holding out for a few months, Baroness de Koenigswarter climbed into her Rolls-Royce convertible, drove across Central Park to a spacious apartment at the (initially) more accommodating Bolivar Hotel, and, seemingly undaunted, resumed her singular role in New York's insular jazz subculture in relative anonymity.

A few years later, however, Nat Hentoff wrote a lengthy profile for *Esquire* magazine heralding de Koenigswarter as "the most fabled figure on the New York jazz scene," and the subject of "more fanciful speculations . . . than anyone in jazz since Buddy Bolden" (a reference to the shadowy, never-recorded New Orleans cornet player often cited as the "first man of jazz"). For the next three decades, Nica, as she was known to the cognoscenti, continued to play a supporting role in what Hentoff called "the inner councils of jazz," and over time, the legend of the "Jazz Baroness" became permanently woven into what remains one of the music's central myths: the decline and fall (and resurrection) of Charlie Parker.

Ironically, almost everything we know about the final days of bebop's tragic hero derives from a three-page statement Nica provided to Robert Reisner for his 1962 compendium of ornithological anecdotes and tributes, *Bird: The Legend of Charlie Parker*. Since Bird's sudden passing had generated a fog of paranoid fabrications and conspiracy theories, she began her account by attempting to debunk them.

As to the rumor that she had surreptitiously shipped off the body of the thirty-four-year-old saxophonist to Bellevue (where it was supposedly tagged "John Parker, age 53"), Nica declared that in fact the doctor who had been treating Bird had arrived within five minutes of his death and the medical examiner had begun official proceedings within the hour. "He had Bird's name, Charles Parker, taken down absolutely correctly," she insisted, and "gave Bird's age as 53, because that was his impression." She didn't correct him simply because "I didn't know." Point by point, Nica sought to set the record straight. Bird had simply shown up at her Stanhope suite, as he had on other occasions; he then collapsed on her doorstep, was treated by her personal physician, Dr. Robert Freymann, and three days later expired while watching a juggler on a TV variety show.

In an effort to confront the fervid speculation that would haunt her for much of her life, she took particular pains to underscore the platonic nature of her relationship with Parker. "We did have a wonderful friendship going," she told Reisner, "nothing romantic." Along the way, she also recounted what has become one of the most treasured anecdotes in the sacred text of Bird lore. As Nica described it, during the doctor's initial examination of Bird, he asked the ailing saxophonist (who had been consuming prodigious quantities of alcohol for months), "Do you drink?" "Sometimes," Bird responded with a wink, "I have a sherry before dinner." Finally she engaged in a bit of mythmaking of her own, describing how, at the exact moment of Parker's passing, a tremendous clap of thunder echoed across the night sky above New York.

For hard-core jazz fans, Nica's narrative has taken on the aura of a bebop Passion play, or *tableau vivant*, each detail reverberating with profound significance. There in the foreground lies the lifeless figure of Charlie Parker, the savior sent to save mankind from the empty commercialism of swing (his crown of thorns the spikes of a heroin syringe); attending to his wounds is the good Dr. Freymann (an extended finger directing the viewer's gaze toward the track marks on Bird's outstretched arm); and finally Nica herself, a modern-day Mary Magdalene (clutching the rent and bloody folds of a double-breasted pinstriped suit). And— as if conceived to invoke the final element of the scene's metaphysical symbolism—painted on the backdrop's cityscape is the graffiti that had mysteriously begun appearing on the walls of Greenwich Village in the days after Parker's death: "Bird Lives!"

Since the baroness's own death, in 1988, a coterie of bebop loyalists and ardent Nicaphiles have also kept alive a Hirschfeldesque caricature of Pannonica de Koenigswarter, fashioned out of little more than a cresting wave of carefully coiffed black hair, an outsized cigarette holder, and a silver flask. A closer look at the forty-year reign of the Jazz Baroness, however, reveals an iconic figure whose extraordinary life was played out at the nexus of gender, race, and class during a transformative period in American popular culture. And while tabloid stories about an attractive European heiress openly consorting with African-American jazz musicians fed neatly into the era's racial and sexual hysteria, in fact the unique bond Nica forged with the jazz community transcended tawdry midcentury stereotypes. According to the bebop pianist Hampton Hawes, Nica's contributions also had little to do with the traditional tropes of noblesse oblige. "I suppose you would call Nica a patron of the arts," Hawes wrote in his memoir, *Raise Up Off Me*, a brutally honest depiction of his life as a jazzman and a junkie, "but she was more like a brother to the musicians who lived in New York . . . There was no jive about her, and if you were for real, you were accepted and were her friend."

In the years before Parker's death, Nica's Rolls-Royce (dubbed the Silver Pigeon) had become a fixture on 52nd Street, and she had developed personal relationships with a widening circle of jazz innovators, including the drummer Art Blakey, the pianist Horace Silver, and the tenor saxophonist Sonny Rollins, all of whom were now making regular appearances on "the Street" and each of whom would soon record a musical tribute to her. While most jazz fans continued to associate her with the scandal surrounding the death of Charlie Parker, Bird was only one of a score of jazz giants who were the beneficiaries of Nica's unwavering friendship and generosity. For example, following *Time* magazine's 1964 cover story on Thelonious Monk—which devoted a sizable portion of its feature to their intense, if unlikely, friendship—Nica became even more closely linked to the brilliant and inscrutable pianist who, two decades later, also died in her home.

Monk's own homage to the fabled Rothschild baroness, simply titled "Pannonica," remains one of the most beloved of all his classic compositions. Although it first appeared on Monk's 1956 Riverside album, *Brilliant Corners*, a somewhat earlier solo version, captured on Nica's reel-to-reel tape recorder, has recently come to light. Here, in a spoken introduction, the usually taciturn pianist identifies the woman who inspired his heartfelt ballad and offers an explanation for her unusual name: "It was named after this beautiful lady here," he explains. "I think her father gave her that name after a butterfly that he tried to catch . . . I don't think he caught the butterfly."

A few years later, when the jazz singer Jon Hendricks added lyrics to Monk's melody for a song he titled "Little Butterfly," Hendricks directly addressed the intangible essence of its subject:

Delicate things, such as butterfly wings,
poets can't describe, 'tho they try.
Love played a tune
when she stepped from her cocoon.
Pannonica, my lovely, lovely, little butterfly.

And throughout her life, just like that elusive butterfly, Nica evaded every attempt to pin her down.

1

A *Weird* Mishbocho

Chastened by her stint in the tabloid spotlight following Bird's death, Nica retreated into the shadows. Though she would periodically emerge to address the jazz press on behalf of one of her favorite musicians, she shunned the media, rejecting virtually all requests for interviews. There were, however, rare occasions when she did let down her guard. In his memoir, *Live at the Village Vanguard*, for example, Max Gordon, the owner of the revered jazz club, recounts a conversation he had with Nica in 1970 during which she abandoned her customary reticence.

Perhaps because they were about the same age and fellow Jews, Nica, who had known Gordon from the time of her arrival in New York, not only opened up to him about her jazz-world exploits but even provided a couple of tantalizing glimpses into her failed marriage and the nature of her relationships with her children and siblings. At one point, while reflecting on her Rothschild lineage, she employed a familiar Yiddishism for "extended family," couched in a classic example of British understatement. "Maybe I do come from a weird *mishbocho*," she confessed, "but we're a close family, Max, believe it or not."

Although Nica may have been more than a little circumspect about her place in the legendary European banking dynasty, her Rothschild identity was a source of great satisfaction for many of the marginalized black jazz musicians whom she befriended. A few years earlier, for example, when Thelonious Monk was being filmed for a cinema verité documentary, the pianist interrupted the casual conversation Nica was having with a couple of hangers-on backstage at the Vanguard in order to offer a slightly skewed rendering of an archetypal Rothschild anecdote. "The royal family came to your grandfather cryin' the blues, and he laid the bread on him to beat Napoleon," Monk declares. "I'll tell everyone who you are. I'm proud of you." Then he turns to address the camera directly. "She's a billionaire," the pianist announces with unmistakable delight. "She's a Rothschild!"

The "grandfather" Monk cited was actually Nica's great-great-grand-father, Nathan Mayer Rothschild, who had been dispatched to England by his father, the family patriarch, Mayer Amschel Rothschild, in the late eighteenth century. And while Monk's hipster version of the family's legendary role in the survival of the British Empire may be something of an overstatement, there is no question about the pivotal role Nica's fore-bears played both in English history and on the world stage.

After leaving the Rothschilds' ancestral home in Frankfurt's Juden-gasse ("Jew Alley"), Nathan settled in Manchester and began a career as a textile merchant. Before long, however, the twenty-one-year-old entre-preneur was actively trading in foreign currency, government securities, and gold bullion on the London stock exchange. By 1811 he had moved his base of operations to the heart of the City of London, inaugurating a new family enterprise, N. M. Rothschild & Sons, at New Court, St. Swithins Lane—not far from the Bank of England—where the head-quarters of the family bank remains to this day. There, enriched with the enormous commissions he made supplying gold bullion to Wellington's army during the last years of the Napoleonic wars, Nathan secured the family a prominent niche in London society. But because Nathan was a Jew still bearing the telltale accent of the Frankfurt ghetto, his attempts to breach the rigid barriers of the British class system did not always go as planned, as illustrated in another well-worn Rothschild anecdote.

In an effort to ingratiate himself with London society, Nathan periodically hosted private concerts in his palatial Piccadilly mansion. One evening, after a recital by a celebrated violinist, he rose and somewhat stiffly offered his thanks to the performer. Then, perhaps in defiance of his guests' barely suppressed smirks of superiority, he reached into his pocket and jingled a handful of coins. "That's my music," he explained. "People listen to it just as carefully, but somehow they don't respect it as much." While succeeding generations would gradually complete Nathan's awkward quest for social status, it's no small irony that a century later, his rebellious great-great-granddaughter blithely turned her back on this life of wealth and privilege in order to devote herself to the music of an often demonized subculture.

By the mid-1800s, Nathan's sons were not only comfortably ensconced in the upper echelons of British society but they had also acquired the traditional accoutrements of power and prestige. Like their old-moneyed Christian counterparts, the Rothschilds took respites from the travails of business in their own huge art and antique-filled country estates. There the male members of the family assumed the role of country gentlemen, entertaining the movers and shakers of Victorian England, from Browning and Tennyson to Gladstone and Disraeli. As one regular guest described the Rothschilds' lifestyle during this period, "The Medicis were never lodged so in the height of their glory."

Nathan's eldest son, Lionel, for example, purchased his historic Hertfordshire mansion, Tring Park (with its four thousand prime fox-hunting acres), for a cool quarter of a million pounds. Although references to the property date back to 1086, the grand seventeenth-century manor house, designed by Sir Christopher Wren, had been a gift from Charles II to his mistress, Nell Gwynn. Not long after settling into his country estate, however, Lionel's effort to breach one of the final frontiers of British power and influence shifted his attention back to London. In 1847 he stood as a candidate to represent the City, the country's financial center, in the House of Commons. Although he won the election handily, he was denied his seat when members of Parliament invoked a law forbidding admittance to those of the Jewish faith.

It took eleven years, but finally, in 1858, after a change in the wording of the oath of office, Lionel was sworn in, on a copy of the Old Testament, as the country's first Jewish MP. That left just one more rung on the ladder: the House of Lords.

It was Lionel's eldest son, Nica's grandfather, Nathaniel Mayer (known as Natty), who would take that final step. By this time, the scions of the Rothschild dynasty had taken their place alongside the sons of their aristocratic brethren as students at Trinity College, Cambridge. So it didn't hurt Natty's campaign to become the first Jewish peer that he had forged a fast friendship with the Duke of Windsor (the future King Edward VII) during their time as Trinity classmates. In 1885, when Queen Victoria named Nathaniel Mayer Rothschild a baron of the United Kingdom, he took his seat in the House of Lords with little of the fuss his father had faced.

Although Natty never shrank from his responsibilities as the unofficial leader of English Jewry, he represented the apotheosis of three generations of cultural assimilation. In his tailored frock coat and top hat, Lord Rothschild became one of the upper house's most strident spokesmen for the status quo, repeatedly railing against political, economic, or social reform. And though even his critics took note of Natty's genuine spirit of philanthropy and unfailing moral rectitude, his rigidity and personal hauteur made him a forbidding presence both in his public affairs and within his own family. By all accounts, Natty's wife, Emma—herself a member of the German branch of the Rothschild *mishbocho*—was even more emotionally restrained than her husband.

The combination of stifling overprotectiveness, extravagant expectations, unbounded privilege, and emotional austerity that characterized life at Tring Park, where Nica's father, Charles, his older brother, Walter, and their sister, Evelina, were raised, provided the ideal environment for a virulent strain of what might be called "Rothschild syndrome." It was a malady to which both brothers fell victim, each in his own way. In her candid memoir of that generation's accomplishments and eccentricities, Nica's sister Miriam observed, "Fate had, in fact, been very unkind to the brothers . . . For one brother had received a crushing overdose of the sense of responsibility . . . while the other had retained an almost infantile insouciance."

As Natty and Emma's firstborn son, Lionel Walter Rothschild was heir apparent to his father's vast fortune, prime candidate for the senior partnership in the family bank, presumed inheritor of the Tring Park estate, and, of course, next in line to the hereditary title, Lord Rothschild. At the age of twenty-one, after completing his education at Cambridge and the University of Bonn, Walter accepted a position at N. M. Rothschild, and ten years later he emulated his ancestors by successfully standing for Parliament. Over time, however, he would fall far short of the family's exacting standards. A lumbering, bewhiskered giant of a man encumbered by a paralyzing speech impediment and an almost pathological shyness, Walter was forever cast into the shadows of his father's favor by his financial ineptitude and entanglement in a web of embarrassing scandals (both financial and sexual).

As it turned out, Walter had an eye for the ladies. Unfortunately, his turbulent romantic adventures with a retinue of ingenues and heiresses usually ended badly, while a liaison with a young housemaid produced an illegitimate daughter. After his death, a cache of his letters was discovered that revealed a blackmail scheme perpetrated by one former mistress lasting over forty years. While tales of Walter's personal indiscretions and financial ineptitude provided amusement for the Edwardian-era chattering class, other exploits made him a familiar figure of derision for the masses as well. Descriptions of the three-hundred-pound heir to the Rothschild fortune driving into the forecourt of Buckingham Palace in a carriage pulled by a team of trained zebras appeared in the local press, as did stories that at home, he could often be seen hitching a ride on the back of one of the giant tortoises he kept on the Tring estate.

As a young child, Walter had exhibited a keen interest in the natural world, as well as a precociously analytical mind. While still in short pants he undertook a comprehensive review of the standard works of scientific literature and initiated an ongoing correspondence with experts in various disciplines. By his early teens he had amassed such an extensive collection of birds, butterflies, moths, eggs, and other specimens that a trained assistant was hired to help him catalogue and care for it.

For generations Rothschild men had been free to devote a sizable portion of their time and discretionary income to their various avocations, so long as these pastimes didn't interfere with their primary allegiance to N. M. Rothschild. In the process many had become celebrated collectors of fine silver, rare coins, championship racehorses, Renaissance art, or ancient manuscripts. In Walter's case, however, what should have been a diversion from the rigors of high finance became an all-encompassing passion. In addition to his team of zebras and his obliging tortoises, Walter's private zoo contained an impressive collection of exotic animals, including an anteater, a flock of emus, a family of dingoes, a tame wolf, and a black walleroo, as well as kangaroos, cranes, cassowaries, capybaras, and a flock of kiwis. Yet this only hints at the extent of his acquisitive obsession.

When he wasn't busy dodging his creditors and concealing his peccadilloes from his parents' prying eyes, Walter devoted his formidable intellect—and the bulk of his personal fortune—to creating the most extensive private natural history museum in the world. Housed on one and a half acres of the Tring Park estate and open to the public, the museum building was a present from his father, Natty, on Walter's twenty-first birthday. Here Walter proudly displayed some 2,000 taxidermied mammals, 200,000 bird eggs, several hundred thousand animal skins (some collected by Captain Cook and Charles Darwin), an equal number of bird skins (later sold to the American Museum of Natural History), and over 2 million butterflies and moths. He not only painstakingly catalogued each specimen, with the help of his curatorial staff, but engaged in original research that resulted in a string of scholarly articles that established Walter Rothschild as one of the leading zoologists of his age. In doing so, he also cast an enormous shadow over at least two generations of the Rothschild dynasty—and not just because of his expansive frame. Walter's intense devotion to the scientific study of the natural world became the dominant influence on his younger brother, Charles (Nica's father), as well as his niece Miriam and nephew, Victor (Nica's sister and brother).

Relegated by his father to a secondary role in the family business and overly indulged by a doting mother, Walter retreated into a permanent state of emotional infantilism. Although there were some twenty unoccupied bedrooms in the Tring Park mansion, including a spacious bachelor's apartment, Walter continued to occupy his old room in the nursery for the rest of his life. When his father died, in 1915, Walter assumed the hereditary title Lord Rothschild, but it was his younger brother, Charles, a self-effacing, guilt-ridden model of rectitude and responsibility, who succeeded their father as senior partner of N. M. Rothschild and became heir (following his mother's death) to the bulk of the family fortune, including Tring Park.

NICA'S FATHER, Nathaniel Charles Rothschild, was born in 1877. Ten years younger than his eccentric brother, Charles became imbued with Walter's passion for the natural sciences. While still a student at Harrow, the precocious young naturalist published a study of the local Lepidoptera, and after entering Cambridge, he spent much of his free time in pursuit of rare butterflies in the unspoiled woodlands of Ashton Wold in Northamptonshire, about seventy miles from Tring Park. Now considered one of the pioneers of the modern conservation movement, Charles managed to convince his father (who owned the property) to set aside the bulk of the area as a nature preserve. Then, in 1900, Natty assigned ownership of the land to his younger son and arranged for a sizable country manor to be built there for him.

By that time, Charles had already embarked on an ambitious agenda of entomological research. Although he lacked his brother's acquisitive mania, he was just as obsessive in his area of specialization: fleas. During his tragically abbreviated life, Charles would amass a collection of more than 30,000 specimens, discover a couple of hundred new species, identify for the first time the rat-borne parasite (*Xendpsylla cheops*) responsible for transmitting the bubonic plague, and publish some 150 scientific papers. Despite his natural disinclination for the family business, Charles committed himself to his day job at the bank and spent much of the night at the microscope.

Periodically Charles also engaged in intensive fieldwork, organizing elaborate expeditions to gather new specimens for his research and exotic additions for his brother's collection. An account of one excursion to Egypt and the Sudan, provided by his friend Raymond Asquith (son of the future prime minister), gives some sense of the vast resources at Charles's command: "We had twenty-two camels, 30 black men of various nations, and one Cingalese boy of 15 brought by Rothschild from Colombo on account of his skill in taxidermy." In 1906, Charles undertook a journey to a somewhat less exotic locale, but he brought home an even more precious prize.

It was on an expedition to Hungary's Carpathian Mountains to collect butterflies and trap mice (for their fleas) that the twenty-six-year-old banker and amateur entomologist met and fell in love with the beautiful and sophisticated local beauty who would become his wife. Seven years his senior, Rozsika von Wertheimstein was one of six children born into a venerable if impecunious family whose ancestors had been the first European Jews to be ennobled. According to Miriam Rothschild's account of her parents' romance, Charles was somewhat circumspect when he approached Rozsika's father to request her hand in marriage. "Do you think I can make her happy in England?" the smitten young Rothschild asked. In response (as Miriam slyly describes it), Rozsika's financially challenged father just "leaned back in his chair and smiled."

It wasn't just Rozsika's striking beauty (dubbed "the Rose of Hungary," she had thick chestnut hair and violet eyes), or her lithe body (she was a national tennis champion and the first woman to master the overhand serve), or her keen intellect (entirely self-educated, each day she zipped through a stack of newspapers in four languages, and she was a devotee of Proust), or her political acumen (she would play a behind-the-scenes role in securing the Balfour Declaration, first announced in a letter to Walter Rothschild as de facto leader of Britain's Jewish community), that captured Charles's heart. As Miriam explains it, his attraction to his future bride had even more to do with the powerful appeal of the entire von Wertheimstein clan, whose light-hearted informality and unaffected good cheer represented such a welcome contrast to "the rich, heavy, constrained, almost regal ambiance that prevailed at Tring."

On February 7, 1907, an entry in the "Court News" column of the London *Times* announced that "the wedding of the Hon. Charles Rothschild, the younger son of Lord Rothschild, with Fraulein Rozsika von Wertheimstein, the eldest daughter of Maj. Alfred von Wertheimstein, of Nagyvarad, Hungary, was solemnized in the Josefstadt Temple in Vienna at noon yesterday." Although the *Times* account described in detail the tasteful service and the "festoons of evergreen and white flowers" that decorated the sanctuary, the event was considerably enlivened by a couple of noteworthy—if less publicized—subplots, either of which could have put a serious damper on the joyous occasion. One was the late arrival of Rozsika's older brother, Victor, delayed by an early-morning duel, which fortunately ended with the loss of only an ear (his opponent's); the other, Nica explained to Nat Hentoff, involved a foiled Communist conspiracy to plant a bomb in the Rothschild-thronged synagogue.

After returning from their honeymoon in Venice, the newlyweds split their time between the recently completed country house at Ashton Wold and a grand Georgian mansion in Kensington Palace Gardens, London. While Charles resigned himself to long days in the partners' room at N. M. Rothschild, Rozsika not only took the reins of the two expansive households but became an active member in London's most elite social circle (one that included Queen Mary, wife of George V). She also bore Charles four children in quick succession: Miriam Louisa, in 1908; Elizabeth Charlotte (known as Liberty), in 1909; Nathaniel Mayer Victor (referred to as Victor), in 1910; and Kathleen Annie Pannonica (nicknamed Nica) in 1913.

A highly sensitive man with liberal political predilections, Charles was an unlikely choice to take on the role of prince of the City. As a surrogate for his disgraced older brother, he assumed his responsibilities at the family bank in New Court with dutiful stoicism, for as one Rothschild biographer put it, "There was not room for two cuckoos in

the New Court nest." Charles continued to experience bouts of melan-
cholia, but his marriage to Rozsika seemed to rescue him from his deepest depressions. Writing to a similarly disposed friend, he gushed of his
newfound peace of mind: "I am so glad . . . that you are really better and
that the 'blues' are getting less. Marry as I have done and you won't have
any at all."

When he extricated himself from the dark shadows that often
engulfed him, Charles was a highly compassionate and affectionate man
whose gentle sense of humor lightened the oppressive formality of Rothschild family life. He also managed to pass on his love of the natural
world to his eldest daughter, Miriam, and his only son, Victor, each of
whom would become world-class scientists and the only siblings to be
made Fellows of the Royal Society.

Initially the joys of marriage and fatherhood kept Charles's blues at
bay, but after he assumed his father's role as senior partner of N. M.
Rothschild (following Natty's death, in 1915), the pressures of the family
business had a devastating effect on the reluctant banker. Within a year,
Charles suffered a physical and emotional breakdown and was forced
to leave for an extended rest cure in Switzerland. He returned home in
1918 but soon fell victim to the influenza pandemic that coincided with
the end of World War I. Although he survived—unlike the 20 million
who quickly died of the disease—he contracted a form of encephalitis
that left him physically debilitated, beset by migraines, and mired in an
unshakable lethargy. In 1923, after five harrowing years, Charles locked
himself in his bedroom and committed suicide.

Shortly thereafter, a grief-stricken Rozsika and her four young children, now between nine and fifteen years of age, joined Walter and his
mother, Emma, as well as a small army of servants and caretakers in
the expansive confines of Tring Park, where, as Miriam described it, the
idiosyncratic extended family became "all boxed up together in a ponderous gilded cage." Of course, there were compensations to be had amid
the stifling grandeur. As always, the Rothschilds' salon remained a magnet for members of the international Jewish political and cultural elite.
One guest in particular made a deep impression on the young Nica,

and many years later she still relished the memory of how Albert Einstein had entertained the family with a repertoire of after-dinner parlor tricks—one of which involved removing his vest without taking off his suit jacket.

Meanwhile, Uncle Walter continued to haunt the estate, both terrifying and arousing the bemused curiosity of his young nieces and nephew, while Emma, the family matriarch, now nearing eighty (and mostly deaf), cast a remote and censorious eye on everything. Rising to the occasion, Rozsika took control, not only running the vast estate with clockwork efficiency but brilliantly managing the family's complex finances as well. It seems that Rozsika had become a Rothschild in more than just name, and the lighthearted von Wertheimstein joie de vivre that had first attracted Charles to his Hungarian bride gradually became subsumed by the remote and oppressive atmosphere of her illustrious in-laws. Many years later, when Chaim Weizmann described Rozsika's deft contribution to the negotiations for the Balfour Declaration, the man who would become the first president of the State of Israel told Miriam, "Your mother was the most remarkable of all the Rothschilds."

In 1960, Nica offered her own, somewhat ambivalent assessment of Rozsika's myriad talents. "She was altogether remarkable," Nica acknowledged. "She dug everything, had tremendous, dynamic charm, and could captivate you in two seconds, but everything I did seemed to be wrong." In fact, Rozsika's uncompromising expectations were grafted onto a rigid post-Victorian child-rearing philosophy that proved particularly intimidating for her youngest daughter. Under her mother's sharp-eyed management, the household's emotional temperature seems to have been permanently set on cool.

One consequence of their father's death was that Nica and her siblings were strictly quarantined from contact with other children. Although Victor would eventually keep faith with Rothschild tradition by attending Harrow and Trinity College, Nica and her sisters were educated at home, every aspect of their micromanaged lives governed by stringently enforced schedules. Decades later, Nica provided a chilling portrait of her sequestered childhood: "I was moved from one great country house to another in the germless immunity of reserved Pullman coaches while being guarded day and night by a regiment of nurses, governesses, tutors, footmen, valets, chauffeurs and grooms."

One of the rare moments of family intimacy was the ritual of evening prayer offered by the three sisters at their mother's bedside. According to Miriam, the girls would kneel each night to offer thanks for their blessings, always concluding with the obligatory supplication "and make me a good little girl. Amen." It was this toxic amalgam of nineteenth-century formality and suffocating familial obligation that both aroused Nica's spirit of rebellion and engendered her existential quest for freedom and acceptance.

Rozsika may have had the most profound role in shaping her daughter's character, but it was her father who had bestowed on her the unique name that would become a signifier for her singular persona—and that would later find its way into the title of a score of celebrated jazz standards. The Latin term *Pannonia* refers to the province of the Roman Empire encompassing western Hungary, which was the home of a rare species of Lepidoptera that Charles Rothschild had acquired on one of his annual collecting trips to the Carpathian Mountains. In this way, Nica's name can be seen as both a symbol of her father's entomological passion and a tribute to the land of her mother's birth. Although she may have chafed at the family's claustrophobic rigidity and social pretensions, Pannonica came to embrace the name as an affirmation of her heritage and identity.

Nine years old when Charles committed suicide, Nica had known her father mostly as a distant presence, since for much of her life he had been either immured in his office at New Court or recuperating from his various maladies in Swiss sanitariums. Among the few memories she retained of her father was the sound of the recordings he regularly played on the family gramophone. Later, all she could recall about them was that they "were not classical."

While Nica and her sisters spent their childhood suffering through the earnest ministrations of governesses and tutors, their brother, Victor, was enduring the rampant anti-Semitism and resisting the "ferocious buggery" of Britain's most elite boarding schools. Later, Victor and his older sister, Miriam, would bond over their mutual fascination with the natural sciences, but he passed along his adventurous taste in music to his youngest sister.

Dubbed the "elusive Rothschild" by his biographer, Victor would be, at various points in his life, a research director of the Cambridge zoology department, a member of MI5 (the British secret service), Winston Churchill's personal envoy to President Roosevelt, a senior executive at Shell Oil, the chairman of N. M. Rothschild & Sons, the head of Britain's Central Policy Review Staff (a.k.a. the Think Tank), and the suspected "fifth man" in the clique of Communist sympathizers known as the Cambridge spies. According to proponents of the Jewish conspiracy for world domination—Victor was not only a key source of the classified documents used to develop the Israeli nuclear bomb but a ringleader in the assassination of John F. Kennedy. He is also the person who introduced his sister to jazz.

A talented amateur pianist, Victor grew up on the works of Bach and Beethoven. But as a youth he became captivated by recordings of American jazz that had arrived in England during the first decades of the twentieth century. Nica quickly absorbed her brother's ardor for the exciting new rhythms, and the music's transgressive spirit would prove the ideal soundtrack for her rebellion against the long legacy of repressive Rothschild values.

FROM THE MOMENT jazz first infiltrated mainstream popular culture, it was perceived as a serious threat not only to the prevailing social order but to the integrity of Western culture itself (just as its African-American roots and association with the nighttime netherworld of urban vice made it a prime target of guardians of old-school morality). Of course, it was precisely such sentiments—along with the music's intoxicating rhythms—that captivated young people on both sides of the Atlantic.

In 1919, the Original Dixieland Jazz Band became the first American jazz band to make its way to England. A white quintet from New Orleans, the ODJB, as they're known by aficionados of early jazz, had made history two years earlier when, much to the consternation of the music's African-American inventors, they entered the Victor company's New York studio to cut what is generally acknowledged to be the first recording of the revolutionary new style. After a riotously successful introduction at London's Hippodrome theater, the ODJB was booked for an extended run at the Palladium, where promoters maintained the band's self-generated myth by billing them as "The Creators of Jazz." Nor was the warm welcome the band received in England limited to the customary throngs of music-hall revelers; they were also embraced by British royalty at a command performance at Buckingham Palace, and by London's upper crust at the Savoy Hotel's posh restaurant.

A couple of months later, the first African-American ensemble arrived in England. The Southern Syncopated Orchestra was a large aggregation of musicians and singers organized by Will Marion Cook, one of the turn-of-the-century pioneers of black musical theater. In 1898, Cook, a college-educated and classically trained musician, had collaborated with the poet Paul Laurence Dunbar on *Clorindy; or, the Origin of the Cakewalk*, the first all-black show to open on the Great White Way. Over the next few years, he would go on to produce a string of successful Broadway shows, including such milestones as *In Dahomey* (starring the African-American vaudeville legends Williams and Walker). In London, Cook's elaborate musical revue was greeted with rapturous reviews, resulting in a five-month stand at the Royal Philharmonic Hall, as well as a command performance for King George V.

By the time Cook's protégé Duke Ellington made his first European tour a decade later, England had its own homegrown jazz scene, much of it emerging from the "hot" dance bands working at the Savoy and other society nightspots. One of Ellington's foremost fans turned out to be the Prince of Wales, an enthusiast of the new sound who also fancied himself something of a jazz drummer. At one private party at the home of the Duke of Kent, the prince even sat in with Ellington's band and struck up a friendship with their great drummer, Sonny Greer. Before long, the two men had established sufficient rapport that Greer, abandoning the usual formalities, took to addressing the future king of England simply as "Wales!"

Many years later, when Nica was reminiscing with Village Vanguard owner Max Gordon about the evolution of her musical taste, she credited Duke Ellington with transforming her into a serious jazzophile. Describing how enamored she had been of Ellington's 1943 suite, "Black, Brown and Beige," she told him, "If you should ask me what record really converted me to jazz, I would have to say it was that one. I didn't know jazz could be so beautiful."

Nica's first close encounter with an actual jazz master had taken place much earlier in her life, when her brother introduced her to the urbane swing-era pianist Teddy Wilson. In the early 1930s, Wilson had gone to England as a member of the Benny Goodman Trio (an ensemble credited with being the first integrated jazz band). When Victor persuaded Teddy to give him a couple of lessons—for a generous stipend of five dollars per session—Nica was allowed to observe. "Afterward he'd play for me," she recalled. "He brought me some records, and I learned about a shop in London where I could buy some more." In the run-up to World War II, Victor made a number of secret visits to the United States, carrying messages from Churchill to President Roosevelt, but he always found time for a quick stop in New York "for another lesson with Teddy." A decade later, when Nica freed herself from the constraints of a troubled marriage, it was Wilson who served as her entrée to the New York jazz community.

NICA'S FIRST OPPORTUNITY to escape the cloistered confines of the Rothschild domicile came at the age of sixteen, when she and her older sister Elizabeth were sent off to a prestigious finishing school in Paris operated by three lesbian sisters ("all wore wigs and made passes at the girls," she told Nat Hentoff) who taught their charges "to put on lipstick, and gave us a little literature and philosophy to go with it." After completing their Parisian polishing, the sisters embarked on a yearlong Grand

Tour of Europe that included a visit to Germany, where Nica briefly studied at the Munich Art Academy, and where (despite their Rothschild pedigree) the sisters experienced firsthand the rising tide of anti-Semitism. After returning to London, the eighteen-year-old Nica was formally presented to King George V and Queen Mary, and she threw herself into the swirl of debutante balls and coming-out parties.

While this period of her life may seem redolent of the nineteenth century, Nica's modernist sensibility, which would culminate in her embrace of bebop's daring harmonies and breakneck tempos, first manifested itself in an attraction to the era's fastest luxury automobiles. Virtually every jazz memoir in which she appears contains at least one vivid account of Nica's high-speed exploits behind the wheel. Of course, now that she was of age, her car (most often a sporty Rolls-Royce) could regularly be found parked in front of one of the chic London nightclubs or after-hours venues featuring the liberating new rhythms emanating from across the Atlantic.

It was there that she befriended the saxophonist Bob Wise, a member of the Savoy Hotel Orpheans who had also played with the pioneering British jazz pianist Arthur Rosebery at London nightspots like the Kit-Kat Club. Wise was an amateur pilot, and Nica soon caught the bug. By the time she was twenty-one, she was flying her own plane, and it was on an early jaunt across the English Channel in the summer of 1935 that Nica met Baron Jules de Koenigswarter, a fellow enthusiast ten years her senior.

A graduate of L'École des Mines de Paris, Jules was then working as the head of financial studies at the Bank of Paris. Although his family had been living in France for over a century, the de Koenigswarters had originally been prominent members of the Austro-Hungarian Jewish aristocracy. Jonas Hirsch Koenigswarter, the family patriarch, who had been born in Kynzvart (Koenigswart), Bohemia, had founded a family bank in the early 1800s, and like the Rothschilds, with whom they had distant familial connections, his descendants had been dispersed to various European business centers (including Frankfurt, Amsterdam, and Vienna), where they established profitable new branches of the family business.

By the middle of the nineteenth century, some of Jonas's descendants had settled in France and quickly gained entrée to the upper echelons of the country's academic and financial elite. One descendant, Louis Jean, became a distinguished legal scholar (and established the still extant Koenigswarter Prize, given annually for contributions to the field), while another, Maximilian, led the family banking business to even greater prominence. Along the way, the de Koenigswarters picked up the hereditary title that, by the beginning of the twentieth century, had passed down to Jules.

Nica must have had a devastating impact on the dashing baron when she stepped from the open cockpit of her private plane to the narrow runway of Le Touquet airfield. Slender, with a high forehead crowned by a cascade of windblown black hair, her penetrating gaze and dazzling smile radiating vitality and charisma—it's no wonder that half a century later, their youngest son, Shaun, recalled that his parents agreed that their initial encounter had been a case of "love at first sight ('*le coup de foudre*,' as we say in French)."

Jules initiated his whirlwind courtship by whisking Nica off on an extensive European tour via his own airplane, with stops in Deauville, Salzburg, Vienna, Budapest, Venice, and Monte Carlo. Three months later, however, when the baron (a widower with a three-year-old son) proposed marriage, a skittish Nica responded by immediately arranging passage on the SS *Normandie* bound for America, where her sister Liberty had recently taken up residence. She landed in New York on September 24, 1935, but didn't get much of a respite; two weeks later, Jules arrived in the city aboard the *Normandie* on its next voyage from Le Havre, and this time he wouldn't take *non* for an answer.

On October 16, the *New York Times* ran a story headlined, "Miss Rothschild Married Here," detailing the distinguished heritage of both the bride and the groom and describing the simple civil ceremony that had been held the previous day in the chapel of the New York City Municipal Building. It was a far cry from the flower-strewn wedding Nica's parents had "solemnized in the Josefstadt Temple in Vienna" surrounded by throngs of Rothschilds and von Wertheimsteins. As for the couple's plans, the *Times* report indicated that "the Baron and Baroness will sail in a few days for a world cruise, after which they will divide their time between Paris and London."

In fact their honeymoon lasted over six months, much of it spent in the cockpit of their small private plane. When an engine gave out over the Gobi Desert, the couple crash-landed and hitched a ride on a camel. While they waited in Yokohama for an outbound ship back home, Jules went on an X-rated shopping spree, purchasing a collection of exotic sex toys which he mailed to London in care of Nica's unsuspecting brother, Victor. Called in to claim the kinky consignment by British Customs officials, Lord Rothschild denied knowledge not only of the shipment but of his sister and brother-in-law as well.

Not long after arriving back in Paris, the twenty-two-year-old Baroness de Koenigswarter discovered she was pregnant. Nica returned to England to give birth, and on July 21, 1936, a son, Patrick, was born in the same London mansion (at 4 Palace Green) that had been the setting of Nica's own entry into the world. Two years later the couple welcomed a daughter, Janka, to the growing family, which also included Jules's young son, Louis, from a prior marriage.

By now the de Koenigswarters had moved into Château d'Abondant, an immense Norman-style brick and stone mansion surrounded by acres of landscaped parkland in the town of Dreux, about an hour's drive from Paris. The château's most notable former occupant had been the Duchesse de Tourzel, the last governess to the children of King Louis XVI and Marie Antoinette. Tourzel had been arrested along with the royal family at the outbreak of the revolution, but eventually managed to escape the mob and take sanctuary at d'Abondant, where she remained throughout the Reign of Terror. So it was that the vivacious baroness once again found herself ensconced in the "ponderous gilded cage" of a bygone era.

IRONICALLY, it was about this time that Nica's brother, Victor, assumed the hereditary title of baron, following the death of Walter Rothschild, in 1937. According to his biographer, however, Victor had decided well before Walter's passing "to be Lord Rothschild in name only." Instead, following his graduation from Trinity College, he accepted a fellowship in the zoology department of his alma mater, thus beginning a distinguished thirty-year career as a scientist and an academic. According to the historian Niall Ferguson, however, it was Victor's exposure to Cambridge's left-wing intellectual climate that was the key factor in his decision to forgo his role as scion of the house of Rothschild.

While at university, Victor was a member of the Cambridge Conversazione Society, better known as the Cambridge Apostles since its membership is limited to the school's twelve most brilliant students. This prestigious brotherhood, dedicated to unfettered intellectual inquiry, has been the college's most selective student club since its founding, in 1820. During its history, notable members of the Apostles have included the mathematician and philosopher Alfred North Whitehead; the novelist E. M. Forster; the poet Rupert Brooke; Bloomsbury bigwigs Lytton Strachey, Leonard Woolf, and John Maynard Keynes; and, more recently, the physician/comedian/director Jonathan Miller. During Victor's tenure, the club was dominated by a faction of Marxist ideologues. Although the young Lord Rothschild was, as his biographer explained, never more than "mildly left-wing," the tangled relationship Victor maintained with fellow Apostles Anthony Blunt and Guy Burgess would cast a long shadow over his distinguished career.

At the beginning of World War II, Victor joined the British Security Service, as did Burgess, Blunt, and their Cambridge colleague Kim Philby, while another of their left-leaning classmates, Donald Maclean, secured a sensitive foreign service position in Washington, D.C. Though Victor served his country with such distinction that he was later awarded the George Medal, England's highest civilian citation, his associates proved to be considerably less patriotic. After Burgess and Maclean defected to the Soviet Union in 1951—on the brink of their arrest as double agents—some suspicion spilled over onto Victor. A few years later, however, when it came to light that Lord Rothschild had also sponsored Anthony Blunt for membership in MI5, where he had functioned as a Soviet mole for decades, Victor became the subject of very public scrutiny.

Periodically Victor attempted to clear his name, but the rumors persisted for decades. In 1980, in the wake of Blunt's death, a renewed round of allegations that Victor was the phantom fifth man in a ring of "Cambridge spies" threatened to taint his reputation permanently. On December 3, 1986, in an act of desperation and defiance, Victor wrote an open letter to the *Daily Telegraph*, printed on the newspaper's front page, challenging the government to "state publicly that it has unequivocal, repeat unequivocal evidence that I am not, and never have been, a Soviet agent." The next day a statement from 10 Downing Street was issued with Prime Minister Margaret Thatcher's terse (and artfully opaque) response to Lord Rothschild's letter: "We have no evidence that he was ever a Soviet agent." Though an accumulation of new information has exonerated Victor, the suspicions persisted even beyond his death, in 1990.

LIKE VICTOR, MIRIAM ROTHSCHILD had been inspired by her father and her Uncle Walter to give her life over to the advanced study of the natural sciences. Widely recognized as a leading authority on the same tiny, wingless parasites that Charles had made his field of specialty, Miriam came to be known as the "Queen of the Fleas." But she was also considered an expert on butterflies and pyrazines and chemical communication, and she was the author of over three hundred scientific papers and numerous books (including a biography of her Uncle Walter and a six-volume illustrated catalogue of her father's personal collection of 30,000 fleas). Later, Miriam headed the Society for the Promotion of Nature Reserves (which had been started by her father at the turn of the twentieth century) and emerged as ardent supported of gay rights (a role that earned her the tabloid handle "the buggers' friend"). The mother of six children, she once confessed, "I got a lot more fun out of my children than I ever had out of describing the backsides of fleas."

By her later years—she died in 2005, at the age of ninety-six—Dame Miriam had become a beloved national eccentric. A vegetarian, she had given up wearing leather and would typically show up at Buckingham

Palace soirees hosted by her close friend Prince Charles wearing an evening dress and a pair of large white rubber moon boots. She wore her
brilliance lightly, and in the freewheeling interviews she gave during her
final years, Miriam seemed to delight in affecting the persona of a particular English archetype: the straight-talking, if slightly dotty, country
matron that might have been played by Benny Hill in drag.

For most of her life Miriam resided at Ashton Wold, the country
mansion that had been built by her grandfather as a coming-of-age present for her father, where a painting of her mother, Rozsika, retained pride
of place above the sitting room's fireplace mantel. But Ashton was also
home to one other occupant, a spectral presence who regularly emerged
from a private wing of the rambling, vine-covered house.

In 1987, the writer Kennedy Fraser was visiting Ashton Wold
in preparation for a *New Yorker* profile of Miriam Rothschild when,
according to Fraser, "Wordlessly, her sister Liberty Rothschild came
in, sat down and played some passages on the piano with great finesse,
then picked up a cup of tea and drifted out." Liberty, born Elizabeth
Charlotte, was the second of the three Rothschild sisters. Resistant to
the science bug that had infected Miriam and Victor, Liberty shared
Nica's artistic sensibility, and her talent. Like Nica, Liberty won prestigious national awards for painting while still in her teens and later
went on to study at the Paris Conservatoire. Nica's bond with Liberty
was strengthened during their prewar tour of the continent, and it is
Liberty's name that appears as "witness" on Nica and Jules's New York
State marriage license.

In early adulthood, however, Liberty was diagnosed with schizophrenia, after which she moved in with Miriam at Ashton Wold. Until her
death at seventy-eight (not long after the publication of the *New Yorker*
profile), the sisters came together each day for lunch. Miriam endured
her sister's occasionally bizarre behavior with good humor, as on the
occasion of a formal dinner during which Liberty had become bored.
"She didn't know that's what it was," Miriam told Fraser, "but she was
bored. So she got an orchid out of the middle of the table and ate it.
Munched her way through it. *Very* slowly. Ha! That stopped us in our

tracks!" Yet, thinking back to her sister's youthful talent, Miriam wistfully admitted, "She was the most gifted of us all."

DURING THE FIRST YEARS of their marriage, Jules made the daily commute to his job at the Bank of Paris while Nica was engaged in the typical demands of any young wife and mother, along with her more exalted obligations as mistress of Château d'Abondant. It was a far cry from the bright lights–big city lifestyle to which she had grown accustomed in the years before her marriage; but if Nica did have any regrets about abandoning the heady excitement of London society, they were to be short-lived. There were exciting times ahead—the German army would see to that.

In September 1939, Jules, a lieutenant in the reserves, was mobilized in the face of an imminent Nazi invasion. Before he left to join his regiment, he sat Nica down to discuss her options if the worst should occur. "He left my mother a map, with instructions," their eldest son, Patrick, recalled. "If the Germans get to this point, take the children and escape any way you can to your family in England." Half a century later, when Nica recalled this moment, she told an interviewer, "I'm not a crier, I can count the times in my life when I cried . . . One time was when war broke out, when my husband was called up. And I can remember that time having a crying jag. I remember we had this enormous lawn . . . and walking and running and crying [and I] couldn't stop."

A few months later, the first Nazi battalions breached the Maginot Line and began advancing toward Paris. As instructed, Nica gathered together her children (four-year-old Patrick, two-year-old Janka, and her eight-year-old stepson, Louis), and, along with a maid and a nanny, boarded the last train of refugees heading to the English Channel and passage home.

Battlefield Dispatches:
From the Front Lines
and
the Home Front

Nica and her weary retinue arrived in London on May 28, 1940. It had taken four tortuous days, during which they had largely gone without food or drink. Meanwhile, along with the rest of his battalion, Jules had retreated to Bordeaux, in the still unoccupied area of southwestern France. Not convinced that his family would find safety even at one of the Rothschild estates in the English countryside, Jules instructed his wife to relocate their children to the United States. On June 11, 1940, Nica and the children set sail from Liverpool.

A few days later, as Marshal Pétain was arranging for the armistice with Germany that established a puppet government in the city of Vichy, General Charles de Gaulle arrived in London, where he began organizing a resistance to Nazi occupation. On June 18, the general made a historic address on BBC Radio, acknowledging the dire circumstances of his homeland while challenging the notion that all was lost: "But has the last word been said? Must hope disappear? Is defeat final? No!" He proceeded to invite all loyal Frenchmen to join him in London. "Whatever happens," he proclaimed, "the flame of French resistance must not be extinguished and will not be extinguished!" Hearing de Gaulle's stirring words, Lieutenant Jules de Koenigswarter embarked for England on a converted cruise ship, the SS *Sobieski*, accompanied by 100 French volunteers and 2,000 Polish troops.

Upon arriving in London, Jules presented himself for service in General de Gaulle's Forces Françaises Libres (Free French). On June 25, he was formally inducted into the FFL, promoted to captain, and assigned to an artillery unit in Brazzaville, the capital of what was then French Equatorial Africa. But as the world confronted the deepening conflict, the Rothschild family faced a sudden personal loss. On June 30, 1940, Rozsika von Wertheimstein Rothschild died of a heart attack in Ashton Wold, the house that she had moved into as a newlywed over thirty years earlier. Absent from the long list of mourners was Nica, who had only learned of her mother's death shortly after her arrival in New York.

ABOUT A YEAR EARLIER, as signs of the impending war were becoming harder to ignore, another ship had steamed into New York Harbor, carrying one of America's greatest jazz musicians home after an extended European sojourn. Although the tenor saxophonist Coleman Hawkins had faded from the consciousness of casual jazz fans during his five years overseas, when he walked down the gangplank on July 31, 1939, a small but enthusiastic contingent from the National Swing Club of America was there to welcome him. Accounts of his arrival indicated that although "his hair had thinned" and he was "somewhat slimmer than the 'Bean' of old," the saxophonist had retained his "air of charming sophistication."

Dubbed the "Father of the Tenor Saxophone," Coleman Hawkins had begun his professional career in 1921, when, at the age of seventeen, he began working with the pioneering blues singer Mamie Smith. Dapper and dignified, with a taste for the good life, Hawkins was among the most musically knowledgeable of his contemporaries (in fact his nickname, Bean, was a nod to his impressive brainpower). Over the next few years, he transformed the tenor sax, which had been considered a novelty instrument in early dance bands and vaudeville orchestras, into the foremost solo instrument in jazz.

By 1934, Hawkins had spent a decade as a star soloist with the Fletcher Henderson Orchestra, an innovative and highly regarded New York–based ensemble. So when Duke Ellington returned home from his first tour of England with stories of the phenomenal reception his musicians had received from British jazz fans, the creatively restless saxophonist was intrigued. It wasn't only the enthusiastic response to their music but the respect and interracial camaraderie the Ellingtonians had encountered in Europe that captured Bean's attention. Ever since World War I, when the regimental band of the all-black 369th Infantry (the so-called Harlem Hellfighters) captivated French audiences with their ragtime rhythms, African-American jazz musicians had come back with similar stories—and some decided not to come back at all.

A few months after Ellington's return, Hawkins booked passage on the *Île de France* to join England's most successful bandleader, Jack Hilton, as a featured performer, and soon the saxophonist was soaking in the ecstatic response of jazz-hungry audiences at the London Palladium. After successful tours of Wales and Scotland, Hawkins set off for a series of engagements in Holland, Scandinavia, and Paris, where he performed with Django Reinhardt, the brilliant Gypsy guitarist, and Benny Carter, another American jazz star who had abandoned his homeland for greener pastures overseas. But by the late 1930s, the warm embrace of his European fans wasn't enough to shield him from the harsh winds of racist ideology blowing across western Europe. Hawkins got out in the nick of time. The pianist Freddy Johnson, one of Bean's regular musical cohorts—and an early jazz expatriate who had been living in Europe since the late 1920s—chose to ignore the Nazi threat; he was arrested in 1941 and spent the next three years in a Bavarian prison camp.

Although there's no documentation of their meeting, it's hard to believe that the jazz-obsessed baroness, who was residing in London and Paris during Hawkins's European odyssey, didn't manage to see him perform, and perhaps introduce herself. In any event, when she went to New York in the 1950s, Bean immediately became one of her closest musical associates. In 1967, when reports of his failing powers circulated through the jazz world, Nica sprang to the saxophonist's defense.

"He is as great a giant today as he always has been," she wrote in an impassioned open letter to *DownBeat* magazine. "He is still blowing everyone off the scene!"

IN KEEPING WITH her Rothschild lifestyle, Nica found refuge for her displaced children on the so-called Gold Coast of Long Island, an area on the North Shore that had long been a summer haven for New York millionaires (as well as the fictional setting for F. Scott Fitzgerald's novel *The Great Gatsby*). It was here that the members of the Guggenheim family, another of the great Jewish financial aristocracies, had established their weekend retreat on a couple of hundred acres overlooking Long Island Sound.

Daniel Guggenheim, the original occupant of the estate, lived in the property's main residence, Hempstead House, a 40-room stone pile built in 1912 as a replica of Ireland's fifteenth-century Kilkenny Castle. The mansion featured an enormous stained glass–lined palm court with over 150 species of rare flowers, an aviary filled with exotic birds, a billiard room with a gold-leafed ceiling, an oak staircase salvaged from a seventeenth-century Spanish palace, and a living room whose artworks included paintings by Rubens, Rembrandt, and Van Dyke. Following Daniel's death, in 1930, his widow, Florence, moved to a more intimate cottage located on the estate, and at the start of World War II, she made Hempstead House available as a reception center for refugee children from Britain awaiting placement in American homes.

At first Daniel's son, Harry—who occupied his own cozy twenty-six-room Norman-style manor, known as Falaise, on eighty acres of the Guggenheim estate—was wary of opening his palatial home to any of the young European evacuees, claiming that it would be unfair to expose them to such opulence, only to have them return to their humble circumstances after the war. But when his wife, Alicia, countered with an offer to find "a child who is accustomed to living the way we live," Harry reluctantly agreed. Not long after, the Guggenheims, who had been made aware of Nica's plight through a representative of the British embassy in Washington, arrived at the Waldorf-Astoria to meet Patrick and Janka. According to Nica, the couple immediately "fell in love with them," and arrangements were made for their temporary custody.

The culture shock Harry feared his young charges might face during their new life at Falaise was immediately dispelled when four-year-old Patrick (who had grown up amid the grandeur of Château d'Abondant) looked up at the impressive cliffside manor with its slate-shingled towers, ornate turrets, and leaded windows and declared, "Oh, what a nice little house."

Although the siblings spent most of their time under the supervision of their nanny and a very proper British butler, they did take full advantage of their luxurious surroundings. Patrick later recalled accompanying "Uncle Harry" to watch his horses run at Belmont racetrack, and, making good use of the stables at Falaise, he became an accomplished rider as well. Janka made friends with the daughter of one of Alicia's friends, and the girls often quietly painted together. "Aunt Alicia was very encouraging," recalled Janka, who eventually became an artist.

Satisfied that her children were in good hands, Nica contacted representatives of France Quand-Même (France Forever), an organization dedicated to providing material support for de Gaulle's resistance. In a 1941 article on the group's efforts, *Time* magazine reported that while a contingent of prominent exiles residing in the United States formed its leadership, the six thousand members of France Forever included "waiters and patrons of Antoine's, Galatoire's and other famed restaurants" in New Orleans' French Quarter. Now a Rothschild was added to the list.

Over several months, Nica worked with the organization to assemble a shipload of provisions and medical supplies, and in December 1940 she boarded a fully loaded Norwegian freighter bound for West Africa. On January 1, 1941, Nica was finally reunited with Jules, who was then stationed in Accra, serving as liaison to the British general headquarters. However, she had yet to make the difficult adjustment to the hardships of life in a war zone. According to one account, Nica "stunned local society when she arrived with a lady's maid, and, since there were no accommodations for European lady's maids, the [native] house boy and cook were unceremoniously ousted from their quarters to make room for her."

Following her induction into the Free French Forces, Nica slowly began to adapt to the rigors of army life. Initially she served as a translator and decoder, but before long she was making radio broadcasts in the heated propaganda war against the Vichy collaborators. Meanwhile, back home in England, her siblings had also begun to take an active role in the fight against fascism.

ACCORDING TO Victor Rothschild's biographer, in early 1939, Nica's brother "casually told his friends that he was off to the United States to seek out his paragon, the jazz pianist Teddy Wilson." In fact, Victor was en route to Washington, D.C., to make contact with high-level government officials, including J. Edgar Hoover, Secretary of State Cordell Hull, Secretary of the Treasury Henry Morgenthau, and President Franklin Roosevelt. The relationships he established on the visit assured him a prominent role when he became Winston Churchill's personal emissary to FDR after America entered the war. As head of Churchill's security detail, Victor was also responsible for insuring the prime minister's safety, which included the onerous task of personally sampling Churchill's cigars and vintage bottles of Armagnac.

Victor's other wartime assignment was one particularly suited to his talents: dismantling bombs. As one of his colleagues put it, "Who else combined nimble jazz-playing fingers with a first-class scientific brain?" For five years, Colonel Rothschild's private research lab (operated at his own expense) developed innovative techniques to identify and disarm bombs that the German army disguised as everything from shaving soap to children's toys to lumps of coal. Over the course of the war, Victor personally defused more than one hundred explosive devices. In one well-publicized case, he dismantled a cleverly booby-trapped box of Spanish onions that had made its way onto a British dock. As he deactivated the complex series of fuses, he calmly narrated each action into a field telephone, so that in the event of a misstep, others might be spared the same fate. "When one takes a fuse to pieces," he explained to his biographer, "there is no time to be frightened. One also becomes absorbed in its beautiful mechanism."

By all accounts, however, Lord Rothschild didn't suffer fools gladly. Handsome and supremely self-confident, he had a veneer of erudition that barely concealed an intimidating ruthlessness. Even his sympathetic biographer admits that, despite his undeniable brilliance and bravery, Victor didn't exactly endear himself to his colleagues. Not unaware of his prickly nature, he jokingly proposed adopting the personal motto "Quick to give—and to take—offence." And while he was often generous to his friends and extravagantly philanthropic, the artist Lucien Freud (whose portrait of Victor's son, Jacob, is on extended loan to the National Portrait Gallery) described him as "appallingly rude and abusive and unreasonable and coarse—absolutely Neanderthal."

Although Miriam Rothschild's service may have been somewhat less conspicuous than her brother's, she also contributed her unique talents to the war effort. Based on her early interest in marine biology, she was initially assigned a project to develop chicken feed from seaweed, as a way of saving grain for human consumption. But within a few months she received a posting that would have a considerably greater impact on the course of the war. Miriam was recruited to join an elite team of scientists who had been assembled at Bletchley Park under the direction of Alan Turing, a mathematician and cryptographer often dubbed the "Father of Computer Science."

This was the so-called Enigma Project, a top-secret effort to crack the Nazi code, whose success was considered crucial to the Allied victory. "I spent two years trying to help decode German wireless messages," Miriam told an interviewer shortly before her death. Yet despite her commitment to the cause, life at Bletchley proved difficult for her. "For me they were the most hideous two years you could possibly imagine, because I was always nervous about secrets getting out." And while she was modest about her own role in the endeavor, Miriam did acknowledge the importance of the project, and agreed with the general assessment that "while we didn't win the war . . . we did shorten it probably by two years with our research."

Miriam also gave over her Northamptonshire residence, Ashton Wold, to serve as a hospital for wounded soldiers and refugees, and a sizable portion of the estate was transformed into a base for the U.S. Army Air Force, which converted the adjacent fields into landing strips. Among the members of the squadron stationed there was Clark Gable, who had enlisted not long after his wife, Carole Lombard, was killed in a plane crash during a war bond drive. "Clark Gable was a very strange person to suddenly find wandering around Ashton Wold," Miriam recalled a half-century later, "but he was amazingly good-looking."

MOVIE STARS LIKE GABLE weren't the only entertainers to answer their country's call. As American audiences watched the latest black-and-white newsreel images of troops in formation marching across the screens of their local movie houses, they might have heard the resonant voice of a narrator trumpeting a headline guaranteed to induce a surge of patriotic pride: "Jazz Goes to War!" With the soundtrack blaring the infectious rhythms of a swing-era big band, viewers learned how members of the nation's jazz orchestras were trading in their slick band uniforms for army khaki or navy blue. It was yet another feel-good story for a nation confronting the malevolent forces of fascism. Of course the reality was considerably more complex.

It's certainly true that hundreds of jazz sidemen and bandleaders, both black and white, joined the ranks of those who fought and died on battlefields around the globe. In fact, less than a year after Pearl Harbor, the jazz magazine *DownBeat* added a new column to its array of entertainment news and features, titled "Killed in Action," to honor the scores of musicians who had made the ultimate sacrifice. And before the war's end, the country was united in mourning for a jazz martyr.

In 1942, Glenn Miller, a lanky, bespectacled trombonist, was the most successful bandleader in America. His live appearances consistently broke box-office records, his thrice-weekly national radio show was among the most highly rated on the dial, and his easy-listening hits, like "Tuxedo Junction," "Chattanooga Choo-Choo," and "In the Mood" (featuring his inventive arrangements and dulcet harmonies), are counted among the best-selling recordings of the pre-rock era. When war was declared, Miller was earning about $20,000 per week. Although at thirty-eight he was too old to be drafted, he enlisted in the U.S. Army Air Force and put together a military band that Miller often declared was the best he'd ever had. In December 1944, after a morale-boosting tour of England, he took off for Paris to celebrate the city's recent liberation, but his plane never made it across the Channel. Miller's disappearance was never solved, but in death he became a symbol for the many other jazz soldiers who never returned home.

While Glenn Miller's African-American counterparts had actually laid the musical groundwork for the swing era, they hadn't reaped its rewards. In segregated America, black bands couldn't book high-profile hotel gigs or get their own corporate-sponsored national radio program, nor were any black bandleaders earning the five-figure weekly paychecks Miller was getting. According to one *DownBeat* writer, "Negro [band]-leaders could make more money running a rib joint." Yet among the one million black servicemen (and women) who reported for duty were scores of African-American jazz musicians—or, as Duke Ellington expressed it, "As before, of course, the black, brown, and beige were right there for the red, white, and blue."

Not that the bitter irony of being asked to fight against a racist ideology overseas while being subjected to the daily outrages of segregation at home was lost on the African-American community. A few weeks after war was declared, a letter to the editor was published in the prominent African-American newspaper the *Pittsburgh Courier*, and what had been an issue of internal debate was quickly transformed into a national movement. Printed under the headline "Should I Sacrifice to Live Half American?," the letter had been submitted by James G. Thompson, a twenty-six-year-old cafeteria worker, who expressed frustration that he would be asked to defend a country in which he was denied many of the basic rights of citizenship. Thompson proposed that this fundamental dilemma could be turned into an opportunity, and that the battle for victory over enemies "from without" could be linked to the struggle for victory against discrimination "from within." He referred to this concept as "the double V."

Based on the extraordinary response of its readers, the *Courier* launched its "Double-V Campaign." On February 14, 1942, the editors ran a statement on the paper's front page declaring that while "we, as colored Americans, are determined to protect our country, our government, and the freedoms we cherish," this fight should be waged on two fronts, "against our enemies at home and abroad who would enslave us." Using large bold-faced caps, it concluded with the rallying cry, "WE HAVE A STAKE IN THIS FIGHT . . . WE ARE AMERICANS TOO!"

The paper quickly came up with an insignia featuring a pair of interlocking *V*'s set against the slogan "Democracy: At Home–Abroad," on top of which perched a bald eagle. Soon posters, button, and pins with the Double-V logo were produced, and clubs formed across the country to support the cause. By the spring of 1942, five other African-American newspapers had joined the campaign, and in October, when the *Courier* took a poll on the question of whether, at this critical moment in history, "the negro should soft pedal his demands for complete freedom and citizenship," almost 90 percent of readers answered "No."

Concerned about the growing strength of the Double-V Campaign, J. Edgar Hoover decided that the publishers who were promoting the movement had committed acts of sedition, and with the approval of President Roosevelt he began preparing indictments for treason. It was only after the influential publisher of the *Chicago Defender* assured the U.S. attorney general that the newspapers would show appropriate restraint in promoting the victory-at-home agenda that Hoover shelved the indictments. By the end of 1942, the coverage of Double-V activities had pretty much disappeared from the pages of the black press.

African-American conscripts and enlistees continued to serve despite the indignity of being in segregated units and the mistreatment of racist commanding officers and fellow soldiers. As a group, however, black jazz musicians had a particularly difficult adjustment. Many were educated, culturally sophisticated, and unconventional individuals who had carved out a niche in the relatively enlightened "business of show." For these men, the prospect of life in the racially polarized and highly regimented military was especially onerous. The experience of the veteran Kansas City musician Charles Goodwin was typical. Drafted in 1941, Goodwin was posted to Hattiesburg, Mississippi where he encountered a reality unlike any he had known. "Boy, I never did run across people like that before in my life," he recalled. "I didn't know anyplace like this existed in America. They treated us servicemen like we was lower than a dog."

Unlike their white counterparts—many of whom had been assigned to cushy special service units providing entertainment for the troops at home and abroad—few African-American musicians were able to secure a spot in one of the black military bands. The trumpeter Buck Clayton, a featured soloist with Count Basie, was one of the fortunate ones. After being inducted in 1943, he was stationed in Brunswick, New Jersey, where he joined other black musicians who provided a rousing accompaniment for troops boarding ships bound for deployment overseas. And though it was against army policy, Clayton even got to moonlight as a sideman on recording dates in the New York studios just across the river. His bandmate the brilliant tenor saxophonist Lester Young wasn't so lucky.

While musicians seeking to avoid induction often feigned physical or mental illness or claimed to be homosexual, most kept one step ahead of their local draft boards simply by staying on the road. This last strategy had worked for Lester Young, at least until September 1944, when, as his biographer describes it, a "much-publicized and long-term stint in Los Angeles . . . proved to be his undoing." One night after the band's set at the Club Plantation, two men approached Young and the Basie drummer (and fellow draft evader) Jo Jones. After treating them to a round of drinks, the pair suddenly identified themselves as FBI agents and instructed both men to report for duty at nine o'clock the following morning.

Even within a jazz world populated by proud nonconformists, Lester Young was sui generis, from his sartorial style (trademark porkpie hat, ankle-length topcoat, and a full-spectrum array of suede shoes) to his

vocabulary (a veritable thesaurus of hipster slang and impenetrable aphorisms), to the unique way he cradled his sax ("cool enough to hold his
horn / at angles as sharp as he was heartbroken," as the poet Al Young put
it). Lester even managed to escape the gravitational force of Coleman
Hawkins's declamatory sound, which had held virtually every other tenor
saxophonist in its sway for a decade. Yet despite his deceptively laconic,
behind-the-beat phrasing and ethereal tone, Lester could swing with such
intensity that even Hawkins challenged him at his peril. In recognition of
Young's supreme status, his closest friend and musical collaborator, Billie
Holiday (whom he had dubbed Lady Day) gave him the nickname Prez,
short for the honorary title "President of the Tenor Saxophone."

On the morning of September 30, 1944, Lester Young showed up at
his assigned induction center—with his horn and a bottle of whiskey—
still hoping he could wangle his way out of service. When that proved
not to be the case, Young went AWOL, showing up later that night at his
brother Lee's gig in the city. He was quickly arrested and returned to his
unit. Somehow the thirty-five-year-old saxophonist managed to survive a
grueling period of basic training, after which he was transferred to a base
in Alabama. A few months later, when a search of his belongings turned
up marijuana and pills, Young readily admitted to being high, and on
February 16, 1945, he was taken before the court martial for "violation of
the 96th Article of War." In addition to the physical evidence, there was
testimony from his company commander describing Young as "unsuited
for the military," and a report from a captain in the Neuropsychiatric Service who had found him to be in a "Constitutional Psychopathic State,
manifested by drug addiction (marijuana, barbiturates), chronic alcoholism and nomadism."

Young was sentenced to one year of hard labor in the U.S. Disciplin-
ary Barracks—a harsh sentence, considering that he had no prior record,
had confessed to his drug use, and had testified at his trial with unswerv-
ing honesty. In fact, according to his biographer, "Young's refusal to lie or
dissemble may have bothered the army officers as much as anything else
he did." Of course, the photo of his white wife, which he had taped to
his locker, may not have helped his case either.

Understandably, Young never talked much about the months he spent in confinement, but the bassist Gene Ramey, who played with him late in Young's career, recalled hearing stories about how the "guards would get drunk and come out there and have target practice on his head." While jazz critics continue to debate the effect "the mad nightmare" of his army experience had on his music, psychologically the saxophonist was never the same again. Although there would be brief periods of stability, his alcoholism grew progressively more severe, and Lester Young died alone, at the age of forty-nine, in a shabby 52nd Street hotel room that looked down onto the entrance to Birdland.

BY THE TIME the Allied forces hit the beaches of Normandy in June 1944, both Nica and her husband had been on active duty for over three years. Jules, a skilled engineer, was initially assigned to modify gun turrets, while Nica contributed her linguistic skills to the anti-Vichy propaganda campaign. Before long, however, the couple left the relative safety of Brazzaville and Accra for the front lines. In late 1941, Jules was given command of an artillery unit of the First Free French division engaged in combat against Axis forces led by General Rommel, the so-called Desert Fox. Serving alongside her husband, Nica used the skills she had first honed at the wheel of a Rolls-Royce to drive ambulances and military jeeps in missions across some of the major battlefields of North Africa.

Nica faced the danger and discomforts of war with equanimity, but in early 1942, she came down with a severe case of malaria and was granted medical leave. Viewing it not only as a chance for some welcome R&R but as an opportunity to visit her children, she departed from Lagos, Nigeria, on the liner *Santa Paula*, bound for New York. But the trip didn't turn out to be quite what the doctor ordered.

A day after the *Santa Paula* docked in Brooklyn, on January 24, 1942, the *New York Times* ran a story about the vessel's perilous Atlantic crossing. Under the headline "Liner Here Safely After Dodging Torpedoes; / Passengers Tell of the Thrills and Spills," the article described how "two days out . . . the vessel was attacked twice within six hours by a submarine," with one torpedo missing the ship "by not more than twenty feet." The remainder of the voyage was uneventful, but as the *Santa Paula* reached the U.S. coast, it narrowly escaped "colliding with two unidentified vessels, both blacked out and zigzagging at full speed." The *Times* also noted that among the passengers there were twelve cases of malaria, one being "the Baroness Pannonica de Koenigswarter, sister of Baron Rothschild."

Following her recuperation and a brief reunion with her children, Nica rejoined her husband in North Africa, where he was now serving as commander of the First Regiment of Marine Fusilliers. In the weeks before the Normandy invasion, Jules led his unit across the Mediterranean to Italy, where he acted as a liaison to the advancing American tank and infantry forces. As they advanced on Rome, the regiment faced heavy resistance, and Jules was cited for bravery under fire. He would go on to provide key combat and logistical support for operations across southern France and into Strasbourg, ending the war with the rank of lieutenant colonel. Among his many other decorations, Jules received both the Croix de la Libération and the Croix de la Legion d'Honneur, the highest military honors awarded by the French during World War II.

After landing in Italy, Nica volunteered as an ambulance driver for the Commonwealth War Graves Commission, which was engaged in the gruesome and risky task of removing and identifying the dead from the battlefields of western Europe. By the war's end, she had gotten as far as Berlin, entering the city in late April 1945, just days before Adolf Hitler committed suicide. Nica retired from active service with the rank of lieutenant in the Free French Forces and was awarded the Médaille de la France Libre for her contributions to the Allied victory.

A few months earlier, in late September 1944, Jules and Nica had been granted a brief leave from active duty. Paris had just been liberated by Allied forces, and the couple returned to the city and took up temporary residence in the second-floor apartment of a Rothschild mansion at 22 rue Galilee, just a few blocks from the Arc de Triomphe. An American army unit was already in possession of the house following the hasty evacuation of the SS officers who had commandeered it during the occupation. Among the soldiers stationed there was a twenty-one-year-old sergeant from Marquette, Michigan, named Frank Richardson. Before being drafted, Richardson had been working as a bank clerk in his small Upper Peninsula town, playing a little piano in a local dance band, and singing in his church choir. Suddenly he found himself in the middle of Paris, billeted in a Rothschild mansion with fireplaces big enough to walk into and an entire floor given over to an elegant ballroom. One night, Richardson recalls, he was playing piano for his buddies when "we heard a knock on the door. We opened it and the baroness came in."

When Richardson finished the song, Nica told him how much she had enjoyed his music and invited him to come up to her suite on the mansion's second floor to play for her again. A few days later, the young sergeant climbed the ornate staircase and discovered that Jules and Nica had quickly decorated their rooms with an array of luxurious furnishings, including a gleaming Pleyel grand piano. After Nica poured him a "generous portion of Courvoisier cognac," Richardson launched into his repertoire of standard pop tunes. "I jazzed up a few, and of course she liked that," he reminisced with quiet pride some sixty years later. Although she was exquisitely dressed and gracious to a fault, Richardson insists that "she had no airs, no pretense at all." In fact, if someone hadn't told him who she was, he explains, there was no way he "would have known she was a baroness, a Rothschild."

When Jules left Paris to resume command of a tank division of the First French Army, Nica was joined by his younger sister Odile, who had finally returned from North Africa to celebrate the city's liberation. "She was my age and spoke fluent English," Richardson remembers, and it didn't take long for the wide-eyed young American GI and the sophisticated French debutante to fall into an unlikely wartime romance. At the time, Richardson recalls, it all seemed pretty simple: "She liked me and I liked her, and that was it." Yet as Richardson somewhat shyly admits, "To be honest with you, she was my first girl."

Along with Nica, who was accompanied by an aide to General de Gaulle, the young lovers hit the nightclubs, and Odile regaled Richardson with stories of her coming-out party (she "wore elbow-length white gloves" and the music was provided by "the jazz great Django Rein-hardt"). Odile also seemed to take particular pleasure in initiating the innocent "ex-bank-clerk from the U.P." (as Richardson described him-self) into the joys of *amour* and the *beau monde*. When they parted, she told him, "You'll never forget me." Six decades later, he still hadn't. Nor did Richardson forget what Nica had told him on the very first night he played piano for her. It was the fall of 1944, and the war was still raging, but as soon as it ended, Nica confided in him, she planned to go to New York "to get in on the jazz scene."

After the war Frank Richardson returned home, went to college, and eventually became a public school principal. He also continued his musical pursuits, playing piano, composing Christmas carols, and sing-ing in his local choir. Yet from his isolated perch in the Upper Penin-sula, he kept abreast of the revolution in the postwar jazz world as well. In 1955 he read an article about the death of the "Bop King," Charlie Parker, in the Stanhope Hotel suite of Baroness de Koenigswarter, and it was only then that he realized Nica "had gotten to New York like she said she would."

WHILE IT IS EASY to romanticize Nica's wartime experience, with its cinematic images of windblown Jeep rides through the deserts of North Africa and the brave and beautiful baroness fighting alongside her dash-ing husband under the banner of the French Resistance, there was no escaping the tragic reality of war, or the incomprehensible horrors of the Holocaust. Even for a Rothschild.

Although most of Nica's extended family managed to avoid the Nazi death camps, one, Elizabeth de Rothschild, the wife of Baron Philippe (owner of vineyards at Château Mouton), was interned at Ravensbruck, where she died of typhus not long before its liberation. Nica's eighty-year-old aunt, Aranka (Rozsika's eldest sister), was beaten to death with meat hooks upon her arrival at the Buchenwald train station. And after refusing to heed her son's instructions to leave Paris with his wife and children, Jules's mother was arrested early in the occupation, and she died sometime later in Auschwitz.

Exposure to the carnage of Europe's killing fields would have called into question anyone's quaint notions about the great humanistic tradition of Western civilization. But like millions of others who had seen their world upended by war, Nica was determined to pick up the pieces of her old life as soon as possible. After reuniting with her children and returning to the serenity of Château d'Abondant, however, she (like so many others) soon realized that the foundation of her existence had been shattered forever. Though few were conscious of it at the time, a new world order was taking shape. In the aftermath of the war, women who had faced the enemy on the front lines or worked on defense plant assembly lines on the home front were expected to blithely resume their domestic routines. While many embraced the return to normality, for some the genie of empowerment simply could not be put back into its bottle. In his 1960 *Esquire* article, "The Jazz Baroness," Nat Hentoff observed that as a consequence of her wartime experiences, "For the first time in her life, [Nica] began to realize her capacity for accomplishing something on her own."

Though it would take her a few years, Nica's struggle for fulfillment, which began on the battlefields of Italy and North Africa, would be realized only after she freed herself from both the constraints of her Rothschild heritage and its eerie echoes in her marriage.

3

New World Order:
The Rise
of
Midcentury Modernism

In the immediate aftermath of the war, neither of the de Koenigswarters seemed eager to retreat to the familiar comforts of the past. Having been immersed in the heightened reality of combat and energized by the proximity to power as a member of de Gaulle's inner circle, Jules was in no hurry to return to his hushed office in the Bank of Paris or to the bucolic splendor of Château d'Abondant. Offered the opportunity to be part of the new government, he accepted a position in the diplomatic service and in 1946 was posted to the French embassy in Norway.

Not long after their arrival in Oslo, Nica gave birth to a third child, a daughter named Berit, followed two years later by a second son, Shaun. After spending five years swept up in the vortex of the century's most momentous events, Nica was thus dropped back into a cosseted existence, tightly circumscribed by domestic responsibilities and the ritualized formality of international diplomacy. Although Jules, a man of punctilious habits and strict schedules, thrived in this exalted atmosphere, his wife soon began to suffocate.

Among the most revealing artifacts of Nica's life from this period is a black-and-white photograph taken outside the de Koenigswarters' Oslo residence. In the background, their son Patrick, a well-groomed boy of ten or eleven, stands alongside a uniformed nanny. Looming in the foreground is an enormous 1928 Rolls-Royce convertible, with a resolute-looking Nica in the driver's seat, her hands grasping the wheel at ten and two, her dark eyes riveted on the viewer's gaze as if she is poised to step down on the accelerator and head off into the unknown.

In 1949, however, when Jules was offered a more prestigious diplomatic assignment, Nica and their newly expanded family set off together for Mexico City. Nica continued to perform her duties, both diplomatic and domestic—she gave birth to a fifth child, Kari, one year later—but her proximity to the United States now provided her with both a refuge from escalating marital discord and an opportunity to fulfill the promise she had made in the afterglow of Paris's liberation: that one day she would "go to New York and get in on the jazz scene."

When Nica arrived in Mexico City, she developed a friendship with a fellow jazz fan who offered to get her the latest records (since Jules made no secret of his antipathy to the style). "I would go to his pad to hear them," she explained many years later. "I couldn't have listened to them in my own house, with that atmosphere!" And it was there, while listening to an album of excerpts from Duke Ellington's suite "Black, Brown and Beige," that Nica claims to have had something of a spiritual awakening, or as she expressed it in an interview near the end of her life, it "was in Mexico, when I was in the throes of the diplomatic life, [that] I got a call."

Although Nica could not bring to mind the title of the specific composition, based on the details of her description, it is likely that her revelation was inspired by the opening section of Ellington's ambitious forty-five-minute magnum opus, a piece that was simply titled "Work." Meant to evoke the first stage of the "Negro's" life in America, the music's plaintive sonorities are gradually brightened by what Ellington described in the liner notes to the original album as "a 'way back' figure—heroic, robust," intended to suggest "the hope that a better day would dawn for his race in this new land." Whether or not she was conscious of it at the time, Nica recognized in Ellington's evocation of suffering and eventual redemption a rallying cry for her own liberation. "I heard that," she recalled of this life-altering moment, "and I really got some message . . . that I belonged where that music was, that there was something I was supposed to do . . . was supposed to be involved in it in some way. And I never really got such a strong message . . . and it wasn't long afterwards that it happened. That I cut out from there and got involved and stayed involved for the rest of my life."

WHILE "BLACK, BROWN AND BEIGE" is now considered one of Ellington's masterpieces, it proved to be a frustrating juncture in the arc of the composer's career. After working for a decade on the loosely programmatic work, subtitled "A Tone Parallel to the History of the Negro in America," the piece premiered on January 23, 1943, at the composer's long-awaited Carnegie Hall debut. The concert, organized as a fund-raiser for Russian war relief, attracted a number of notable figures from beyond the swing-era fan base, including First Lady Eleanor Roosevelt. And in addition to hard-core fans and members of the jazz community eager to celebrate what was also the twentieth anniversary of Ellington's band, a number of classical music critics were in attendance, attracted both by his ambitious program and by the prestigious venue.

Jazz had made its debut on the Carnegie Hall stage five years earlier at a historic 1938 concert by Benny Goodman's big band, which climaxed with an incendiary version of "Sing, Sing, Sing" that had the sell-out crowd dancing in the aisles. It was an evening that also included performances by smaller groups drawn from Goodman's pioneering interracial ensemble (featuring Lionel Hampton and Teddy Wilson); and in yet another bold assault on the prevailing racial barriers, the program concluded with an all-star jam session comprising members of the Ellington Orchestra along with a couple of Count Basie's stalwarts, like Lester Young, who had recently arrived in the Big Apple from their Kansas City stomping grounds.

Though Benny Goodman and Duke Ellington may have shared a postracial vision of jazz—Duke Ellington famously declared that there were really only two valid musical categories, "good and bad"—Duke had entered Carnegie Hall on a mission to overcome an even more difficult hurdle. For unlike Goodman, who was content with being a pop star, Ellington was committed to forging a modern, distinctly American music that could stand alongside the great works of European classical music. "Black, Brown and Beige" marked his boldest effort to do just that.

The premiere of Ellington's composition succeeded in uniting the jazz and classical music critics at Carnegie Hall. Both declared it a failure. The record producer and jazz impresario John Hammond (who had masterminded Goodman's 1938 Carnegie concert) bemoaned Duke's attempt to discard "the blues form in order to make music of 'greater significance,'" while the *New York Herald Tribune* critic Paul Bowles wrote that Ellington's composition had simply proven that "the whole attempt to view jazz as a form of art music should be discouraged." Ellington was heartbroken and never performed the piece in public again.

Ironically, just a few weeks earlier—and only a few short blocks from Carnegie Hall—a jazz quintet was making its debut at the bottom of a crowded bill at the Onyx Club on 52nd Street. Its members were also making a conscious effort to create music that was both modern and American, but they were taking an approach very different from the maestro's.

Frustrated by rigid swing-era conventions, the young musicians at the Onyx Club sought to reinstate the primacy of improvisation; inspired by more adventurous elders, like Coleman Hawkins, they looked beyond the standard jazz chord structures to unlock a new world of harmonic possibilities; by reclaiming the music's polyrhythmic roots, they extricated themselves from the straitjacket of swing's dance-oriented rhythms; and, unwilling to accept the restrictive role of entertainer or wear the mask of minstrelsy, they demanded to be accepted as artists. As the band's coleader Dizzy Gillespie memorably put it, "We felt like we were liberated people, and we acted like liberated people."

At the time, John Birks Gillespie was a twenty-seven-year-old trumpeter whose blazing talent had already won him a reputation as one of the hottest new soloists on the scene and whose subversive antics (he had supposedly thrown spitballs at vocalist Cab Calloway from his perch in the trumpet section) had already earned him his enduring nickname. Dizzy's hastily assembled band was not only integrated racially (the pianist, George Wallington, was white), but its members included both seasoned swing-era pros (the bassist and coleader, Oscar Pettiford, and saxophonist Don Byas) and an adventurous neophyte (the nineteen-year-old drum prodigy Max Roach). Although he would quickly replace some of the group with more like-minded associates, the "opening at the Onyx Club," Dizzy proclaimed in his autobiography, "represented the birth of the bebop era."

There are many versions of how the onomatopoetic label "bebop" first became attached to the new jazz style Dizzy brought to 52nd Street, but the consensus is that it didn't originate with the musicians themselves. They simply described what they were doing as "playing modern." In the early 1940s, only a handful of New York–based musicians were involved in the revolutionary new style, and perhaps a couple of hundred jazz insiders even knew it existed. Prior to Gillespie's 1943 Onyx Club debut, one of the only places one could hear the emerging bebop revolution was an out-of-the-way Harlem hangout called Minton's Playhouse. It was there, in after-hours jam sessions, that a corps of jazz insurgents had begun to devise a new approach to playing jazz and to embody a new attitude about their role as musicians.

Located at 210 West 118th Street, adjacent to the Hotel Cecil—a favorite refuge for musicians visiting the Big Apple—Minton's Playhouse had a couple of things going for it, beginning with its favorable location near Harlem landmarks like the Apollo Theater. And since the club's owner, Henry Minton, was also the first black delegate to the New York chapter of the American Federation of Musicians, the uptown nightspot was able to skirt union rules that restricted clubs from featuring the free-wheeling jam sessions that had always been the lifeblood of jazz innovation. But it was the hospitable nature and entrepreneurial skills of the club's manager, Teddy Hill, that were most responsible for attracting the local talent and big-name stars that made the place so special.

Although the pay was negligible ("I never got paid," Dizzy Gillespie asserted), Teddy Hill treated the musicians well, and as Dizzy also recalled, "There was always some food around." Hill assembled an energetic young house band to serve as a foundation for weekly jam sessions that attracted high-profile performers like Coleman Hawkins, Lester Young, Benny Goodman, and Roy Eldridge. As the veteran pianist and arranger Mary Lou Williams (who would become a mentor to the modernists as well as a lifelong friend of Nica's) recalled, "Sometimes you couldn't get into Minton's for the musicians and instruments."

Eventually the small stage got so crowded with ambitious young guns looking to make their rep that the Minton's mainstays began to develop strategies to shut them out. "On afternoons before a session," Gillespie explained, "Thelonious Monk and I began to work out some complex variations on chords and the like, and we used them at night to scare away the no-talent guys." But soon, he went on, the collaborators became "more and more interested in what we were doing *as music*." Painstakingly, Gillespie and the other core members of Minton's band— including Kenny Clarke, a relentlessly innovative drummer who was the band's de facto leader; Charlie Christian, a brilliant twenty-one-year-old electric guitarist who had recently been recruited by Benny Goodman; and Thelonious Monk, an obscure twenty-two-year-old pianist—devised the rhythmic and harmonic revolution that would shatter swing-era orthodoxies. Before long they were aided in this endeavor by a Kansas City–based saxophonist who had recently arrived in New York.

In 1939, Charlie Parker was a nineteen-year-old alto saxophonist who had already honed his skills as a sideman in a couple of blues-oriented big bands, been married and had a kid, picked up a permanent nickname (Yardbird, or simply Bird), and acquired what would become a lifelong heroin habit. While the in crowd at Minton's was conducting its nightly experiments, Parker was washing dishes at a Harlem nightclub so he could listen to the piano god Art Tatum and sitting in at Clark Monroe's Uptown House, another Harlem after-hours spot. "I'd been getting bored with the stereotyped [chord] changes that were being used all the time," Parker remembered, "and I kept thinking there's bound to be something else. I could hear it sometimes but I couldn't play it."

The story of Bird's breakthrough—like most everything else in the saxophonist's short, turbulent life—has become a cornerstone of bebop mythology. It was December 1939, and Parker was jamming in the back room of a third-tier joint named Dan Wall's Chili House with a local guitar player named Biddy Fleet. As they were working their way through a popular swing-era tune, "Cherokee," Parker began pushing the song's unusual chord structure into ever-expanding new variations. Suddenly, he claimed, "I could play the thing I'd been hearing." At that moment, he would later recount, "I became alive."

On a brief return to Kansas City, Bird secured a spot in a band led by the pianist Jay McShann that was about to hit the road for a gig at Harlem's "Home of Happy Feet," the Savoy Ballroom. Word soon spread about the band's hot new saxophonist. But hearing Parker's hard-edged keening sound, startling inventiveness, and dazzling virtuosity for the first time proved to be a sobering experience. According to the trumpeter Howard McGhee, "We all stood there with our mouths open because we hadn't heard anybody play a horn like that. [He] was playing stuff we'd never heard before." When the crowd from Minton's came by to check him out, they recognized the obvious affinities of Parker's unique approach to their own musical innovations. As the drummer Kenny Clarke put it, Bird "was running the same way we were, but he was way out ahead of us."

A few months later, Parker and Gillespie were hired by the bandleader Earl Hines and began sharing musical ideas that would be crucial in advancing the modernist agenda. Gillespie contributed some of the advanced harmonic concepts he had picked up at Minton's (mostly from Monk), while Parker introduced him to the rhythmic restructurings he was using to recast standard melodic lines. The pair would soon emerge as bebop's dynamic duo and establish such a profound rapport that Dizzy famously described Bird as "the other half of my heartbeat."

Bebop had yet to make its way into the mainstream, but its essential elements—cascading streams of evenly divided eighth notes, a sizzling beat carried by the drummer's ride cymbal (punctuated by explosive "bombs" from the bass drum), improvisations that surged across bar lines, and chord progressions that extended far beyond the standard jazz vocabulary—had become fairly well established by the early 1940s. But when bebop finally found its way onto disk in 1945, following a two-year recording ban called by the musicians' union to secure jukebox and radio royalties, listeners were shocked not only by the new style's rhythmic and harmonic advances but by the disorienting speed at which it was played. In fact, bebop's incendiary tempos, reflective of the rapid social transformations and technological advances that had emerged by the beginning of the war, would be a key element in a broader modernist movement in the arts that was taking shape in New York City during this period.

Just as the beboppers at Minton's were devising a transgressive form of popular music, a few blocks away, in Columbia University dorm rooms and the bars of upper Broadway, the founding members of the Beat Generation were forging a free-associative, confessional style of writing that subverted conventional concepts of form and craft. A little further afield, in the cold-water flats and abandoned industrial lofts of lower Manhattan, the pioneers of abstract expressionism were overturning centuries-old artistic traditions to create works that embodied the prevailing values of speed and spontaneity. If, as the nineteenth-century critic Walter Pater proposed, "all art constantly aspires to the condition of music," in the mid-1940s, the music to which New York's most forward-leaning writers and painters aspired was jazz.

LIKE MANY MEMBERS of his generation, Jack Kerouac had been enthralled by the dynamic rhythms of the swing-era big bands he listened to on the radio as a teenager. Of course, what he heard was the result of the same racial segregation that was imposed on most areas of American life. The national radio networks, as well as most of the independent local stations, were vigilant in protecting the homes of the dominant culture against the intrusion of any and all soundwaves of African-American origin. That left a lineup of all-white big bands, ranging from "sweet" orchestras playing lush arrangements of popular songs to "hot" bands who provided a propulsive soundtrack for even the most fervent jitterbugs.

After graduating from Lowell High School in 1939, Kerouac left the red-brick Massachusetts mill town for New York City, where he had been awarded a football scholarship to Columbia University. In order to bolster his academic credentials and put on a few pounds before his freshman season, Jack was encouraged to spend a year at Horace Mann, a Columbia-affiliated prep school popular with New York's middle-class intellectual elite. It was there that he met Seymour Wyse, a sophisticated young jazz buff and proto-hipster who served as Kerouac's guide to the riches of African-American culture. Interestingly, Wyse, like Nica's children, was a Jewish evacuee of the London Blitz, and like Nica herself, he had been captivated by the recordings of the black jazz bands that had found an enthusiastic audience on the other side of the Atlantic.

Under Wyse's tutelage, Kerouac was introduced to top-shelf black bands led by Fletcher Henderson, Duke Ellington, and Count Basie, whose star soloist, Lester Young, would become one of Kerouac's greatest musical inspirations. From a perch in the balcony of the Apollo Theater he also got to hear the exuberant Jimmie Lunceford band and for the first time experienced black music live and in person. Soon Jack was writing a jazz column in the Horace Mann newspaper, and in a review celebrating the "real jazz" to which he had been recently converted, he identified a set of musical values that would eventually become the foundation of his literary philosophy and revolutionary prose.

In the article, the seventeen-year-old Kerouac, who had already committed himself to becoming a writer, expressed his new enthusiasm for a form of jazz that "has not been prearranged—free-for-all ad lib," and he celebrated "the outburst of passionate musicians who pour all their energy into their instruments in the quest for soulful expression and super-improvisation." A decade later, after an abortive academic career, a brief stint in the merchant marine, and a literary apprenticeship that culminated with the publication of a sprawling, Wolfean novel (*The Town and the City*), Kerouac abandoned traditional ideas about the writer's craft (of carefully honed revisions and painful quests for *le mot juste*) to create a freewheeling jazz-inspired style.

During his freshman year at Columbia, Kerouac also fell in with another precocious jazz buff and Horace Mann alum, Jerry Newman, who had already been won over by the modernists at Minton's, located a couple of blocks from the university's uptown campus. Taking advantage of Kerouac's enthusiasm for the music, Newman recruited him to assist in a private recording project. With the tacit approval of the management and musicians, Newman had begun documenting the jam sessions, both at Minton's and at Clark Monroe's Uptown House, on an unwieldy hundred-pound "portable" recording device.

The acetate disks Jerry Newman produced are among the only recordings of the evolution of bebop at its source. A few years later, when these sessions were released on Esoteric Records, Newman's independent label, a particularly catchy improvisation by Dizzy Gillespie (on the chord changes of the pop tune "Exactly Like You") was simply titled "Kerouac," in honor of the aspiring novelist. One of only a handful of white regulars on the scene, Jack often bragged that the first time he smoked weed was when Lester Young shared a joint with him outside Minton's Playhouse.

Beginning with Kerouac's career-making second novel, *On the Road*, jazz became a vital element in his fictional milieu but, more important, the essential influence on his writing. Called upon to explain the sources of his dynamic prose style, Kerouac wrote an essay titled "Essentials of Spontaneous Prose," which made explicit his links to the jazz musicians he had been exposed to since his arrival in New York. He likened his creative process to "*blowing* (as per jazz musician) on the subject of image," and equated his use of "the vigorous dash separating rhetorical breathing" to a "jazz musician drawing breath between outblown phrases." His new mantra: "Tap from yourself the song of yourself, *blow!—now!—your* way is your only way."

Kerouac's principles of spontaneous prose and its explicit links to the improvisatory ethos of jazz became the foundation of Beat Generation literary theory. In 1959, when Allen Ginsberg was asked about the rhetorical innovations of his great Beat anthem, "Howl," he cited the influence of both Kerouac *and* Lester Young: "Lester Young, actually, is what I was thinking about . . . 'Howl' is all 'Lester Leaps In.' And I got that from Kerouac. Or paid attention to it on account of Kerouac, surely he made me listen to it." Of course it was Ginsberg who had famously dubbed Kerouac's transformational method of composition "spontaneous bop prosody" in the first place.

Having rejected contemporary literary conventions as well as middle-class morality, Western religion, the military-industrial complex, and the era's heterosexual hegemony, the Beats turned to black culture as an anti-dote to the spiritual and aesthetic enervation of the cultural mainstream. By valorizing the "instinctive" and "anti-intellectual" wellsprings of their creativity, however, Kerouac also opened himself to accusations that his descriptions of black jazz musicians were distorted by "primitivism." Though this criticism certainly has some validity, Kerouac was remarkably prescient in recognizing the sociological transformation that musicians like Monk, Parker, and Gillespie represented. In his essay "The Beginning of Bebop," for example, Kerouac argues that the irreverence and ironic detachment of these pioneering African-American musicians—their rec-ognition of "the goof of life," as he put it—made them "not only misplaced in a white nation but mis-noticed for who they were."

Among his peers, for example, Charlie Parker was considered "an intellectual" (Miles Davis) as well as "a great philosopher" (the bassist Milt Hinton). As Hinton explained it, Bird didn't always conform to the stereotype of bebop's tragic hero. "For some reason, we always got into [talking about] politics," Hinton told the jazz critic Ira Gitler. "Between sets we would play classical music—we would talk about politics and race and really deep things like the solution for blacks in America." According to Davis, Bird "used to read novels, history, stuff like that. And he could hold a conversation with almost anybody on all kinds of things." Nor did Bird's legendary virtuosity mystically emerge from some deep wellspring of the African soul, a natural manifestation of black consciousness; it was in fact the consequence of obsessive practice and unwavering dedication.

Nor, truth be told, were Kerouac and the other Beat Genera-tion writers simply sounding their barbaric yawps over the rooftops of Greenwich Village in ecstatic bursts of inspiration. Not only had they deeply immersed themselves in the great works of world literature (from Whitman and Melville to Dostoevsky and Rimbaud), but they had also engaged in wide-ranging explorations of literary form and theories of rhetoric. As the critic and cultural historian Ann Douglas has pointed out, during the course of his career Kerouac initiated "the most extensive experiment in language and literary form undertaken by an American writer of his generation."

AS KEROUAC WAS DEVISING a theoretical framework for his radical writing style, the painter Jackson Pollack, who had forged his own artistic innovations during this period, was struggling to articulate a new set of aesthetic principles. In a statement that reads like a free-form Beat poem, Pollack declared, "Technic [*sic*] is the result of need—new needs demand new technics—total control—denial of the accidental . . . energy and motion made visible." And just as Kerouac's "spontaneous bop prosody" sought to liberate his writing by embracing the improvisatory approach of "a tenor man drawing a breath and blowing a phrase on his saxophone," Pollack's gestural abstract expressionism was an attempt to transcend the controlling force of consciousness to achieve unimpeded immediacy and directness. Not coincidentally, Pollack was also an avid jazz fan.

According to his wife and fellow artist, Lee Krasner, Pollack's controversial "splatter" or "drip" paintings of the mid-1940s were made to the accompaniment of a jazz soundtrack. "He would get into grooves of listening to his jazz records—day and night . . . for three days running," she told an interviewer. "He thought it was the only really creative thing happening in this country." By 1950, when Pollack painted his gesture-field masterpiece, *Autumn Rhythm*, his swirling splatters and arabesques seemed to pulse with the cadences of a Charlie Parker solo.

But when the Museum of Modern Art issued a CD anthology of Pollack's record collection (in conjunction with a 1999 retrospective), many listeners were surprised by its conservative playlist. Since Pollack had begun concocting his action-oriented abstractions just as the beboppers were forging their dissonance-laced musical experiments, the assumption has always been that the artist was consciously transposing the explosive syncopations of modern jazz directly onto the canvas. But based on Pollack's own collection, a motley assortment of disks by Jelly Roll Morton, Louis Armstrong, Count Basie, Artie Shaw, and Billie Holiday, New York's foremost cutting-edge artist had yet to make the leap to musical modernism.

In truth, the familiar cross-genre analogies linking New York City's post–World War II artistic avant-gardes can be pushed only so far. The beboppers, Beats, and abstract expressionists may have all contributed to forging the era's "culture of spontaneity," but these artistic movements were not always promoting the same aesthetic agenda. For example, when Kerouac slipped a 120-foot-long roll of paper into his typewriter and launched into the three-week prose jag that produced *On the Road*, he may have been channeling the headlong riffs of Bird or Lester Young, but he wasn't engaged in a frontal assault on the European canon. The battle for a distinctly American literature had already been waged—and won—by the Beat Generation's spiritual forefathers, from Walt Whitman to William Carlos Williams. But in 1943, when Jackson Pollack finally took up his brush to fulfill a long-delayed commission from Peggy Guggenheim for a 160-square-foot mural for her New York apartment, his night-long assault on the empty canvas (a rhythmic burst of calligraphic swirls) was energized by his consciousness of a mission that went beyond even the immense borders of the painting itself.

Often referred to as the only purely American art, jazz had been embraced by the fathers of European modernism during the first decades of the twentieth century. Cubists and surrealists from Paris to Zurich, who viewed America—land of the skyscraper, advertising, and the movies—as the engine of modernity, had heralded jazz as the soundtrack of the modern age. Decades later, however, most American artists still looked to Europe as the primary source of cultural legitimacy. A native of Cody, Wyoming, Jackson Pollack seemed to go out of his way to flaunt (at least publicly) his disdain for the lingering Europhilia of his contemporaries. So while his colleagues at the Art Students League were all thrilled that the great Matisse (who had titled a recent series of exuberant collages *Jazz*) might pay them a visit, Pollack notoriously exclaimed, "What do we need those Europeans for!" He then launched himself into the forefront of a movement that would transform America (and particularly New York City) into the art capital of the world.

In his seminal 1952 essay "The American Action Painters," the critic Harold Rosenberg, an early champion of the new generation of New York–based artists, challenged the notion that Pollack, Willem de Kooning, Franz Kline, Philip Guston, and others, were simply participating in a formalist exercise played out in pigment on a flat picture plane (as his chief rival, Clement Greenberg, contended). Instead, according to Rosenberg, each time they picked up a brush, these painters were engaged in a heroic, existential confrontation. "At a certain moment," he memorably observed, "the canvas began to appear to one American artist after another as an arena in which to act—rather than as a space to reproduce."

While Rosenberg's art-world dictum can be applied to the dynamic creative process of the Beat Generation writers and bebop jazz musicians, it also offers a valuable prism through which Nica's life can be seen as yet another expression of the era's cultural zeitgeist. Just as many of New York's most adventurous painters, writers, and musicians had come to conceive of their art as "an arena in which to act," Nica was poised to play out a similar confrontation on the canvas of her own life. And as Rosenberg proposed in his essay, what mattered most—for Nica as much as for her artistic counterparts—was "the revelation contained in the act."

A FEW MONTHS after Nica's arrival in Mexico City, she began making periodic trips to New York, where, through her connection to Teddy Wilson, she gained entrée to the jazz community and developed friendships with musicians from across the entire spectrum of jazz history. In 1951, as she came to the end of one New York getaway, Nica decided to drop by Wilson's Harlem apartment on her way to the airport. In passing, he asked her if she was familiar with a young pianist on the scene named

Thelonious Monk. "I had never even heard of Thelonious," she later admitted. According to Nica, Wilson told her, " 'You can't leave without hearing, "'Round Midnight," ' and he galloped off to get the record."

Listening to the recording on Wilson's phonograph would prove to be a decisive moment in Nica's life. "I couldn't believe my ears," she recalled in an interview a few months before her death. "I had never heard anything remotely like it; I made him play it to me twenty times in a row. "Round Midnight' affected me like nothing else I ever heard." When she described the experience to Max Gordon, she confessed, "The first time I heard Thelonious play "Round Midnight,' I cried." In fact, Nica got so caught up in listening to the record that she missed her flight and didn't return home for a couple of weeks. "And that was that," she told Max. "I asked him [Wilson] to send me anything Thelonious made to Mexico."

By the early 1950s, Nica and Jules were becoming increasingly estranged. According to their eldest son, Patrick, while his parents' marital difficulties were partly the result of their diverging values, they were also deeply rooted in Nica's fraught relationship with her mother, Rozsika. "My father was a very controlling person," Patrick suggested. "He reminded my mother of her own domineering mother. He was adamant about punctuality, while Nica was notorious for being late." Nor did it help, he added, "that my father had no particular interest in the subjects that fascinated her: art and music. He would quip that they were not serious matters."

For her part, Nica joked that the only music her husband enjoyed was military marches—what she described to Nat Hentoff as "the kind with drums." Then she described how Jules would sometimes take out his frustration over her habitual tardiness by destroying her most prized possessions. "He used to break my records when I was late for dinner," she told Hentoff. In a conversation with Max Gordon backstage at the Village Vanguard, she summarized the situation even more succinctly: "Jazz," she declared, "didn't do my marriage any good."

As the mother of five young children, Nica's decision to extend her next New York excursion indefinitely was an act of existential self-assertion at least as consequential as any being played out by the modernists in New York. And though Monk's early masterpiece may have precipitated Nica's departure for the Big Apple, by marrying an aristocratic Jewish banker with deeply held traditional values, Nica had found herself trapped in an environment whose austere rigidity was not unlike the one she had chafed against as a child.

Somehow it always comes back to the *mishbocho*. At least, that's been the moral of many of the most enduring Rothschild narratives, including the following. One day, the story goes, Nathan Rothschild, the founder of the English branch of the family, is approached by his young son, who wants to know how many nations there are in the world. "There are only two you need to bother about," Nathan replies. "There's the *mishbocho*, and there are the others." This constricted notion of "the family" would remain a potent force in every Rothschild generation; for Nica, however, it became a straitjacket from which she would ceaselessly struggle to escape.

But when Nat Hentoff questioned her about her motivation for abandoning her enviable social status in order to cast her lot with a brotherhood of (mostly) black jazz musicians, Nica's response cut through the fog of speculative psychobabble and racial ruminations; it also confirmed how her own formative experiences had prepared her to recognize the essential message of jazz: "It's everything that really matters, everything worth digging," she declared. "It's a desire for freedom. And in all my life, I've never known any people who warmed me as much by their friendship as the jazz musicians I've come to know."

There is also little question that in abandoning the consolations of the traditional nuclear family for a new life within the jazz *mishbocho*, she, like so many of the musicians she idolized, would pay a considerable price for her freedom.

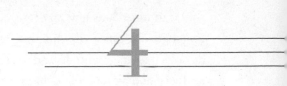

Nica's Dream:
The Birth of
the Jazz Baroness

In 1953, after two years of round-trip forays, Nica's long-deferred dream of living in New York became a reality. Although her husband, Jules, also made the journey from Mexico City to take up his new post as ambassador of France to the United States and Canada, the couple decided to live apart. Their children, except for Janka, a teenager who had a close bond with her mother, remained with Jules, while Nica and her daughter settled into an elegant, antiques-filled suite at the Stanhope Hotel on the Upper East Side.

Nica arrived in the jazz capital of the world just as the music was experiencing a painful period of transition. Over the previous decade, the confident rhythms of the swing era had faded away, and the sense of community that had been forged on the dance floor of the Savoy Ballroom had come apart at the seams. Weakened by wartime attrition, entertainment taxes, and rationing, the big bands that had dominated the jazz mainstream were displaced by a youthful corps of (mostly) draft-deferred modernists.

By the early 1950s, bebop had moved from Minton's to midtown and found its way onto a series of recordings that introduced the new sound to musicians and jazz fans across the country. The vast audience that had coalesced around the celebrated big bands of the previous decade had fragmented. And as the jazz devotees diverged into insular factions passionately debating the authenticity of the New Orleans tradition or the spurious pretensions of bebop, jazz itself was rapidly being displaced from its perch on the Hit Parade and the airwaves. Pop vocalists who had cut their teeth as featured performers in the swing-era orchestras dominated the record charts, while local stations on the edges of the radio dial introduced a rollicking new style of dance music called rhythm and blues, which became the music of choice of the younger generation.

On 52nd Street, the marquees no longer featured the roster of jazz greats, from Billie Holiday and Coleman Hawkins to Charlie Parker and Thelonious Monk. Now one was more likely to encounter billboards promoting Zorita, the exotic snake dancer. So many jazz clubs had either closed or become seedy burlesque houses over the previous few years that *Variety*, the entertainment newspaper, rechristened Swing Street "Strip Row." The historic bebop haven the Three Deuces hung on longer than most, but by the middle of the decade, only Jimmy Ryan's, a Dixieland oasis, and the Hickory House, a piano bar, were still featuring any jazz. However, not long after declaring, "The Street Is Dead: An Obit," the music magazine *Metronome* ran another story suggesting that rumors of the midtown jazz scene's demise may have been at least somewhat exaggerated; its headline: "Jazz Is Dead on 52nd Street and Very Much Alive on B'way."

Broadway had long been home to a variety of popular music venues, from dance halls like Roseland and upscale cabarets like the Latin Quarter to movie palaces like the Strand and Paramount, which featured big-name performers between daily screenings. By the early 1950s, however, a short stretch of the famed thoroughfare, just east and west of 52nd Street, had also become the setting for new nightspots that showcased the stars of bebop. The first to open was the Royal Roost, a former fried chicken emporium, which wittily billed itself as the Metropolitan Bop-era House. It was quickly followed by Bop City, a short-lived club that added pop and R&B to its bebop menu, and by the notorious Charlie Parker–themed venue Birdland, which immodestly touted itself as "The Jazz Corner of the World."

Undaunted by the recent upheavals in her life and in the local jazz culture, Nica threw herself into Big Apple nightlife. After purchasing a sporty Rolls-Royce, she began making the rounds of the local jazz clubs and forging bonds with the men who inhabited them. Soon she had also picked up a new nickname, "the Baroness," conferred on her by a musical fraternity that already had both a Duke and a Count.

Now forty years old, Nica projected an aura of international chic. Despite having had five children, she retained a shapely figure that was enhanced by a designer wardrobe of elegantly tailored suits and little black dresses set off by a collection of tasteful accessories. "You could tell by her pearls—four strands of very good pearls. She was a *vrai* Rothschild," recalled Jean Bach, a fashion-conscious jazz fan and local radio producer who maintained a lifelong friendship with Nica. Like so many others who had close encounters with the Baroness, Bach can still conjure up the lingering scent of her expensive perfume; and if the photos from this period are any guide, Nica's recent liberation had turned up the wattage of her dazzling smile to match the big-city lights.

Nica also made an immediate and lasting impression on the reserved British-born pianist (and future host of the long-running NPR show *Piano Jazz*), Marian McPartland, who was leading a popular trio at 52nd Street's Hickory House. One night, McPartland was taking a break between sets when she noticed the Baroness sitting in her Rolls outside the entrance to Birdland. Nica invited the pianist into the car and whispered that she had something she wanted to show her. It was an expensive-looking leatherbound book; but when Nica opened it, Marian saw a bottle of whiskey tucked into a niche cut into its pages. After a couple of drinks, she headed back to the club, but the memory of the Baroness stayed with her. "Nica had long black hair hanging down her back and a very upper-class British accent," McPartland recalled four decades later. "And she would swear away. I used to get so amused by her."

Another doyenne of New York's jazz scene who can still recall Nica's arrival is Phoebe Jacobs, who—at least initially—was not impressed. Jacobs, a jazz-world insider who has worked most of her adult life as a publicist, promoter, and freelance manager for such major figures as Benny Goodman, Louis Armstrong, Sarah Vaughn, and Peggy Lee, was born in the Bronx in 1918. At ninety, Jacobs still retained her classic "New Yawk" accent, and she salted her stories of the jazz demimonde with earthy epithets and vintage slang. She remembers being introduced to Nica in the Stanhope's bar by a mutual friend who was also living in the hotel at the time. At first glance, however, the Baroness failed to live up her image as a glamorous Rothschild heiress: "I didn't particularly care for her mink coat. I mean, my mother's coat was ten times more fashionable."

While the Baroness's exotic automobile heralded her appearance on the scene with the intended fanfare ("That lady's here with the Rolls!" Jacobs remembers the doorman at one club announcing), Nica's passionate engagement with the insular jazz community also aroused considerable suspicion. According to Jacobs, musicians were soon asking each other, "What does this broad want?" or, more pointedly, "Who's she makin' it with?" And after columnists like Walter Winchell began to seed their surveys of goings-on about town with not-so-subtle swipes at Nica's race-blind associations, veteran members of New York society would note her entrance at El Morocco or the 21 Club with barely suppressed smirks.

At the same time, Jacobs believes that Nica's illustrious heritage made it considerably easier for her to overcome the negative innuendoes than it might have been. "Her name was magic for her," Jacobs contends; but before long, it had also become apparent that her devotion to the music was genuine and deep. "If you were a jazz musician, honey, you were on her love list." After witnessing Nica's numerous acts of kindness and generosity, Jacobs realized that the Baroness was nothing less than a woman on a mission. "Anyone who needed her, she was going to be there," she explains, "and her resources were endless."

Phoebe Jacobs had a prime vantage point from which to observe Nica's progress within the subculture of New York nightlife. When Jacobs was about ten years old, her father ("a bootlegger and gambler") opened a jazz joint called the Club Calais, while her maternal uncle, Ralph Watkins, a former big-band saxophonist whom she describes as "the Jewish Rex Harrison," had already become one of New York's most prominent entertainment entrepreneurs. During 52nd Street's golden age, Watkins operated a string of clubs, including Kelly's Stable, a popular venue featuring both swing-era giants and bebop pioneers. Over the next two decades he would have a significant stake in the Royal Roost, Birdland, the Embers, and Basin Street East as well.

According to Jacobs, who began working as a coat-check girl in her uncle's clubs while still in her teens, Watkins was a devoted Anglophile who had his suits custom-made in London and also owned a Rolls-Royce. Although he was a popular host and well-liked by the musicians (a rare phenomenon), he wasn't a "schmoozer." But whenever Nica dropped by, Jacobs recalls, the two of them "would sit in his office and talk for hours. He had a lot of regard for her." He also went out of his way to dispel some of the more unsavory rumors about the British-born jazzophile. "You've got to be grateful for this woman," Watkins would lecture wary musicians. "She's like a lighthouse in a storm."

The only thing that Jacobs still has trouble comprehending was Nica's obsession with Thelonious Monk. "I mean, people used to *avoid* Thelonious Monk!" she exclaims with undiminished incredulity. "We thought he was a kook!" In fact, a decade after he helped lay the foundations of the modern sound ("Monk is the guy who started it all," the drummer Art Blakey once declared), the pianist remained a tough sell even within the hard-core bebop fan base. And as other members of the Minton's vanguard were churning out hot new disks for specialized independent labels, Monk's unorthodox piano style and uncompromising aesthetic vision delayed his own recording career for years.

On the rare occasions when Monk was hired as a sideman, there was usually flak about his spare, angular piano style, his "weird" chords, or his "bizarre" behavior. After booking Monk for a gig on 52nd Street, Coleman Hawkins faced a barrage of complaints. "I used to get it every night," Hawkins recalled. " 'Why don't you get yourself a piano player?' And, 'What's that stuff he's playing?' " Blue Note, an adventurous indie label, finally did sign Monk to a record contract in the late 1940s, but immediately met resistance even from their most reliable distributors. When Lorraine Gordon, who at the time was married to Blue Note co-owner Alfred Lion, took the first batch of Monk records—including his classic composition "'Round Midnight"—to a Harlem record store, the owner told her flat out, "He can't play, lady. What are you doing up here? The guy has two left hands."

MONK'S BLUE NOTE recording of "'Round Midnight" may have sparked Nica's desire to settle in New York, but by the time she made her move to the city, it was virtually impossible for her to hear him perform it. And this wasn't only because of his outsider status within the modern-ist mainstream. In 1951, Monk had been caught up in a drug bust, and while it's generally agreed that the heroin actually belonged to his friend and protégé Bud Powell, Monk took the fall.

For sixty days, Monk languished in a cell on Rikers Island; more con-sequentially, the authorities used the arrest to revoke his "cabaret card," a New York State license required to work in any entertainment venue that sold alcohol. Six years would pass before Monk was able to get his card restored. "Every day I would plead with him," his wife, Nellie, recalled, 'Thelonious, get yourself out of this trouble. You didn't do anything." But Monk refused to compromise his integrity by informing on his friends. "I have to walk the streets when I get out," he insisted. Thus began what Nellie referred to as the "un-years."

During this period, Nellie, who was making forty-five dollars a week working in a tailor shop and at other low-wage jobs, became the Monk family's main source of income. "Thelonious had trouble get-ting work even before he lost the card," she observed philosophically. "Therefore, it wasn't a sudden total calamity." And even during the most difficult times, Thelonious and Nellie took strength from each other. "We felt each of us was doing the best he could," she told Nat Hentoff. And despite their desperate financial situation, Thelonious always maintained his self-respect and equanimity. "He didn't get bitter,"

Nellie recalled. "Anybody else with less strength would have snapped." For years, she explained, "There was no money, no place to go. A complete blank. He even had to pay to get into Birdland."

Ironically, while Monk was relegated to the sidelines on a bum rap, Nica had no trouble getting her daily dose of jazz from bands that harbored one or more of the dozens of junkies who populated the bebop movement. While there are a lot of theories about why heroin became the scourge of the postwar jazz scene, one of the primary factors was the sheer availability of the drug. At the end of World War II, the Sicilian Mafia reopened the supply lines from Turkey and began assiduously marketing the drug, mainly in the black community. This is the historical basis for the scene in *The Godfather* when the five families approve a new trafficking scheme despite Don Corleone's objections. "In my city," one of the other dons announces, "we would keep the traffic in the dark people, the coloreds. They're animals anyway, so let them lose their souls." And since many of New York's Mob-connected nightclubs, including Birdland, often functioned as drug supermarkets with a live jazz soundtrack, the musicians were easy targets.

Meanwhile, in cities across the country drug squads were often deployed to intimidate black jazz musicians, a policy fueled by a toxic blend of racism and sexual hysteria. As Harry Shapiro points out in *Waiting for the Man: The Story of Drugs and Popular Music*, "Black musicians were prime targets for harassment. The police hated seeing black and white together, especially if a white girl was on the arm of a black musician. Successful musicians driving new cars could expect regular shakedowns and the sudden appearance of drugs in the car once the officers had done their search."

Heroin's ascendancy during the bebop movement can also be seen as both a symptom of the bebopper's marginalized role in the pop music mainstream and an emblem of hipness worn (along with berets, shades, and goatees) by a generation of black jazz modernists who were challenging the vestiges of minstrelsy they associated with their big-band predecessors. For their white cohorts, the drug became a way of symbolically connecting to their musical heroes. As the young white trumpeter Red

Rodney ruefully explained, "Heroin was our badge . . . It gave us membership in a unique club, and for this membership, we gave up everything else in the world."

More than anyone, it was the movement's supreme hero who became the face that launched a thousand junkies. Having grown up in Kansas City, a major distribution center for heroin, Charlie Parker had been an addict since he was seventeen. While every young jazz musician coveted Parker's creative genius and personal charisma (which were unattainable), anyone could simply shoot up and "be like Bird." Red Rodney, who played in Parker's band during the early 1950s, was only one of many who tried. A roll call of the decade's heroin addicts, black and white, would include Gerry Mulligan, Jackie McLean, Stan Getz, Chet Baker, Miles Davis, Art Blakey, Billie Holiday, Milt Jackson, Art Pepper, Fats Navarro, Anita O'Day, Tadd Dameron, Wardell Grey, Dexter Gordon, and Hampton Hawes. And that's just scratching the surface.

By entering the world of New York's jazz modernists, the Baroness had joined a highly dysfunctional subculture. "Don't forget," Phoebe Jacobs declared, "we're talking about some guys who were alcoholics, who were drug addicts and led some pretty sick, distorted lives." Yet Nica was able to see past these shadows to their genius, and heard only the beauty they created. And she willingly accepted the harsh consequences of her choice. According to Jacobs, "She knew she wasn't going to get acceptance [from conventional society], and she said, 'Who needs it?' " As Jacobs describes it, Nica was simply pursuing personal fulfillment. "Don't think for one moment that she was sacrificing anything, man. It gave her an opportunity to play a role that she wanted for herself, and she did it with style and grace. It takes a lot of class—and she had that!"

Yet of all the charges that were leveled against Nica during these years, the most pervasive and problematic criticism has focused on her response—or lack of it—to the era's heroin epidemic. Even sympathetic members of the jazz community who weren't caught up in the hysteria of the times wondered how she could shut her eyes to the self-destructive behavior of the musicians she befriended. As the wife of one club owner put it, "I wouldn't say she isn't a good friend, but I would say she's not a good friend for someone who needs some lecturing rather than permissive acceptance."

Suspicions about Nica's role in bebop's drug-ravaged jazz scene even filtered into a 1959 short story titled "The Pursuer," by Julio Cortázar, about a heroin-addicted alto saxophonist named Johnny Carter. Although the enigmatic and amoral character Tica (a.k.a. "the marquesa") is depicted as both deeply attuned to the music and "absurdly generous," it's she who bears the brunt of the blame for the hero's downfall. "I'm sure as can be," says the story's narrator, "that the marquesa was the one who got the junk for him." While in fact Tica is no more complicit than other members of the saxophonist's inner circle, her unique ability to emerge unscathed from the wake of Carter's self-destructiveness makes her an object of resentment: "Tica's doing very well," says one. "Of course, it's easy for her. She arrives at the last minute and all she has to do is open her handbag, and it's all fixed up."

In her defense, Nica claimed that she had tried to persuade musicians to "kick," but with little success. "I used to think I could help," she told Nat Hentoff in their 1960 interview, "but no one person can. They have to do it alone." Eventually, however, she did learn to put some limits on her unconditional acceptance. "I had to find out for myself that one has to stay away from them. Addiction makes them too ignoble, and you can't be safe around them." What she could do, however, was provide them with a safety net.

Among those who had reason to grateful for this effort was the young pianist Hampton Hawes, who had come to New York from L.A. with a glowing musical reputation and a serious heroin habit. In his autobiography, *Raise Up Off Me*, Hawes explains that the Baroness had "a number you could call from anywhere and get a private cab. If I was sick or fucked up I'd call the number and the cab would come and carry me directly to her pad." Hawes soon discovered that this was just the beginning of her benevolence. "She'd give money to anyone who was broke, bring a bag of groceries to their families, [and] help them get their cabaret cards, which you needed to work in New York." Although there was never a shortage of speculation about her motives, Hawes saw things more simply. "The only important truth," he came to realize, "is that she loved music and musicians and dedicated her life to them."

Nica's Stanhope Hotel suite quickly became a nonstop jazz salon, as performers dropped by after gigs to talk, spin records on her top-of-the-line hi-fi, and order up from room service. The pianist Horace Silver recalls a typical visit in his autobiography, *Let's Get to the Nitty Gritty*: "She had a huge record collection, and Doug [Watkins] and I made it a point to visit her around dinner time, because she always invited us to eat. We ordered filet mignon from the restaurant downstairs, and the waiters wheeled the meal in on a trolley and served it to us." As another of her well-fed guests confessed, "We didn't dig going up there just for the meal, but it was a ball to be waited on like that."

Another charter member of Nica's inner circle was Freddie Redd, a young bebop pianist who had arrived in New York a few years before the Baroness, following a stint in the army. By the time Nica began making the scene, Redd had already been sitting in with the likes of Bird, Bean, and Blakey—three of her all-time jazz heroes. As the pianist tells it, he and Nica quickly became "hang-out buddies." She would show up at his gigs, and when he wasn't working, she'd drive up to his apartment around midnight and honk her horn, and he would come down (either alone or with his wife) and they'd head off into the night. When the clubs closed, they'd wind up in Nica's hotel's suite to sip some Chivas Regal ("That was her favorite"), listen to records, and talk till dawn.

Nica never revealed much about herself, but over time Redd did learn a little about her privileged childhood and her wartime exploits. "Nica brought a whole other level of sophistication to the scene. She always knew just what to say and what to do," he remarked many years later. "Everybody loved Nica—I mean, she was irresistible! We needed somebody like her. I mean, she was a real patron. She gave us so much assistance and respect. It was wonderful."

Before long, the musicians began to repay her many kindnesses in one of the few ways they could—by dedicating compositions to her. Within a few years of her arrival, an entire medley of tunes had been written in her honor by grateful musicians including Freddie Redd ("Nica Steps Out"),

Gigi Gryce ("Nica's Tempo"), Kenny Drew ("Blues for Nica"), and Kenny Dorham ("Tonica"). Two of the other tunes written for the Baroness have taken their place among the most durable standards in the jazz repertoire: Thelonious Monk's haunting ballad "Pannonica" and Horace Silver's Latin-tinged classic "Nica's Dream." As Silver explained, "She loved the music and she loved the musicians," and these tunes were simply a "tribute to her because she was so good to us." Not that Nica's open-door policy sat very well with the Stanhope management, especially considering the dark-hued demographic of those who came to call.

Located on the corner of Fifth Avenue and 81st Street, directly across from the Metropolitan Museum of Art and Central Park, the Stanhope Hotel was the epitome of restrained elegance, a world apart from both the tumult of midtown tourist joints and the upscale glitz of the Plaza and the Waldorf-Astoria. The slender, fifteen-story, neo–Italian Renaissance limestone tower, which opened in 1926, was designed by Rosario Candela, a Sicilian immigrant who had a knack for creating buildings that reflected (in the words of architecture critic Paul Goldberger) "the greatest traditions of old money." On the basis of his grand residential buildings along Park and Fifth Avenues, Candela has been given credit for "the most magnificent assemblage of extraordinary apartments ever produced by any architect." Over the years, the Stanhope became the refuge of royalty (Prince Rainier of Monaco and his princess, the former Grace Kelly, made it their New York headquarters) as well as a discreet setting for romantic trysts (movie tough guy Edward G. Robinson supposedly settled his mistress there for a number of years). Somewhat later, its reputation for discretion made the hotel the fictional setting for intimate liaisons in works by John Irving, John Guare, and Anne Rice, and in a couple of episodes of *Sex and the City*.

Once Nica's guests made it past the disapproving stares of the concierge and up to her suite in the service elevator they were forced to use by the hotel management, they found themselves in a world unlike any they had ever known. Hampton Hawes never forgot his own awestruck first visit: "A lot of paintings and funny drapes, a chandelier like in an old movie palace, Steinway concert grand in the corner. I thought, 'This is where you live if you own Grant's Tomb and the Chase Manhattan Bank.' " For black jazz musicians, who were typically refused accommodations in considerably more modest lodgings, the silver service carts, filet mignon, and crystal chandeliers provided a rare taste of the Rothschild lifestyle—as did Nica's silver Rolls-Royce, which also found its way into a more than a few of their memoirs.

But it wasn't just the Rolls that stuck in musicians' memories. What comes across most vividly in their recollections was the hair-raising thrill of riding in a car with the Baroness behind the wheel. By all accounts, Nica was both an irrepressible speed demon and a skillful driver. "She always drove as if she were competing at Le Mans," her son Patrick told one interviewer, "and she paid very little attention to traffic rules." In fact, his father was so concerned about her recklessness that he had a clause placed in their divorce agreement stipulating that none of their children could be in the car while she was driving—"a condition that was largely ignored," according to Patrick.

Over the previous two decades, Nica had journeyed across much of the globe. She had traveled from the cloistered opulence of the Rothschilds' country estates to the gilded elegance of Château d'Abondant and from the blood-soaked battlefields of North Africa to the insular hush of French embassies in Norway and Mexico. But according to Phoebe Jacobs, "it was only when she settled in New York"—at the age of forty—"that she first started to be born." As Jacobs explains it, "She wasn't born in London. She was nobody in London—she was the daughter of royalty. In America she became *somebody*. Here in America she was accepted for herself, she made a place for herself."

THROUGHOUT THIS PERIOD, Nica visited England regularly to see her siblings and old friends, and in the fall of 1953 she provided logistical support for Teddy Wilson's first solo tour of England and Scotland. In what would be a prelude to the notoriety she would soon generate in the New York gossip columns, the Baroness became fodder for the British tabloids just by showing up to meet Wilson at the airport

("Blues Man Gets the Blue Rolls" was the headline of one article). In his memoir, however, Wilson describes with relish the royal treatment he received as Nica personally drove him across the country to each of his performances. "I saw it at its best," he wrote, "because we were riding in a new Rolls-Royce, a four-door sedan, with the sunroof open, at highway speeds."

Nica also happened to be in London in the spring of 1954, when she received exciting news: Thelonious Monk had just been booked to perform at the upcoming Paris Jazz Festival. Monk was something of a wild card in the lineup of more familiar American and European acts on the bill. According to Monk's biographer, Robin Kelley, he had been "a last-minute addition to the program [and] none of the advance publicity mentioned Monk or prepared the way for his unique brand of jazz." Though some of the pianist's recordings could be found in Left Bank record stores, Monk was an obscure figure for French fans, most of whom were either swing-era diehards or aficionados of the traditional New Orleans style (so-called Dixieland jazz), which they considered the essence of authenticity.

But Nica couldn't have been more thrilled. She immediately booked a flight across the Channel and arrived at the elegant Salle Pleyel just in time for what would be Monk's first European concert. As it turned out, she may have been one of the few people in the three-thousand-seat concert hall who wasn't completely appalled by what took place when Monk came onstage. In Robin Kelley's account, both Monk's music ("His chords were shockingly dissonant, the melody unfamiliar") and his accompanying physical gestures ("He grunted, sweated, both feet flailing wildly underneath him in a macabre stationary dance") left most members of the audience believing that the pianist's performance was "more circus than concert." A review in the leading French jazz journal, *Jazz Hot*, disdainfully referred to Monk as "a kind of court jester to modern jazz," and concluded with the rueful verdict "To witness a man making a fool of himself and his music as I had just done, a man committing artistic suicide, was no such pleasant sensation."

From the Baroness's vantage point in the Salle Pleyel, however, Monk's performance had been nothing short of a triumph. While she grudgingly acknowledged that the pianist had "played too modern" for some members of the audience, Nica believed that most "were really grasped by it." But Monk was stung by the hostile reception he received from the French audience. "They're not really listening to what I'm playing," he complained at a postconcert party. And to be fair, the pianist (who was unable to bring along his own sidemen) had been given little time to rehearse his challenging compositions with his French band, and, nervous about his European debut, he had been drinking considerable amounts of scotch both before and during the performance.

Scheduled to appear again the following evening, a chastened Monk rigorously rehearsed his band, laid off the alcohol, and turned in a sharply focused performance. While some critics noted the improvement, according to Kelley, the audience's "attitude toward Monk remained unchanged." In any case, when he got to his dressing room, his spirits were considerably buoyed by the warm greetings of an old friend, Mary Lou Williams.

A brilliant pianist and creative arranger, Williams was one of the few prominent female instrumentalists of the swing era. After earning the title "the Lady Who Swings the Band" back in the 1930s, when she performed with Andy Kirk and his Clouds of Joy, a decade later Mary became a mentor to the modernists at Minton's, especially Thelonious Monk. But in the early 1950s, discouraged by her inability to find work—or get a fair hearing for her ambitious compositions—Williams moved to Paris, where she became a member of the city's thriving African-American expatriate community, which included Richard Wright, James Baldwin, the actor Canada Lee, and an aggregation of jazz musicians ranging from the New Orleans jazz patriarch Sidney Bechet to the pioneering bebop drummer Kenny Clarke. Alone and far from home for the first time, Thelonious had phoned Mary shortly after his arrival in the City of Light.

Meanwhile, aware of Williams's longstanding connection to Monk, Nica had also contacted Mary when she landed in Paris to arrange an introduction to her elusive hero. "I went backstage afterwards," she recalled, "and Mary Lou Williams introduced me to him. That is how I met him." It was, as they say, the start of a beautiful friendship—one that Monk's biographer has described as "the most significant relationship in Monk's life outside of his family."

It would also be the start of Nica and Mary's own enduring friendship. Over the next quarter century, until Williams's death in 1981, the two women established an intimate bond based on their appreciation of jazz as an artistic and spiritual force and their mutual efforts on behalf of the jazz community. While the two women saw each other regularly when they were both living in New York City during the 1960s and '70s, they also maintained an ongoing correspondence in which they shared their joys and frustrations and expressed their affection and support. As for her meeting with Monk, Nica claims that they "hit it off" from the start, and since Monk wasn't scheduled to leave Paris for another week, the unlikely duo "hung around for the rest of the time he was there and had a ball."

It was during this first flush of Monk-inspired mania that Nica had what she called "a brain wave." She would rent London's Albert Hall (which seats eight thousand people in Victorian splendor) "for six Sundays in a row to put on these fantastic concerts" of Monk's music. Unfortunately, Nica's enthusiasm considerably outpaced her experience as a producer, and when she ran into difficulty obtaining Monk's labor permit, she found herself "stuck with Albert Hall for six Sundays in a row and no one to put on." While she was chagrined that she had to pay the hall's steep fee in full, she was even more distressed because "Thelonious was very disappointed."

Once they were both back in New York, their relationship deepened and the pianist became a familiar presence in Nica's Stanhope suite. Hampton Hawes describes how on a visit to the Baroness during this period, he heard "a low rumbling sound, the whole place shaking with it." Peeking through the doorway, "he saw a body layed [sic] out on a gold bedspread, mudstained boots sticking out from a ten thousand dollar mink coat." It was then that Nica came rushing up, "finger to her lips as if I'm about to wake a three-week-old baby from its afternoon nap. 'Shhh, *Thelonious* is asleep,' " she scolded.

THELONIOUS SPHERE MONK, JR., was born in Rocky Mount, North Carolina, in 1917, but when he was three years old his family joined the Great Migration to New York City. His father, a laborer and amateur pianist, was soon forced to return home when the cold New York winter caused a flare-up of his asthma. According to Robin Kelley, Thelonious Sr. never returned; not long after he arrived back in Rocky Mount, he began exhibiting symptoms of bipolar disorder (an illness his son would inherit) and he was admitted to a mental asylum, where he remained until his death. So his wife, Barbara, an affectionate and devout woman, moved the family into a cramped apartment nestled in an Upper West Side enclave known as San Juan Hill and found work as a domestic.

The largely working-class black community was often beset by crime, violence, and racial tensions along the fault lines of adjoining white neighborhoods. Yet there was a small-town solidarity among the hard-pressed residents, and the rhythms of bouncing basketballs and kids pounding out their piano lessons could be heard across the open courtyards. Thelonious contributed more than most to this syncopated soundtrack.

When he was eleven, his sister, Marion, began taking weekly piano lessons, but it was Thelonious who was most powerfully drawn to the instrument. Tall, confident, and charismatic, he soon earned the respect of his peers for his skill on the court—and at the keyboard.

Monk later claimed that he learned to read music simply by looking over his sister's shoulder, and before long he was picking out the melodies of the gospel hymns his mother sang around the house. Once he started taking lessons, the true nature of his talent emerged. Within two years, he had made his way through the standard repertoire of Mozart, Bach, Beethoven, Chopin, and Liszt, impressing his teacher, Simon Wolf, with his dazzling musicianship. "I don't think there will be anything I can teach him," Wolf declared when asked about the boy's progress. "He will go beyond me very soon."

By this time, however, Monk had been completely won over by the sounds of jazz that he heard on the radio and in the clubs and theaters that dotted the neighborhood. By the age of fourteen he had formed a band with a couple of friends, and they began earning pocket money playing at local amateur shows and rent parties. Although Monk was an average student, he managed to gain entry to Stuyvesant, the city's premier high school for math and science. And while initially his grades indicated that he could meet the school's rigorous academic demands, by the middle of his sophomore year his attendance was beginning to deteriorate as his musical career gained steam.

Monk brought his formal education to a close when he was seventeen. After signing on as an accompanist for a traveling evangelist, he toured the South and Midwest, performing at churches and revival meetings. Later, when he was asked to describe this formative experience, he simply said, "She preached and healed and we played." On a stop in Kansas City, Monk showed up at a jam session where he caught the attention of Mary Lou Williams, the city's reigning piano queen. Williams later recalled that even at this point in his apprenticeship, Thelonious's unique approach to the instrument was already well established: "He was playing the same style then as he is now." Not long after returning home, Monk became a Minton's mainstay, playing alongside the greatest jazz musicians of his generation. He also began writing some of his classic compositions, including "'Round Midnight."

Although he was barely out of his teens and had never played in any of the big-name big bands like the rest of the Minton's regulars, Monk is often credited with being the "architect" of the new sound. Night after night, older and more experienced jazz musicians gathered around his piano for enrollment in the ad hoc Thelonious Monk Institute of Advanced Harmony. But while he may have been a musical visionary and a generous teacher, he was also exquisitely sensitive, and under stress he would either withdraw into reclusive silence or get swept up in manic jags that could last for days. And his piano style was as idiosyncratic as his personality. His harmonic substitutions and off-kilter phrasing were so distinctive that his music proved difficult for both listeners and other musicians.

Teddy Hill, who operated Minton's Playhouse, summed up the attitude of many musicians on the scene. "I always used to be so disgusted with him," Hill declared, "and yet you never knew such a likable guy . . . Everybody liked the guy . . . Everybody wanted him [in their band], but everybody was afraid of him. He was too undependable. He'd just rather mess around at home." So after helping to give birth to bebop, Monk watched as Bird, Dizzy Gillespie, and others took his concepts (and compositions) into the clubs on 52nd Street and onto recordings. As Hill described it, "Monk seemed more like the guy who manufactured the product rather than commercialized it." He also had a theory for why that was the case. "One reason for it," Hill explained, "is that he was living at home with his own people . . . Dizzy had to be on time to keep the landlady from saying, 'You don't live here anymore.' Monk never had that worry."

Monk relished the comforts of home and the security of his family. Despite their strained financial circumstances, his mother, Barbara, had always created a warm and inviting atmosphere in the family's two-bedroom ground-floor flat. And when Thelonious was growing up, kids from the neighborhood would regularly gather around the piano as he entertained them with everything from gospel hymns to pop standards. Looking on shyly from the back of the crowd was a bright-eyed girl a couple of years younger than Thelonious, Nellie Smith, who happened to be the sister of his best friend, James (known as Sonny). "I was about twelve when I heard him play," Nellie told Robin Kelley a few years before she passed away. "A lot of young girls used to go to his house. His mother would let them in. Of course a lot of the girls had a crush on him." But as it turned out, she was the one who captured his heart.

Eventually the Monk apartment at 243 West 63rd Street would become a place of pilgrimage, as aspiring musicians made their way to Monk's home for musical instruction and his cryptic words of wisdom. In 1947, when Lorraine Gordon arrived with her then-husband, Alfred

Lion, to scout out Monk for a possible Blue Note record deal, she recognized the apartment's spiritual ambiance: "Monk's room was right off the kitchen. It was a room out of Vincent van Gogh somehow—you know, ascetic: a bed (a cot really) against the wall, a window, and an upright piano." Oh, and taped to the ceiling directly above his narrow bed—something probably missing from van Gogh's room at Arles—a small photograph of Billie Holiday.

IN 1954, WHEN NICA first entered the modest apartment on West 63rd Street, Barbara Monk had only recently passed away. Thelonious was now the head of his own young family, and he proudly introduced them to his new friend. There was Nellie, his childhood sweetheart, who had moved into the Monk home in 1948; their five-year-old son, Thelonious, known as Toot; and Toot's one-year-old sister, Barbara, known as Boo Boo. The crowded home continued to radiate warmth and familial solidarity, but after three years without a cabaret card Thelonious's career had bottomed out. The sudden appearance of a Rothschild baroness couldn't have come at a better time.

Monk's son was too young to recall Nica's first visit. But when asked about the consequences of her arrival in the Monk household, Toot immediately sought to set the record straight. "Contrary to popular mythology," he asserts, "she was never my father's mistress or anything, and actually, at the end of the day, Nica supplied an extra helping hand for my mother, and they both watched out for Thelonious." As he describes it, rather than being a ménage à trois, the relationship among Nellie, Thelonious, and Nica was more like the Three Musketeers'. As he put it, "Nica was abundantly clear that Thelonious was in love with Nellie, but that was OK, because she loved him anyway."

Thelonious also took the baroness up to the Bronx to meet his brother-in-law, Sonny Smith, and his wife, Geraldine, who were raising their seven children in a fifth-floor tenement walk-up on Lyman Place. Their daughter, Jackie Smith Bonneau, remembered hearing about "this 'special person' who lived in a hotel in Manhattan" even before Nica made the arduous climb up to their apartment. According to Jackie, it wasn't unusual for Thelonious to shepherd people who mattered to him, including band members and musical colleagues, up to their apartment with little more in the way of explanation than "We're going up to Sonny's, Nellie's brother." That's simply the way he was, she explains. "He took you into his life and created his own world."

Jackie recalled her uncle's sense of pride when he presented his new friend to the family, and she imitated the Baroness's posh British accent as she was introduced to even the youngest of the seven kids: "It's so nice to meet all of you. It's so wonderful. I've heard so much about you." Meanwhile, Thelonious walked off to poke around the apartment, leaving Nica to her own devices. "She was just fascinating," Jackie recalled. "She was so lovely, and so down to earth." A few months later, the teenaged Jackie also got a taste of Nica's legendary generosity. "He told her when my birthday was," she explained, "and she went out and bought me all these records and things."

While Jackie understands why people continue to be confounded by the curious trio, she believes that somehow both Nellie and Nica found a way to put aside all traces of possessiveness in pursuit of a higher purpose: the artistry of Thelonious Monk. She also suggests that in doing so, the Baroness was able to transcend both her Rothschild heritage and her noble title (what Jackie calls "pedestal stuff") in order to "connect to a life force beyond flesh and *things*."

Looking back at Nica's role in the life of his family as well as in the larger jazz community, Monk's son, Toot, now realizes that her contributions went far beyond the material support she provided. "Nica's story is so integral to the emotional survival of so many of the musicians," he explains. "What she really provided was belief in them. She brought a credibility that musicians really needed and appreciated." For his father, who had been so underappreciated during this period, the validation from a Rothschild heiress and member of the upper echelons of Europe's cultural elite was particularly potent.

Nica, on the other hand, left no doubt about the attraction Monk

held for her. In the mid-1960s, when Monk was recording for Columbia Records, she sent his producer, Teo Macero, a collection of recent
musings she titled "Some Thoughts About Thelonious (for what they're
worth . . . !)." One of them begins: "I have known four great men in my
life . . . Professor Einstein, Charlie Parker, General de Gaulle, and Thelonious Monk . . . *on second thought you can leave out the first three . . . !!!*"

While Nica's prescient recognition of Monk's creative brilliance
speaks to her modernist sensibility and "big ears" (jazz jargon for a listener's musical acuity and taste), her ability to recognize the genius behind
his façade of eccentricity can also be traced back to her childhood. In
Monk, a large, imposing figure whose shyness and verbal constraints ("I
needed an interpreter to understand what he was saying at the beginning," she admitted) masked a unique talent, she may have made out
a shadowy reflection of her Uncle Walter, the ponderous, tongue-tied
Rothschild scion who rode about the Tring Park estate of her childhood
on the back of a giant tortoise but who was also a world-class scientist and (according to Nica's sister Miriam) someone who possessed a
"smudge of mad genius."

Whatever its ultimate source, however, Nica's devotion to Thelonious was so ardent—and enduring—that his son finds it particularly
ironic that the Baroness has become so indelibly linked in jazz mythology
to Charlie Parker, someone with whom she had a rather casual friendship that lasted little more than a year. In Toot's telling of the story, the
moral of Nica's relationship with Bird can be summed up by the old
adage "No good deed goes unpunished." "Charlie Parker died in Nica's
home because Nica was being true to the person she'd always been!"
Toot explains, with more than a little intensity. "Charlie Parker, when
he could not knock on *anybody's* fucking door in the world because he
had fucked over *everybody*, he could knock on her door and she would
open up and she would let him in." But, he continues, there was just
one problem. "Unfortunately, the motherfucker dropped dead on her and
she's been paying the price ever since."

• • •

ON MARCH 15, 1955, when the front page of New York's *Daily Mirror* broke the news of Bird's demise—"Bop King Dies in Heiress's Flat"—most readers may have been titillated by the story's heady mix of miscegenation and modern jazz on the Upper East Side, but in isolated pockets of hipness across the country, fans and fellow musicians were devastated by the sudden loss of a jazz genius. In the days that followed, some defiantly scrawled the mantra "Bird Lives" on the walls of Greenwich Village, while others, looking for someone to blame, found in Nica an ideal target for their anger and sorrow.

A McCarthy-era climate of character assassination, combined with familiar Rothschild conspiracy theories and racial paranoia, soon fueled incendiary rumors about the Baroness's role in Bird's death. "The rich white bitch killed him" was how Toot vividly characterized the attitude of some in the black community. Among those who voiced suspicion about Nica's pernicious influence was Charles Mingus, the virtuoso bassist and composer, who stormed through the jazz world for half a century, leaving a trail of brilliant music, smashed furniture, and bruised relationships in his wake.

Despite Mingus's lingering hostility, the Baroness later sought to heal the breach in their once cordial relationship by creating a small abstract drawing (now in the collection of the Institute of Jazz Studies at Rutgers University). About the size of an LP cover, the work appears to be a tempest of stylized question marks through which Nica threaded an overture for reconciliation: "There are no plots, Mingus . . . Only those that originate from within . . . Be honest!! You've always known that, haven't you?"

In the days after Bird's death, however, there were other dark mutterings in the jazz community—about hospital shenanigans, falsified identity forms, and conflicting cause-of-death statements. It's no wonder that when the Baroness finally did provide her behind-the-scenes description of Bird's demise, in Robert Reisner's 1962 anthology, *Bird: The Legend of Charlie Parker*, she began with an emotional outburst of pent-up frustration. "I'm sick of this 'shipped the body off to the morgue' business and 'laid unknown,' for how long, for that is ridiculous." Nica then shared with Reisner a bittersweet account of Bird's final days that belies his tragic hero persona while subtly deflecting her own demonization.

Nica explained that when Parker arrived at the door of her Stanhope suite, he suddenly began to vomit blood. She called her physician, Dr. Robert Freymann, who lived just a few blocks away, but when the doctor arrived, Bird claimed he was feeling better and expressed his eagerness to set out for his gig at a Boston jazz club. Despite the doctor's insistence that he be taken to a hospital for treatment, Bird remained adamant. He had been through a series of hospitalizations over the previous few years (including a stint at a California drug treatment center and a recent stay at Bellevue for a suicide attempt), and he'd had enough of them. After some back-and-forth, they reached a compromise: the Baroness volunteered to care for Bird, and the doctor would come by a couple of times a day to check on him.

Nica and her sixteen-year-old daughter, Janka, took turns nursing Parker around the clock—mostly supplying him with pitchers of cold water. "His thirst was incredible," Nica explained. "It couldn't be quenched. Sometimes he would bring it up with some blood, and then he lay back and had to have more water. It went on like this for a day or two." Meanwhile, Dr. Freymann, who had diagnosed the saxophonist as suffering from advanced cirrhosis and stomach ulcers, did the best he could; he gave Parker a shot of penicillin (which seemed to offer some relief) and left instructions that Bird not be allowed to leave except in an ambulance.

On the third day, Parker was well enough to collaborate with the Baroness on a little surprise for Dr. Freymann, whom he had come to like and respect. According to Nica, "Bird wanted the doctor, who had been a musician, to listen to some of his records." So they put together a program of Bird's recent recordings with strings—mostly popular songs with Bird's alto soaring through the lush arrangements. "The doctor was very impressed," Nica reported, and "Bird got a great charge out of that." The next day, he was feeling so much better that Freymann agreed to let him get up and watch a little television. It was Saturday night and *Stage Show*, the Dorsey Brothers' variety program, would be on. Nica and her daughter got Bird into an armchair, wrapped him in blankets, and turned on the TV.

Among the performers that night was a team of comic jugglers whose act ended with a cascade of tumbling bricks and gales of laughter. Suddenly Bird began to choke, and then he collapsed. Nica rushed to the phone to call the doctor as Janka tried to reassure her: "Don't worry, Mummy. He's all right now." But when she checked his pulse, Nica knew better. "I didn't want to believe it. I could feel my own pulse. I tried to believe my pulse was his. But I really knew that Bird was dead." Then there was a huge clap of thunder, a cosmic coincidence that long reverberated in her imagination. "One can imagine all sorts of things alone with death," the Baroness told Nat Hentoff in a 1960 interview. "It's dramatic enough without special effects. Yet I did think I heard a clap of thunder as Bird passed away. I convinced myself finally that I hadn't until I talked it over with my daughter, and she heard it too."

The emotionally resonant depiction of Nica's brief friendship with Charlie Parker also offered a sharp contrast with the caricature promulgated by jazz-world backbiters. She recalled how Parker had occasionally dropped by her apartment to hang out—"We'd talk about everything under the sun. Bird knew about everything and then some"—or to play "peggity" (Chinese checkers) with her daughter, or just to listen to some of his favorite records. She also made clear how abject and desolate these final years were for Bird. She described one evening when she saw the saxophonist standing in front of Birdland in the pouring rain because "he just had no place to go." Sometimes, Parker told her, when he couldn't find someone to take him in, "he would ride the subways all night."

As the stories of Bird's death played out in the tabloids and within New York's jazz subculture, the lurid reports of Nica's role in the scandal had dire consequences closer to home. Having heard the news linking his estranged wife to the death of the notorious Bop King on Walter Winchell's radio show, Nica's husband filed for divorce. Under the circumstances (drug-addicted, African-American jazz musician dies mysteriously in apartment of diplomat's wife), Jules's success was a foregone conclusion. A few months after gaining custody of their three minor children, he remarried and—after completing his diplomatic chores in New York—went on to serve as French ambassador to Indonesia and Peru. Eventually, Jules returned to Paris and a position in the Ministry for Foreign Affairs. Following his retirement, Jules de Koenigswarter moved to Spain, where he died in 1995.

THOUGH CHARLIE PARKER'S death would become a convenient symbol for the end of bebop's golden age, in reality jazz had been moving in new directions for several years. In 1948, for example, Miles Davis (who had made his New York jazz debut as a nineteen-year-old sideman in Parker's band) began experimenting with a new spare style that offered a soothing respite from bebop's overheated intensity. He formed a nine-piece ensemble that included French horn and tuba (in addition to the typical small band instrumentation) and—collaborating with adventurous young arrangers including Gil Evans, John Lewis, and Gerry Mulligan—began to produce a series of sophisticated and impressionistic recordings. In 1957, twelve of the tracks were collected on an LP whose title, *Birth of the Cool*, reflected an abrupt change in the emotional temperature of jazz.

While Davis and his colleagues were orchestrating an alternative to the abstractions of bebop, others were attempting to reclaim jazz's populist roots. Beginning in the early 1950s, a corps of young performers including Art Blakey, Horace Silver, the tenor saxophonist Benny Golson, and the trumpeter Lee Morgan transplanted some of the harmonic advances of the modernists into the fertile soil of the blues and infused it with the ecstatic spirit of gospel music to create a soulful sound dubbed "hard bop." In its muscular intensity and emotional power, the style also drew from the new genre of dance-oriented black popular music known as rhythm and blues, which had recently infiltrated the nation's airwaves.

For a while, midcentury jazz split into two distinct and often divisive styles: "cool jazz," viewed as emotionally restrained, intellectual, and grounded in European harmonies (played mostly by white musicians based on the West Coast), and "hard bop," touted as a return to the emotionally direct, African-based roots of jazz (dominated by black musicians based on the East Coast). Although the dichotomy was never so neatly defined, the escalating civil rights movement had begun to engender racial tensions within the jazz community, creating not-so-subtle color-coded categories that made one's choice of jazz genres a political act. A jazz omnivore, the Baroness never engaged in the passionate factionalism that preoccupied so many of the era's fans, but she did have her favorites—and one of them was a newly formed quintet that would turn out to be the seminal band of the hard-bop movement.

The Jazz Messengers were a collaborative African-American quintet led by Art Blakey, a bosom buddy of Thelonious Monk who was the drummer on the pianist's early Blue Note records, and Horace Silver, a talented young pianist and extraordinarily gifted composer. By the mid-fifties, the band had created a hard-driving ensemble sound that would set a standard for small-group jazz for decades to come. Despite their improvisational brilliance and potent blend of blues-based funk and Latin-tinged lyricism, the Messengers got off to a rocky start. And as she had done so many times before, Nica was there to help.

The Baroness's support for the Jazz Messengers began with their wardrobe; she bought them all matching Ivy League suits, shirts, ties, and shoes. "I thought that would help them get jobs," she confessed to the Village Vanguard's owner, Max Gordon. "I was out of my mind." Misguided or not, the sartorial accoutrements Nica provided weren't her only contribution to the survival of the Jazz Messengers. When the band was stranded in Ohio after a tight-fisted club owner refused to pay them for a weeklong gig, one phone call to the Baroness was all it took. As Silver recounted in his autobiography, "She wired us some money so we could pay our hotel bills and return to New York. Once again we were befriended by Nica."

Nica's other efforts to move past the trauma of Bird's death were complicated by a campaign of intimidation initiated by the Stanhope's management, which was none too pleased by the discreet hotel's association with the recent bebop scandal. First, the manager uprooted the Baroness from her airy penthouse suite and moved her to a dark cubicle on the second floor at a hugely inflated rate, which she stubbornly refused to pay. It wasn't that she didn't have the resources ("I had lots of bread then," she told Hentoff in an interview for his 1960 *Esquire* article), but she simply refused to be bullied. While the actual figure is veiled in secrecy (like so much else about her private life), Nica's annual trust fund was not inconsiderable; one estimate placed it at about $200,000, although her eldest son, Patrick, was considerably more vague. "My mother was comfortable," he declared in a 2008 interview. "She had a trust fund, but she always had money worries."

The standoff was finally resolved by Nica's brother, Victor. Using the diplomatic skills he had honed while serving as Churchill's wartime emissary to Washington, Lord Rothschild negotiated a settlement: he agreed to pay off his sister's substantial debt, but she would be allowed to vacate the premises at her convenience. So a few weeks later, seemingly undaunted by her recent tribulations, the Baroness got into her silver Rolls, drove across Central Park to the more accommodating Hotel Bolivar, purchased a new Steinway grand (with Thelonious Monk's guidance), and resumed her singular role in New York's insular jazz subculture.

Since Monk was still coping with the creative and financial hardships imposed on him by the loss of his cabaret card five years earlier, he gratefully accepted Nica's hospitality. For long periods he camped out at the Bolivar, working on new tunes, including his tribute to the Baroness ("Pannonica") and a quirky ode to her new domicile ("Ba-lue Bolivar Ba-lues-are"). But there was another reason Monk became such a fixture at the Baroness's during this period. A catastrophic fire had gutted his West 63rd Street apartment, destroying his piano, along with copies of many of his compositions, and forcing the family to take refuge in the Bronx with Nellie's brother, sister-in-law, and their seven children. It would be six months before they could return home. Inevitably, the situation took a severe toll on Monk's emotional well-being.

In truth, even when he wasn't in crisis, Monk's psychological state could be precarious. He often experienced difficulties coping with the demands of daily life, something his wife had recognized even before they were married. Yet not only was Nellie perhaps the first person (outside his own family) to appreciate Thelonious's unique artistry, but she happily accepted the sacrifices that would be required to nurture it. With Nica's arrival, Nellie had acquired a staunch ally in these efforts; now, another loyal comrade was about to sign up in the cause.

WHEN HE RAN INTO Monk at the Café Bohemia in the fall of 1955, Harry Colomby was a slight, soft-spoken high school English teacher in his mid-twenties. It was about 1:30 in the morning, and Colomby had gone to the Village jazz club looking for Art Blakey, whom he had booked for an upcoming concert with the Jazz Messengers at Far Rockaway High School, the New York City public school where he was employed.

Colomby had fallen in love with Monk's music when he first heard the obscure pianist on a Coleman Hawkins recording made a decade earlier. "I never heard piano like that," he recalled in a 1980s interview, and he recognized immediately that "this was something special." In fact, Harry had already had a personal encounter with the pianist through his older brother, Jules, a serious jazz buff who had recently cofounded an independent label, Signal Records, with a couple of fellow fanatics, Don Schlitten and Harold Goldberg. Coincidentally, Jules had hired Monk as a sideman for a band led by the saxophonist Gigi Gryce, and among the tunes they recorded was Gryce's own tribute to the Baroness, "Nica's Tempo."

Although Harry didn't find Blakey at the Bohemia, he spotted Monk at the bar and sidled up to say hello. To Harry's surprise, Monk remembered their recent meeting, and after exchanging some pleasantries, he asked the young teacher for a ride uptown so he could visit his pal Art Blakey. "I don't know whether it was destiny or whatever," Colomby reflected years later.

After a quick visit with Blakey, during which Colomby was able to confirm plans for the Jazz Messengers gig, Monk asked Harry if he would give him a lift up to Nellie's brother's place in the Bronx. By now it was close to 3:00 in the morning, and even as he pictured himself falling asleep in front of his 7:30 English class, Colomby, inspired by his proximity to his idol, launched into a long riff about Monk's unique music, his integrity, and his enormous artistic potential. The pianist abruptly turned to him and asked, "Do you want to be my manager?" "I said yes quickly," Colomby remembered, "before either of us would have a change of mind."

After the two men shook hands (the only contract they would ever have), Colomby turned to Monk and said, "I don't know how rich we're going to get, but I'll guarantee you this: that you'll be recognized and appreciated in your lifetime." When he woke up a few hours later, however, he was suddenly struck by the reality of his impulsive early-morning pledge. "I had no idea," he confessed years later. "I had no idea what the money was, I had no idea what these guys were getting . . . I knew they worked someplace . . . I had no idea at all." Then he sat down with Nellie, only to discover the full extent of the challenge he had taken on.

"I spent like a whole night, I remember, with his wife," he recalled. "She was giving me all the information. All night." Monk had a contract with a low-budget indie record company, but his records weren't selling; his music was considered unorthodox, and stories of his unreliability and strange moods had tarnished his image; and when he wasn't being simply ignored by the jazz press, he was often the subject of ridicule. Then there was the slight problem of Monk's cabaret card, without which he couldn't work in any nightclub in New York City, his hometown and the jazz capital of the world.

But when Colomby looked at Monk, all he could see was a king. "There was this regality about him that made me like him so much more, knowing how little money he had . . . his bearing was always kingly." As Colomby describes it, once again his trepidation quickly gave way to a sense of duty. "Here is this great genius whom I look up to as a demigod—a maligned, weird guy . . . I'm going to be in a position to help this guy. I suddenly feel totally responsible for him." Wisely, however, Harry didn't give up his day job.

It took him a while, but as Colomby shuttled back and forth between Monk's apartment and the Bolivar, he also began to make sense of the baffling domestic arrangement Monk, Nellie, and Nica had constructed.

And he quickly shed any preconceptions he might have had about the nature of the pianist's relationship with the Baroness. "I am convinced, I would almost guarantee, that it was never anything physical," Colomby declared. In fact, having observed Monk's obliviousness to the sexual overtures he received from attractive young women in jazz club back rooms, he adds, "They talk about jazz musicians liking wine, women, and song. Well, with Thelonious it was just wine and song."

Colomby believes that at least initially, Thelonious had seen Nica as little more than an "ideal fan," but soon, he explains, each of them "found that they had more in common, [were] more kindred spirits, than they suspected in the beginning." In fact, despite the disparities of race, nationality, and class that separated them, Monk and the Baroness were bound by a shared and unshakable self-belief: it was what permitted Monk, who had virtually nothing of material worth, to maintain his musical integrity in the face of unrelenting critical rejection and commercial failure; and it was what enabled the Baroness, who had abandoned a life of unimaginable wealth and social status, to remain true to her own nature despite an onslaught of condemnation and ridicule from all quarters.

Just as Colomby's status as a teacher was a source of pride for Monk ("he thought it was cool"), the Baroness seemed to bestow on the impoverished pianist an imprimatur of success. "Something about her, a cachet if you will—driving her great English cars, and being a painter and living in nice hotels, being a Rothschild—that was special," Colomby suggests. "I suppose it was flattering." He believes that Nellie was equally captivated by the exotic creature who had found her way into their world. "Nica had a certain presence in the room, a certain sound or look that gave her a certain theatricality, and I think Nellie enjoyed that . . . Nellie perceived Nica as a friend, as someone she could trust, someone she could rely on." And considering Thelonious's alternating bouts of depression and manic jags that might keep him awake for days at a time, Nica also provided Monk's wife with much-needed respite. "Nellie, you know, would be relieved sometimes when Nica was around, when Thelonious was a little difficult," Colomby recalls.

Aware of Monk's financial straits, Colomby occasionally slipped a five- or ten-dollar bill under an ashtray during his visits to his apartment. While his paltry teacher's salary of seven thousand dollars a year necessarily limited his largesse, the Baroness was under no such constraints. Nica not only had the wherewithal to help the family meet its basic needs, but she also presented the pianist with an extravagant token of her affection—a brand-new 1956 two-tone Buick Special. Monk was over the moon. "It's a prize-winning model!" he boasted to Colomby.

No matter how much Monk benefited from Nica's generosity, however, Nica always contended that she was the one who gained the most from their friendship. In spite of her legendary family name, her ample trust fund, and her gleaming Rolls-Royce, she seemed to bask in Monk's reflected glory. "I think when Nica walked into a nightclub with Thelonious Monk, she felt elevated and proud—she was very proud of that," Colomby asserts. And despite Monk's considerable hardships and vulnerabilities, it was Nica who claimed to be the beneficiary of *his* strength and support.

Colomby believes that the trauma of Bird's death and the ensuing tabloid scandal had taken a considerable toll on the Baroness. She had always been something of a drinker (her silver flask figures in as many jazz-world anecdotes as her expensive cars), but now alcohol seemed to have become "a problem." Although they rarely talked about personal matters, Colomby recalls a conversation in which Nica described how Thelonious had helped her get her drinking under control. "She was drinking too much at the time . . . and somehow needed something, some kind of strength to get her away from it. And she said that he provided that." Although she was somewhat vague about the exact nature of Monk's intervention, Colomby understood exactly what she meant. "There was something about his personality—you just wanted his approval in some way. He had that kind of presence."

Monk also encouraged Nica's own creative endeavors. On his frequent visits to the Bolivar, Colomby remembers seeing evidence of Nica's artistic pursuits. "There were a lot of paintings scattered around the floor," he recalls, "bright, colorful, abstract works that were from her

Mexican period, when she was living there with her husband." Colomby disclaims any expertise as an art critic, but he believes "she was very good, very talented." Although he describes the rug in Nica's makeshift bedroom studio as "covered in paint," when the Baroness discussed her technique with Nat Hentoff in their 1960 interview, it turned out that her art was as unconventional as her life. "The truth is, I use somewhat weird ingredients," she revealed, "anything from scotch to milk to perfume. Anything liquid that happens to be around." She also told the jazz writer about the exhibition of her paintings in a 1958 group show at New York's ACA Gallery, explaining that she "only entered because Thelonious dared me." In an amusing—and revealing—footnote to the story, Nica's son Patrick remembers that although all of her works at the show sold, his mother "spent the next year trying to buy her paintings back, because she hated the thought of being parted from them."

It was also during this period that Nica purchased one of the new Polaroid cameras that had recently come on the market and discovered another outlet for her creativity. For the next fifteen years, she would use a succession of the company's latest instant-print models to take intimate behind-the-scenes photographs of hundreds of musicians in New York jazz clubs and jam sessions.

FOR A WHILE, Nica's life at the out-of-the-way Hotel Bolivar was a private musical paradise. "[Monk] would be up there playing piano all day long," she explained to an acquaintance many years later, "and at night we would go out around the clubs, and then all the musicians would come back with us to the Bolivar and we would have these fantastic jam sessions until nine the next morning." Naturally it was too good to last.

Harry Colomby recalls that he was home marking a stack of student essays when he got a phone call from Monk's wife: on their way to the Bolivar, Thelonious had suffered a mental breakdown and didn't even seem to know who she was. Harry rushed out of his Queens apartment, but by the time he got to the hotel a doctor was already on the scene. It

turned out to be Dr. Freymann, the physician who had attended Charlie
Parker during his final days at the Stanhope. Monk's condition was soon
stabilized, but the episode proved to be a harbinger of things to come. A
few days later, while driving the new Buick Nica had given him, Monk
got into a minor accident with another vehicle. No one was hurt and
there was little damage to either car, but when the police showed up, he
was in a catatonic state, so an ambulance was called. The car was taken
to the local precinct, and a handwritten note placed on the windshield
told the rest of the story: "Psycho taken to Bellevue."

There would be a number of conflicting theories about Monk's medical condition, and over the years he was subjected to a range of treatments, including massive doses of Thorazine and shock therapy, with
varying degrees of success. Nellie and Nica also explored a variety of
nontraditional remedies to treat his symptoms. Nellie administered her
own blends of organic fruit and vegetable juices, and Nica took Monk to
Dr. Freymann's Upper East Side office for his designer "vitamin" injections, a high-potency formula combining vitamin B_{12} and a hefty dose of
amphetamine.

Periodically Harry Colomby was recruited to drive Monk to Freymann's East 78th Street office, and he can still recall his first glimpse of
the doctor's waiting room, the seats filled with an assortment of "wealthy
East Side dowagers and junkies on the nod." Colomby came to believe
that the Jewish physician, who had fled Germany not long after the Nazis
came to power, was sincere in his efforts, and that by defying the prevailing code of the 1950s medical establishment, Freymann was providing a
well-meaning alternative treatment for heroin addicts.

Despite his confidence in the doctor's good intentions, eventually
Colomby began to wonder whether Freymann's intravenous cocktails
were doing Monk more harm than good. And he was not the only one. By
the late 1960s, Dr. Freymann had come under the scrutiny of the New
York State Medical Society for "unprofessional conduct," and in 1973,
a *New York Times* investigative article headlined "Two Doctors Here
Known to Users as Sources of Amphetamine" provided an even greater

measure of notoriety. This article noted that Dr. Robert Freymann, along with Dr. John Bishop and Dr. Max Jacobson (who had infamously prescribed his own amphetamine-laced injections for President Kennedy), had become a known figure within New York's elite underground. While acknowledging that it was "not illegal to give patients amphetamines," the *Times* confronted Freymann with accusations of malpractice made by some former patients, and the doctor was both unapologetic about his pharmaceutical protocols and proud of his roster of satisfied clients. "I have a clientele that is remarkable, from every sphere of life," he boasted. "I could tell you in 10 minutes probably 100 famous names who come here." Although the doctor mentioned no names, it later turned out that the list of his clients included not only Monk, the Baroness, and a big band's worth of jazz musicians but a couple of Warhol superstars and perhaps a sixties rock icon or two.

In 1966, when the Beatles album *Revolver* was released in the United Kingdom, it marked a creative breakthrough for the band, one that reflected both their audacious use of recording studio wizardry and their experiments with mind-altering substances. A track called "Dr. Robert" certainly reflected these recent preoccupations. The song, written by John Lennon, was a jaunty multitracked refrain paying tribute to the obliging sixty-year-old physician of the title, who could "pick you up" with just a sip from his "special cup." As Paul McCartney later explained, the band had heard about Freymann on one of their early visits to New York. "We'd hear people say, 'You can get anything off him, any pills you want.' The song was a joke about this fellow who cured everyone of everything with these pills and tranquillizers. He just kept New York high."

A year later, when shooting began on *Ciao Manhattan*, Andy Warhol's cinematic exploration of downtown debauchery (starring his latest "superstar," Edie Sedgwick), the cast and crew were making such frequent use of Dr. Freymann's services that a charge account for the production was opened at Freymann's office. And in yet another homage to the accommodating physician, a scene was written into the film in which "Dr. Roberts" administers his famous vitamin cocktail into the unprotesting posteriors of Edie and her companion (Warhol veteran Baby Jane Holzer). In 1971, Edie Sedgwick died of drug-related causes at the age of twenty-eight, a few months before the film was released. Three years later, Freymann was expelled from the New York Medical Society for malpractice.

Having been subjected to the hostile scrutiny of the mainstream media herself, the Baroness was not inclined to rush to judgment; and as someone who had experienced condemnation from various guardians of the social status quo, she may also have identified with those who challenged the prevailing orthodoxies. Ultimately, however, it was Dr. Freymann's caring and sensitive treatment of Bird and Monk that won Nica's respect and loyalty, and he remained a trusted friend and confidant of the Baroness until his death, in 1987, only a few months before her own passing.

NOT LONG AFTER Monk's release from his brief stint in Bellevue, he was back to his old self—a baffling amalgam of unsettling silences, epigrammatic epiphanies, and astonishing creativity—and he quickly reclaimed his place of honor at the Baroness's Bolivar jam sessions. Night after night, her hotel suite was filled with many of the greatest jazz musicians in the world. "Sonny Rollins and Art Blakey and Bud Powell, Kenny Dorham, Hamp [Lionel Hampton] . . . everybody you can think of used to come up there and jam," Nica recalled.

When Monk's producer at Riverside Records, Orrin Keepnews, stopped by the Bolivar one night to talk to the Baroness about a Charlie Parker tribute he was helping to organize, they were forced to retreat to her car. "Her apartment was too full of musicians and too noisy for her to be able to talk to me," Keepnews explained. Although Nica couldn't understand why her neighbors were all complaining—she thought they should be grateful to be "hearing this fantastic music they would never hear again in their lives!"—before long the hotel management insisted that the Baroness find other accommodations.

Meanwhile, armed with little more than his reverence for a neglected genius, Harry Colomby had been chipping away at the music industry's resistance to Monk, and by late 1956, his persistence had begun to pay off. As one old-school booking agent told him, "Well, if you have nerve enough to be Monk's manager, I guess I have nerve enough to try and book him." He offered the pianist a couple of out-of-town gigs, and Monk surprised many when he established himself as a reliable performer and a popular act. Then Colomby turned his attention to reclaiming Monk's cabaret card, the key to his reentry into the Big Apple jazz scene.

Monk and the Baroness
Each
Find a Home

Like the glory days of Hemingway's Paris, the Baroness's New York jazz salon was a movable feast. After being evicted from her Upper East Side aerie at the Stanhope, Nica had made the ten-minute journey across Central Park and resumed her nightly soirees at the Bolivar. Within the year, however, she had worn out her welcome there as well. So in the spring of 1957, the Baroness and her eighteen-year old daughter, Janka, who had inherited her mother's love of jazz and fascination with the men who made it, packed up the paintings and the piano and moved again, this time to the Algonquin, the landmark midtown hotel that had indulged the improprieties of Dorothy Parker, Robert Benchley, George S. Kaufman, and other members of New York's hard-drinking literary set back in the 1920s. Soon the sounds of jazz once again filled Nica's hotel suite.

Aware of the historic value of the music being created in the privacy of her living room, Nica purchased a top-of-the-line Wollensak reel-to-reel tape recorder, and she immediately began using it to document jam sessions, rehearsals, and live performances. Monk's son, Toot, who makes a couple of appearances on the tapes as a teenager, considers the four hundred hours of Nica's meticulously annotated tape recordings (amassed over the course of fifteen years) "the greatest inside look at what was going on in the personal, creative side of that generation of jazz musicians." The so-called Pannonica Collection, which remains in the possession of Nica's children, has never been made available either to the public or to jazz scholars.

One of the earliest tapes made at the Bolivar documents the visit of the twenty-five-year-old saxophonist Sonny Rollins, who had recently been hired to play on Monk's first album of original compositions for Riverside Records (Reel 15: "Sonny Rollins & Nica Talk; Thelonious Plays 'Darn That Dream' "). A few months later, another saxophonist who would rise to fame in Monk's band, was also captured by Nica's microphone (Reel 14: "Coltrane Learns 'Monk's Mood' at Algonquin, April, 1957"). A partial list of the jazz greats who show up in the Pannonica Collection includes Charles Mingus, Larry Adler, Horace Silver, Art Blakey, Sun Ra, Milt Jackson, Elvin Jones, Lionel Hampton, Barry Harris, Elmo Hope, Kenny Drew, and Donald Byrd. Typically, interludes in the music are filled by the small talk of a multigenerational roster of musical geniuses, along with members of the Monk and de Koenigswarter families. One reel even features a guest appearance by Nica's brother, the baron, identified on the label of Reel 25 as "Teddy Wilson's Favorite Pupil (Victor)."

Harry Colomby recalls that Victor Rothschild had been making regular visits to New York during this period, often accompanied by his personal accountants, in order to keep tabs on his sister's trust fund, a task that typically necessitated his financial intervention. "He had to always bail me out of these hotels when I was thrown out," Nica recalled. While she made sure that her brother got to know Monk, the amateur jazz pianist and former member of the British Security Service never did appreciate the pianist's modernist aesthetic; "utter fucking crap" was his candid assessment. "He may have spied on Thelonious's music," Nica once quipped, "but he sure didn't catch on."

Nica's sister Miriam, busy with her entomological research, her environmental activism, and her six children, managed to make only one visit to New York during these years. Naturally Nica was eager to introduce her sister to Monk, but when she got to 63rd Street to pick him up for their planned get-together, she could tell Thelonious "was high as a kite." Though Miriam had been "dying to hear him play," Nica saw that "nothing on earth would make him sit down at the piano." The Baroness was more than a little disconcerted at the turn of events, but her sister took it all in stride. "She was frankly cool about it, and said, 'Don't worry, I understand,' you know, 'He's a genius,' and all that stuff."

Although Nica's long-distance relationship with her siblings may have been cordial, over time she was being systematically written out of Rothschild family history. For example, her great-niece, Hannah Rothschild (the daughter of Victor's son, Jacob), wasn't even aware of her existence until she was in her late teens. The first time Hannah recalls hearing about her great-aunt was on a visit to Victor's home, when, in an effort to further her cultural education, he played her a couple of recordings by his favorite jazz pianists, Teddy Wilson and Art Tatum. Following the listening session, he turned to her and casually suggested, "If you ever go to New York, you should look up your aunt . . ." Hannah consulted a Rothschild family tree and saw, to her astonishment, that "there was this person I'd never even heard of." Not long after, on a visit to her great-aunt Miriam's house, she came across a leather photo album with the name *Pannonica* embossed in gold across the cover, "and I opened it up and there's this little girl from nought to about the age of nine or ten." As to why Nica had been jettisoned from the official history of a family populated by eccentric characters, Hannah can only speculate. "Miriam and Victor in their own right were such stupendously accomplished people," she explains, "but they were also quite nervous and they weren't overly confident, and they didn't particularly like to share the limelight."

Hannah also believes that Nica's brother and sister harbored considerable resentment toward their younger sister because, as they took on the often onerous responsibilities that went along with the Rothschild name, "what they saw from the other side was somebody having a jolly nice life, thank you." Nor did they fully appreciate the true nature of

Nica's embrace of the jazz life. "We can see, with the value of hindsight, what Nica did," her great-niece points out, "but they didn't realize that." For Victor and Miriam, Nica was simply "the one who got away."

DURING THE SPRING of 1957, Thelonious was spending most of his time at Nica's comfortable new digs at the Algonquin Hotel, obsessively working on a new composition. Although the renovation of the Monks' fire-damaged apartment had been completed and a rented Steinway baby grand filled the living room and most of the kitchen, Thelonious found it difficult to spend much time there. Nellie had recently entered the hospital, with a thyroid condition that would require major surgery followed by a protracted period of recuperation. Thelonious sought escape from his paralyzing anxiety at Nica's piano.

After working tirelessly for weeks, he completed what remains his most heartfelt composition, and the only tune he always performed straight through exactly as composed: a stately ballad for his ailing wife. Initially he titled the piece "Twilight with Nellie"; most likely it was the bilingual Baroness who proposed the French translation, "Crepuscule with Nellie," and Monk, no doubt pleased by this evocation of romance and sophistication, concurred. Nica also managed to capture the evolution of the composition on her tape recorder, as borne out by the tantalizing notation for Reel 21 of the Pannonica Collection: "Thelonious, The Birth of 'Crepuscule,' May 1957."

Nellie eventually made a full recovery, but the experience left Thelonious shaken and only exacerbated his emotional vulnerability. According to Harry Colomby, "He was just going crazy. He was walking around drunk and dangerous." On visits to the Algonquin, his anxieties occasionally precipitated bouts of mania that tore him away from the piano. As Nica described it, "Thelonious started walking around the corridors on other floors in the hotel, and he would be wearing a red shirt and shades and carrying a white walking stick. He would push open the door and stick his head in and say, 'Nellie.'"

Needless to say, many of the elderly ladies who accounted for a sizable percentage of the hotel's long-term residents were none too pleased. "They started sending for their trunks from the attic," Nica remembered, "saying they were cutting out." As for the hotel's legendary tolerance for artistic eccentricity, Nica soon discovered that even the Algonquin had its limits. "They were supposed to be broader-minded and like having geniuses there," she explained, "but Thelonious turned out to be one genius too many for them." Informed that the pianist was no longer welcome at the Algonquin, the Baroness continued to slip him past the front desk and whisk him up a flight of stairs to the elevator. It worked for a while, until one occasion when the elevator doors opened and left them face-to-face with the night manager. For the third time since settling in New York, Nica would have to seek other accommodations. "I obviously wasn't going to stay there if Thelonious wasn't allowed," she explained.

Harry Colomby's loyalty to Monk also remained as strong as ever. When he wasn't working to secure Monk short-money out-of-town gigs or keeping track of his guest appearances on sessions for friends like Art Blakey and Sonny Rollins—or teaching his high school English classes—Colomby was putting all his efforts into getting back Monk's cabaret card.

New York's system for licensing cabarets—defined as "any room, place or space in the city in which any musical entertainment, singing, dancing or other similar amusement [takes place in conjunction with] the business of directly or indirectly selling to the public food or drink"—goes back to the 1920s. The legislation was really just another response to jazz-age fears about the racial mixing taking place in the urban nightspots featuring so-called hot music. In the 1930s, the New York City Police Department joined forces with the New York State Liquor Authority to issue licenses for the city's nightclubs both high- and lowbrow; a decade later, its purview was expanded to cover not just the venues themselves but those employed therein.

Ostensibly the requirement that chefs and waiters be photographed, fingerprinted, and issued a "Cabaret Employee Identification Card" was meant to prevent "undesirables" from infiltrating establishments perceived to be breeding grounds of vice and criminality. But according to Maxwell T. Cohen, a lawyer who would later spearhead a successful challenge to the police-card system, the new licensing rules were actually a reaction to another of the era's great dangers, the Red Menace. As Cohen pointed out, "It was thought that many of the unions were dominated by Communists, particularly the waiters' union," and the card was "seen as a way of weakening the unions." Within a few years an extensive bureaucracy had been established for the distribution of licenses to waiters, bartenders, cooks—and musicians.

The license, which had to be renewed every two years, required payment of a two-dollar fee, collected by the police and quietly deposited in the department's pension fund. Even more remunerative, however, was the unofficial income generated by a pervasive system of not-so-petty graft, bribery, and blackmail. In some cases, a couple of bucks passed under the table to a department representative might undo the revocation of someone's card, while in others, thousands of dollars changed hands. Maxwell Cohen explained that if club owners challenged the system, the police "responded in the only way possible—constant inspections, summonses, threats, and suspensions." By the mid-1950s, the cabaret cards of many of the era's greatest jazz musicians (including Bud Powell, Jackie McLean, J. J. Johnson, Billie Holiday, and Thelonious Monk) had been revoked or suspended, almost exclusively for drug-related offenses. In many of these cases, the consequences proved tragic.

Not long before his death, Charlie Parker wrote a letter to the State Liquor Board expressing his desperation following the suspension of his cabaret card. "My right to pursue my chosen profession has been taken away, and my wife and three children who are innocent of any wrongdoing are suffering," he began. After detailing the difficulties he was having affording medical treatment for his infant daughter, Pree (who died not long after), Bird explained that he had "made a sincere effort to be a family man and a good citizen." He beseeched the board to "give me and my family back the right to live." Soon two detectives showed up at his apartment with an offer to restore his card if he agreed to finger other high-profile users, but Parker refused to name names. Eventually he was able to reclaim his cabaret card, most likely through the Mob-connected backers of one of the big Broadway jazz clubs that wanted Bird's name on their marquee. For Harry Colomby, the problem was that nobody seemed to want Thelonious enough to do the same.

After an initial attempt to reclaim Monk's card fell through, Colomby lined up letters of support from critics and other upstanding members of the jazz community and filed his own affidavit saying that Monk was drug-free (a lie, he later admitted, that caused him more than a few sleepless nights). In the spring of 1957, a Nica-funded lawyer secured a new hearing, and this time, according to Monk's biographer, Robin Kelley, "it worked. Monk promptly headed down to 56 Worth Street, the Police License Division, where he was fingerprinted, photographed, and relieved of two bucks. He walked out with card number G7321, a license to work, and a job."

Those aware of both the corruption of the cabaret-card system and the depth of Nica's pocketbook have always assumed that she provided a generous under-the-table contribution to some police officer's private pension fund. But while she was certainly eager to help recoup Monk's license, Harry Colomby knew enough to prevent her direct involve-ment in the process. "She would have been an obstacle, if anything," he declared, "a rich white woman looking for a cabaret card for Monk!" Years later, when she was asked how Thelonious had managed to reclaim his card, the Baroness confirmed Colomby's account. "I have no idea, really," she admitted. "Mainly we found out everything we could and got all the lawyers onto it and ended up pushing it through."

It turns out that the key to Colomby's success was the promise of a gig he had secured from Joe Termini, the owner with his brother, Ignatze (a.k.a. Iggy), of a shabby bar on the northern edge of the Bowery, a mile-long avenue that had been the city's skid row for over a century. The brothers had inherited the saloon from their father, Salvatore, after their return from World War II, and they had kept the place pretty much as it had been when he was running it: there was a battle-scarred bar along one side of the dimly lit room, a couple of rickety tables, sawdust on the floor, and plenty of watery beer and jug wine to satisfy the local clientele.

• • •

HUDDLED IN THE SHADOWS of the Third Avenue Elevated line, the Terminis' Bowery Café was one step up from the fictional Village gin mill of *The Iceman Cometh*, Eugene O'Neill's epic about a ragtag collection of lushes and losers who subsist on a combination of cheap booze and their "pipe dreams" of a brighter day. But if someone had told the Termini brothers that their dreary dive would soon become the haunt of internationally renowned artists and prizewinning writers, it would have seemed like the biggest pipe dream of them all.

By the time Colomby enlisted the Terminis in his campaign to secure Thelonious Monk's place in the forefront of modern jazz, their out-of-the-way hole in the wall had already seen some big changes. In 1955, the city tore down the train tracks that loomed above the Bowery streetscape, and once again the sun shone down on the brick façades of the mostly abandoned nineteenth-century tenements and warehouses. Soon Joe and Iggy noticed that their bar was attracting some unusual new customers. Drawn by the cheap rents and the light, artists had begun to settle in the area; looking for a quiet place to gather for a drink, they found a congenial haven at the Terminis' ramshackle tavern.

In 2008, with his ninetieth birthday only a few months away, a frail and soft-spoken Iggy Termini marveled at how his Bowery saloon had been abruptly transformed into a latter-day Lapin Agile, the down-at-the-heels cabaret in Montmartre that had served as a clubhouse for Picasso, Modigliani, and other turn-of-the-twentieth-century modernists. As Iggy made clear, once again "the artists were the ones who started it all." He credits the painter Herman Cherry, who had come to New York to study with Thomas Hart Benton at about the same time as Jackson Pollack, with establishing the place as a watering hole for the downtown art crowd. "He helped us quite a bit," Iggy recalled. "It was his idea to put up the posters"—a reference to the wall of overlapping flyers and one-sheets promoting local art exhibits and performances that shows up so often in photos of the club.

Another of the new arrivals in the neighborhood was a merchant sea-
man and amateur pianist named Don Shoemaker, who had been host-
ing jam sessions in an upper-floor apartment next door to the Terminis'
place. Tired of running up and down the stairs for pitchers of beer, Shoemaker told the brothers that if they put in a piano, he would provide
free music. A few weeks later, a secondhand upright was sitting across
from the bar and the requisite license was hanging on the wall, certifying
that the Five Spot Café (renamed in honor of its location at 5 Cooper
Square) was legally permitted to feature live music in accordance with
the provisions of the city's cabaret laws.

By the summer of 1956, some of Herman Cherry's Cedar Tavern
cohorts—including such leading abstract expressionist painters as Franz
Kline, Willem de Kooning, Jack Tworkov, Joan Mitchell, and the sculptor
David Smith—began making the fifteen-minute walk from their Greenwich Village headquarters to the Bowery saloon. While it wasn't exactly
what you'd call a jazz club, word of Shoemaker's informal performances
spread, and soon the joint was packed with art-world music fans in paint-
splattered jeans. In a 1989 interview with the discographer and DJ Phil
Schaap, Joe Termini reflected on his initiation into the jazz life. "In the
beginning, I didn't understand anything," he told Schaap during a Monk
birthday broadcast on WKCR. "Then I was nodding my head along with
everybody else."

While the Terminis may have been jazz neophytes, they soon had
some expert guidance in the person of David Amram, an exuberant
twenty-five-year-old French horn player who had just returned from
Europe, where he had served a tour of duty in the armed forces and
spent a year in Paris hanging out with the current crop of American
expats. Within a week of his arrival in New York in the fall of 1955,
Amram had enrolled in the Manhattan School of Music to study classical composition, found a cozy sixth-floor walk-up (for forty-eight dollars
per month) on the Lower East Side, and been hired by Charles Mingus,
who was lining up a new band for a gig at the Café Bohemia. Amram
was immediately caught up in the exhilarating energy of New York's mid-
fifties music scene, but he also felt the pall that had been cast by Charlie

Parker's death just a few months earlier. "In a way," he wrote in his mem-oir, *Vibrations*, "the jazz world was tied together because of this loss;" and Amram—who had heard the news of Bird's demise in Paris—experienced it more personally than most.

Amram had been living in Washington, D.C., before leaving for his army service in 1952. One night he went to hear Charlie Parker at the Howard Theater, and following the show, he went backstage to meet the saxophonist. The pair hit it off, and Amram invited Bird to his basement apartment, where they talked and listened to classical records while Amram cooked some Jewish soul food—borscht, sour cream, and dumplings. "He loved it all," Amram recalled. During the rest of Parker's weeklong run at the Howard, the new friends got together a few more times; one night they were joined by what Amram described as "the cream of Washington's hip underground," and Parker's young, drug and alcohol-free acolyte suddenly felt very uncool. "To console me, Bird said something I'll never forget. He said, 'David, the hippest thing is to be square.'"

Three years later, Amram found himself in the beating heart of hip, and he fit right in. Mingus's gig at the Bohemia attracted throngs of fans and fellow musicians, and to Amram's delight he "was able to get into the groove right away." One night Monk came by to hear the bass player's new band, and, impressed by Amram's ability to swing so freely on the cumbersome French horn, he took the trouble to introduce himself. Amram was thrilled to meet one of his greatest musical heroes, but when Monk asked to exchange phone numbers and invited him to get in touch "anytime," he was ecstatic. The very next day, when Amram finished class, he rang up the pianist, and Monk proved as good as his word. "Hey, Dave," he replied to Amram's eager overture, "come on over."

They soon fell into a familiar pattern. Amram would leave the Manahttan School of Music at the end of the day and head over to West 63rd Street for after-school sessions with Monk. "We would sit around for hours talking and listening," the composer remembers. "His remarks and comments on music were unbelievably perceptive." On other occasions, Monk would head down to Amram's East Village apartment and they'd spend "the whole day jamming, talking, eating, and generally hanging out."

One night Monk took his young friend up to the Bolivar to meet Nica, and Amram got his first taste of a scene unlike any he'd ever experienced. After entering her enormous suite, he was introduced to Nica and Janka ("She was lovely—just a teenager"). Then he sat down as Monk walked over to a beautiful Steinway and "played the piano all night." From his very first visit, Nica made Amram feel like part of the family. "She was just this incredibly warm and gracious person," he recalls fondly. "She was far from what you would think of as some kind of millionairess or countess or arts patron with an iron grip on your psyche. She was just such a lovely person—you just felt right at home *immediately* and didn't want to leave." Many times, he didn't. Sometimes he just crashed on her couch, but mostly he would get into the flow and—like everyone else— stay up for two or three nights in a row. "It was like there was no time, in the traditional sense. A day might be thirty-six hours long, followed by a six-hour rest period. Nobody slept much."

Jazz musicians who knew Nica have provided similar accounts of her schedule: her day would typically start at four or five in the afternoon; she would bathe, listen to some records, perhaps work on one of her art projects, and then rush off to catch the last set at one of her favorite jazz clubs. Although the Baroness loved to spend time browsing in record stores, the only one that stayed open late enough was Colony, a Broadway landmark located near Birdland, which didn't close until four in the morning. "Sometimes, in fact, I've kept them open until five while I was digging the new releases," she confessed to Nat Hentoff. And as Hentoff came to learn firsthand, when you set up a meeting with the Baroness, you needed to set your watch to "Nica time." Once after she agreed to an interview with Hentoff and then failed to show up three times in a row, a car arrived at his apartment, four hours after their scheduled appointment, with a note of apology from the Baroness, in verse, hand-delivered by a chauffeur. It read in part:

I swear that I am
Much more touched than you'd know
By the kindness that you show
And so flattered that I am
Worth an hour of your time
That perhaps is why
I keep goofing. I'm shy.

For the indefatigable David Amram, however, the day-for-night life-style of New York's jazz community just meant additional opportunities to talk, jam, and hang with his heroes; and like everyone who was admitted to Monk's inner circle, he soon became privy to the very special bond between Thelonious and Nellie. "The love was so strong in that apartment," he observed after his first visit to West 63rd Street, "it was almost like the heat was turned up." He also realized that "Nellie was also crazy about Nica. They were really close." And, Amram insists, "Nellie understood that if Monk was over there, he was there just to play music."

Although Nica typically receded into the background in social situations, Amram soon became aware of her wide-ranging interest in literature, art, ballet, and history. "She was like a brilliant, worldly, sophisticated woman," he recalls, "but she was the kind of person who was into making everyone else feel at home—and feel good about themselves." And it was only in passing that he picked up tantalizing tidbits about her past. "She never talked about herself," he remembers, "except occasionally when she would say, 'When I was . . . ,' and then she'd mention some fantastic place where she was, or some incredible world-renowned figure that she knew. But she would only do that as part of the passing conversation. She wasn't a name-dropper."

DURING HIS TIME IN PARIS, Amram had fallen in with a circle of American artists, including the vibrant and volatile modernist painter Joan Mitchell. "Joan had kind of taken me under her wing," he remembers. "She was a few years older and *really* sophisticated." So when

Amram announced that he was planning to return home, Mitchell told him, "When you go to New York, go to the Cedar Tavern." It was here that he reunited with a couple of acquaintances from his Paris days and made friends with artists such as Franz Kline, David Smith, Alfred Leslie, Norman Bluhm, Larry Rivers, and Herman Cherry, all of whom had recently begun hanging out at the Five Spot. Like them, Amram was struck by the joint's creative ambiance and relaxed vibe. "There were no microphones, no lighting, everybody was smoking, everybody was sitting there—black and white people all hanging out together."

More than anyone else, it was Amram who recognized the natural affinity between the painters, poets, and jazz musicians. "The struggle painters had was like that of jazz musicians," he explained. "People still thought that if art wasn't from Europe, it was worthless. Jazz was an accepted art form in Europe in the fifties, but only a small group of people recognized it here." Through his conversations with Kline, de Kooning, and the others, Amram also began to have a greater appreciation for their revolutionary aesthetic. "The painters taught me to see again," he acknowledges, "and this taught me to hear."

In November 1956, the freewheeling modernist aesthetic that was evolving at the Five Spot was put to the test when Amram took a new musical acquaintance down to the club and turned him loose on the Terminis' beat-up piano. About the same age as Amram, Cecil Taylor was a classically trained African-American piano prodigy whose musical taste extended from the work of swing-era veterans (particularly Duke Ellington) and the architects of jazz modernism (especially Thelonious Monk) to that of the most venturesome masters of contemporary European classical music (including Bartók and Berg). Raised in a middle-class neighborhood of Queens, New York, Taylor had benefited from the tutelage of a culturally sophisticated mother, who had exposed her son to the tap dancing of the Nicholas Brothers, the singing of Ella Fitzgerald, the philosophy of Schopenhauer, the big-band arrangements of Mary Lou Williams, and the poetry of Langston Hughes.

Somehow, it all came out in his music: a cacophony of roiling syncopations, percussive polyrhythms, and dissonant tone clusters all played with an unbridled physicality that belied Taylor's small stature and bespectacled studiousness. When he was unleashed on the Five Spot keyboard, however, what also came out was a random selection of the piano's internal mechanisms. The instrument was already on its last legs, but it was the Terminis' baby. The brothers were furious, and as Amram recalls, they took it out on him. "Joe Termini, God bless him, said, 'I can't have that guy play, he broke my piano!' " While Amram tried to placate him by offering to fix the instrument, Joan Mitchell had an even more effective strategy. "Look, we think this guy's a genius," she told Joe on behalf of her fellow artists, "and if he doesn't come back, we're not going to come back." After taking a minute to contemplate the mass exodus of his new clientele, Termini relented.

Later, when he was asked by the *New York Times* how the Five Spot came to feature such "far out" jazz musicians as Cecil Taylor, Termini explained that his customers enjoyed them, because "most of them were abstract artists and they were pretty far out too." In Taylor's spontaneous free-form improvisations and vibrant splashes of dissonance, Mitchell, de Kooning, Grace Hartigan, and the others recognized the aural equivalent of their own artistic explorations. As Amram put it, "The painters not only made the Five Spot grow from a Bowery bar into a jazz center, but they created its atmosphere. They were genuinely interested in the music and they felt what we were doing was serious music."

For the next five weeks, Taylor and his quartet held forth to a growing crowd that included veteran jazz fans and curious scene-makers. While some were able to hear beyond the jarring cacophony and appreciate the band's rigorous modernity and passion, many others headed for the exits. Ironically, many of the naysayers dismissed Cecil Taylor's music using the same turn of phrase that had been hurled at the modernist painters: "My kid could do that!" Taylor's stint at the Five Spot may have been primarily a *succès de scandale*, but as far as the Terminis were concerned, that was good enough. From then on, the erstwhile Bowery bar owners were in the modern jazz business.

In January 1957, David Amram took the tiny Five Spot stage with a "chamber jazz" ensemble built around the sound of his French horn. The place was packed with the usual suspects, along with a host of curiosity seekers drawn to the club by the hype over Cecil Taylor's recent engagement. For the next three months, attendance at the club far exceeded its official capacity (seventy-six persons), and the mainstream press began to pay attention. Midway through Amram's booking, *Esquire* sent the photographer Burt Glinn to do a feature for the magazine. In addition to a full-page shot of Amram in action, the article focused on the notable members of the city's "New Bohemia" that had made the place its headquarters. One photo featured club regulars crowded around a table in animated conversation. The identifying caption: "In a corner of the Five Spot (left to right) are sculptor David Smith; Frank O'Hara, a poet; Larry Rivers and Grace Hartigan, both artists; an economist, Sidney Rolfe; dancer Anita Huffington; and Bill Hunter, a neurosurgeon. Bar jumps till four a.m."

When Harry Colomby went to check out the Five Spot, he saw the club's cramped confines as its greatest virtue. "I was looking for a small place that [Monk] could have an extended engagement in, rather than just a week or two," he recalls. "I wanted to find a place where he could sit down and play for months and months and months. And I wanted a small place because I wanted to make sure that it always looked crowded, that it had a feeling of excitement." Joe Termini would later admit that he really didn't know much about Monk at that point—"I'd heard of him," he told the disk jockey Phil Schaap—but he was open to giving the pianist a shot. Joe's guarantee of a gig paved the way for the restoration of Monk's cabaret card, and an opening night was scheduled for early July. It would be Monk's first full-scale New York nightclub booking in over six years.

The timing couldn't have been better. A well-received engagement by Charles Mingus had further solidified the Five Spot's reputation as the city's hippest jazz joint, and Monk's brand-new Riverside LP, *Brilliant Corners*, had just received a glowing five-star review by Nat Hentoff. Writing in *DownBeat*, Hentoff praised the "Monk-idiomatic melodic twists and pragmatic, this-is-how-I-hear-it chord structure" of his new compositions, and called listeners' attention to the pianist's Zen-like ability to "dominate by the force of his personality." The review ended with the blurb-worthy declaration "This is Riverside's most important modern jazz LP to date."

Naturally, this came as no surprise to Nica, who had not only been privy to the album's creation but had provided the inspiration for two of its most striking tunes, "Pannonica," Monk's homage to her, and his quirky blues honoring her hotel sanctuary, "Ba-lue Bolivar Ba-lues-are." For months, Monk had commandeered Nica's Steinway as he honed his new compositions until they met his rigorous standards, and then taken his bandmates to the Bolivar to rehearse them.

FIREWORKS LIT UP the sky the night Thelonious Monk made his return to the Big Apple jazz scene. OK, so it just happened to be the Fourth of July, and along the Bowery, the only bright spot in the murky thoroughfare was the dim glow from the window of the Five Spot Café. Though the historic significance of Monk's opening night may have escaped the notice of most New Yorkers, for a small circle of intimates, including Nellie, Nica, David Amram, and Harry Colomby, it was a profoundly moving moment.

"I was exhilarated beyond description, that's all I could say," Colomby recalled in a 1987 interview. Not only was he thrilled that Monk would now be able to perform again in the city he loved so much, but he felt a tremendous sense of personal vindication that his impetuous promise to Monk two years earlier had borne fruit at last. "I thought we were on our way to achieve what we started out, and what I kind of promised I would try to do—that was to get him recognized in his lifetime."

Monk's Five Spot performances became a magnet for jazz fans and fellow musicians, most of whom had never had the chance to hear the pianist play in person. "They were people that heard *about* him, that were hearing him for the first time," Colomby recalled, "and what I felt was there was kind of—what is that called? A conversion. I mean, he was always respected by a handful of musicians, but the people didn't know, the world didn't know, and here was an opportunity for the world to see and to hear."

A couple of weeks into the gig, the Terminis realized they were onto something big. The brothers junked their secondhand piano and had Monk pick out a shiny new Baldwin grand; they reconfigured the awkward interior of the club to create a bigger bandstand (and squeeze in about a dozen additional paying customers); and they began tentatively to jack up their prices. Reassured that he now had a commitment for a long run, Monk formed a new band, made up of some of his favorite sidemen, including the saxophonist John Coltrane, who had just come off his first big-time gig with Miles Davis. Over the next seven months, the Five Spot Café became the center of the jazz universe and the Thelonious Monk Quartet, featuring John Coltrane, emerged as one of the legendary bands in the history of jazz.

Although the first set at the Five Spot was scheduled to begin at about 9:15, Monk believed jazz was best heard, as the title of his most famous composition put it, "'round midnight." Besides, it took a while to pick out his wardrobe for the evening, and Monk had to look sharp! For the most part it fell to Nica to get him from his West 63rd Street apartment down to the club on the Lower East Side, and it typically required all her prodigious feats of automotive daring to arrive before the crowd got too restive. The Baroness was aided in this endeavor by a recent, rather extravagant acquisition.

After losing a couple of late-night drag races with other jazz-world hot-rodders, Nica traded in her Rolls-Royce for a brand-new Bentley S1 Continental Drophead Coupe, whose top speed of 120 miles per hour made it the fastest four-seat production model of its time. The car, dubbed the Bebop Bentley, makes an appearance in the memoirs of various musicians, including one by the pianist Hampton Hawes. It was about three in the morning, and Nica was driving Thelonious, Nellie, and Hampton down Seventh Avenue when Miles Davis pulled alongside in his Mercedes-Benz sports car, "calling through the window in his little hoarse voice . . . 'Want to race?'" After expressing her willingness to take up the challenge, Nica turned around to announce "in her prim British tone: 'This time I believe I'm going to beat the motherfucker.'" We don't know who won the contest, but Nica continued to barrel through the city in her beloved Bentley for the rest of her life. In 2001, when Christie's featured it in a fine-car auction, the Bebop Bentley sold for a cool quarter of a million dollars.

The Terminis were usually pulling out their hair as they waited for Monk, but the fans stayed and drank more beer, and as Monk rushed up to the bandstand—often still wearing his coat and hat—the packed club burst into thrilled applause. Nat Hentoff believed that more than anyone else, Monk was responsible for the Five Spot phenomenon. "The Five Spot was different," he explained to the journalist Dan Wakefield. "Monk gave the club an aura." In doing so, Hentoff contended, the Five Spot earned its place in jazz history as "the most significant jazz club since the clubs of Chicago in the twenties where Louis Armstrong played." For Nica, whose silver Bentley shone like a permanent beacon at the club's entrance, "there'd never been anything like the Five Spot."

Over the course of Thelonious Monk's extended engagement, the founding members of the Five Spot scene (Willem de Kooning, David Smith, Larry Rivers, Herman Cherry, David Amram, and others) were joined by an astonishing cross-section of the city's cultural cutting edge. There was Jack Kerouac, whose novel *On the Road* would be published later that year; the poet Frank O'Hara, who served as a vital link between the writers and artists, gays and straights, and bohemias uptown and downtown; and Allen Ginsberg, whose poem "Howl," published a year earlier, had made him the most famous and controversial poet of the era. Other regulars included the playwright, poet, and black-arts-movement pioneer LeRoi Jones (who, with his wife, Hettie, had recently moved directly across the street from the club), Leonard Bernstein (fresh from rehearsals for *West Side Story*), and the photographer/filmmaker Robert Frank (who was completing his groundbreaking photo-essay, *The Americans*).

The Five Spot also attracted jazz musicians from across the country, some of whom had never had the chance to hear Monk perform live. In addition to old friends like Dizzy Gillespie, Max Roach, and Charles Mingus, many younger musicians trekked to 5 Cooper Square. One of them was a twenty-one-year-old bass player named Buell Neidlinger. Unlike many of the others, however, Neidlinger was no stranger to the Five Spot itself, since he had been the bassist in the Cecil Taylor band that had stirred up so much controversy there earlier that year; and since he lived in a Bowery loft a block away, he didn't have to travel as far as most to get there.

Neidlinger had arrived in New York in the early 1950s, after a year at Yale, to get in on the city's Dixieland revival, a fad in which studious white devotees re-created vintage New Orleans and Chicago jazz. Before long, however, he had fallen in with a coterie of adventurous musicians who turned away from nostalgia to chart the future of jazz. Among these was the soprano saxophonist Steven Lacy (another revivalist refugee), who had first introduced the young bass player to Cecil Taylor. As Neidlinger explains it, "I went from being a Dixieland musician to being the bassist in the band that was the forerunner of modern jazz."

Aware that Neidlinger lived nearby, the Terminis would periodically call on him to bring one of his instruments down to the Five Spot when Monk's bassist, Wilbur Ware, showed up without his ax. As a result, Neidlinger established a personal relationship with Monk, often accompanying him out to the small courtyard behind the club between sets, where they bonded over a variety of controlled substances. Occasionally Neidlinger would also get a call from the Baroness, when one of her jam sessions was in danger of flagging for want of a bass. Typically Nica would race down from the Algonquin to the Bowery to pick him up, cramming his bass into the back seat of her Bentley; other times, when she couldn't tear herself away from the scene, she would just send a cab. This soon began to seem more trouble than it was worth. But when Neidlinger suggested to Nica that she buy a bass to keep around for such situations, and even offered to help her pick out a serviceable instrument, she looked at him as if he were mad. "With all these pawn-shop freaks here?" she responded in her high-toned British accent. "I can't do that!"

As someone who had his own struggles with addiction, Neidlinger understood what she meant. "I think they probably robbed her blind," he reflected. Yet he believes that for Nica, such issues were, as the musicians put it, just part of paying your dues. "Nica knew what hip was," Neidlinger explained, "but I don't know how she learned it." Decades later, when asked what else he recalled of his nights with the Baroness, he thought for a moment: "I remember the sound of her voice, and her unobtrusiveness."

Some former Five Spot regulars still retain visions of the Baroness making a grand entrance with a retinue of hangers-on, but most share Buell Neidlinger's recollection of someone who was content to fade into the background. For hours she would sit, alternately riveted by the music and engaged in animated conversation, snapping Polaroid photos or quietly drawing. Charles Turyn, a young jazz devotee who was working as a waiter at the club during this period, remembers Nica sitting with Sonny Rollins, casually doodling on the back of one of the "minimum cards" that were placed on each table. Glancing down at her small abstract sketch, Turyn blurted out, "Oh, Georges Braque!" She turned to Sonny proudly: "Even the waiter knows!" According to Turyn, "From then on, I was her guy in the place."

Occasionally Nica would lug her tape recorder down to the club to document Monk's repertoire as it evolved during the pianist's multimonth engagements. One evening she decided to play disk jockey, and as Monk kicked off the set with "Crepuscule with Nellie," the Baroness leaned into the microphone. On the tape, her voice, its ripe British accent shadowed by sultry, whiskey and smoke-cured inflections, cuts through the conversational hubbub and clinking glasses. "Good evening, everybody. This is *Nica's Tempo*"—the title of her imaginary radio show, lifted from a tune written for her by Gigi Gryce—"and tonight we're coming to you direct from the Five Spot Café, and that beautiful music you hear is coming from Thelonious Monk and his quartet: Charles Rouse on tenor saxophone, Roy Haynes on drums, and Ahmed Abdul Malik on bass." It's her only intrusion into a rare contemporary recording of Monk's historic appearance at the club.

Although the nine-year-old Toot may not have been there that particular evening, he often accompanied his father and Nica on their drive to the Five Spot, and he still recalls some of the amazing stories she told along the way. Conjuring up the fairy-tale world of her Rothschild childhood, Nica recounted the visits she made with her father to the vaults of the Bank of England, where the guards would challenge her to pick up one of the gold bars, or described how Albert Einstein, on one of his visits to the Rothschild mansion, had entertained her family with after-dinner parlor tricks. Toot also remembers tagging along on some of Nica's late-night missions of mercy. "We'd drop him [Monk] off at the club, and then me and Nica would go off in her Bentley up to some street in Harlem to save somebody. I was with her all the time, going to *this one's* house to bring him some food, or we'd have to run around all day because *he* didn't have a horn, but Nica was going to buy him a horn." Based solely on what he personally witnessed, he considers Nica "one of the greatest artistic benefactors in the history of the world." Toot also believes that the enormous respect the Baroness received from the musicians transcended both her Rothschild pedigree and her role as a wealthy patron of the arts. "Nica really, really knew the music," he insists. "That's one of the things the musicians loved about Nica—that she really knew, as if she was a musician herself." It's a perspective shared by many others in the jazz community, including Dan Morgenstern, the respected critic (and director of the Institute of Jazz Studies at Rutgers University).

Morgenstern, who had immigrated to New York from Denmark in the late 1940s, was just making his bones as a jazz writer when he was introduced to Nica at the Five Spot. Over the next couple of decades, the Baroness—a voracious reader of jazz history and criticism—would become one of his most dedicated readers, just as he would become a loyal defender of her role in the jazz community. "To me, she was a real patroness," Morgenstern explained, "a really warm-hearted person." And as for the notion in some quarters that Nica was little more than a dilettante, Morgenstern insists, "She really understood the music. We would have little talks when I would run into her and whatever she had to say was very perceptive." Nor did he find her as parochial in her taste as many jazz aficionados. "She wasn't limited; she could appreciate different styles. So to me, she was a terrific lady!"

That's certainly how she struck the jazz vocalist and songwriter Jon Hendricks, who had first met the Baroness in the clubs on 52nd Street not long after her arrival in New York. A serious student of twentieth-century African-American history and culture, Hendricks introduced a racial component to the divergent theories about Nica's devotion to jazz and its creators. "She understood what culture is, and so she approached *our* culture in that way," the singer contends. "To her, Thelonious and Bird were not just 'hip jazz musicians,' they were great cultural artists, and she treated them in that way."

Hendricks had started his professional career as a child performer in a Toldeo, Ohio, jazz club featuring the piano genius Art Tatum. In the early fifties, when Bird was passing through the Midwest, he caught Hendricks's act and encouraged the young singer to go to New York. By 1957, as Monk was packing them in at the Five Spot, Hendricks was recording his first album with a groundbreaking vocal trio he had formed with the bebop-inspired singers Dave Lambert and Annie Ross. Over the next few years, the group, known simply as Lambert, Hendricks and Ross, would propel Jon into the upper echelons of the jazz world, but at that point he was still scuffling. Since he was living in a fifth-floor walk-up on East Sixth Street (around the corner from the Five Spot), Hendricks regularly dropped by to check out the scene. Too broke to pay the cover, he would press up against the front window, until one rainy night Joe Termini pulled him inside. "Anybody who loves this music as much as you should be in here," Joe told the singer as he led him to a stool at the end of the bar.

Once inside the club, Hendricks got a chance to renew his acquaintanceship with the Baroness. "Every time we met, we'd find a little quiet spot and chat," he recalls. After the war, Hendricks had studied English and writing at the University of Toledo on the GI Bill, and he prides himself on his wide-ranging erudition. "I was able to speak with her on many different levels," he explains, "and she liked to speak to me for that reason." To Hendricks, she was the epitome of cultural sophistication and grace. "She remained a lady through everything," he declared, "and was always meticulously herself." Meanwhile, Monk—with whom Hendricks also developed a close and enduring bond—would acknowledge his presence with the affectionate greeting "How you doin', muthafucka!"

Following in the footsteps of *Esquire*'s prescient piece about the club's role in New York's "New Bohemia," *The New Yorker*, which had recently added the Five Spot Café to its weekly survey of the city's prime music venues, sent a reporter to interview Monk. According to Jon Hendricks, who witnessed the exchange, it had been pouring all night, the rain beating against the club's storefront windows:

> *Reporter:* Tell me, Mr. Monk, do you think the rain will have an
>   influence on your playing?
> *Monk:* I hope so!

Typically, Thelonious Monk's singular aphorisms have been cited to embellish demeaning caricatures of the pianist or to illustrate his eccentricities. But Hendricks, a dedicated collector of Monk's bon mots, has a different perspective. "Monk was deep," he explains. "I don't think the depth of this man was probed by anybody. His mind was formidable." And rather than dismiss his Zen-like declarations ("Two is one," "It's always night or we wouldn't need light"), Hendricks believes that in fact Monk was "telling you something very valuable. I began to understand things a lot more deeply just from talking with Thelonious."

Not long after Bob Dylan arrived in Greenwich Village in the early 1960s, he also had the opportunity to experience Monk's offhand insights. In his memoir, *Chronicles: Volume One*, Dylan describes how, one afternoon while wandering around the Lower East Side, he was drawn into a jazz club by the sound of some bluesy keyboard riffs. It was Monk, all alone, "a big half-eaten sandwich left on top of his piano." When Monk took a break, Dylan casually mentioned that he "played folk music up the street." The pianist didn't miss a beat: "We all play folk music," he responded. "Even then," Dylan observes, Monk "summoned magic shadows into being."

In Nica's 1986 article, "A Remembrance of Monk," published in the *Daily Challenge* (a Brooklyn-based African-American newspaper) a few years after the pianist's death, the Baroness offered her own perspective on the Wit and Wisdom of Thelonious Monk. "As a man, he was exactly like his music," she wrote. And while he usually preferred to communicate entirely though his music, according to Nica, whatever he did say "would come up from some bottomless well of wisdom and dry humor."

Based on her personal experience, however, she admitted that it "could take you years to get the full meaning of those little three-word sayings of his—if you were lucky enough to ever get it at all."

For the members of New York's cultural vanguard who flocked to the Five Spot during Monk's long tenure, the pianist's ineffable persona became a repository of aesthetic and spiritual sustenance, from which they drew inspiration for their own art. One of the regulars who was drawn into Monk's gravitational pull was Norman Mailer. "The place was incredibly small, and you could sit about five feet away from Monk's hands on the keyboard," he recalled of his nights at the jazz club. "It was a special time there, getting high and listening to music. I've never since had mental rides like I had then."

Monk's Five Spot debut happened to coincide with the publication of Mailer's controversial essay "The White Negro: Superficial Reflections on the Hipster" in the journal *Dissent*. The essay's most provocative section focused on the author's depiction of "the Negro" as the archetypal "American existentialist," whose exclusion from the "sophisticated inhibitions of civilization" had rendered him the embodiment of "hip." Drawing on his recent interest in the theories of Wilhelm Reich, Mailer described how the primal sexual power of the black male fueled a music that "gave voice to the character and quality of his existence, to his rage and the infinite variations of joy, lust, languor, growl, cramp, pinch, scream and despair of his orgasm. For jazz," he declared, "is orgasm." Nor was the author content to simply experience these potent forces vicariously. As his biographer Carl Rollyson explains, Mailer took action on two fronts: he built himself an "orgone box," and he rented a saxophone "in order to 'honk' along with the music of Thelonious Monk. Although he could not play the instrument, Mailer believed he was in tune with it, that he was 'hip.'"

The Beat pioneers Jack Kerouac and Gregory Corso, and their African-American counterparts LeRoi Jones and Ted Joans (the poet and artist credited with creating the graffito "Bird Lives"), were also fixtures at the Bowery jazz club. But it was Allen Ginsberg, who lived only a few blocks away, on East Second Street, who became a Five Spot favorite. Joe Ter-

mini immediately took a shine to the impecunious poet, often letting
Ginsberg bypass the club's modest cover charge. Like Mailer and Kerouac (who had first turned Allen on to Monk), Ginsberg viewed Monk
as a jazz guru.

One night Ginsberg presented Monk with a copy of his recently published Beat manifesto, "Howl." A week later, when the poet returned to the
Five Spot, he asked Monk what he had thought of his account of "Angelheaded hipsters . . . floating across the rooftops of cities contemplating
jazz." The pianist responded succinctly, "It makes sense." Ginsberg was so
struck by Monk's spontaneous witticism that over the years, the exchange
became one of his favorite anecdotes. Naturally, Monk also found his way
into Ginsberg's writing. In his 1965 poem "Who Be Kind To," a long, Whit-
manesque expression of universal compassion, Ginsberg added Monk's
name to his catalogue of those deserving the world's beneficence:

> Be kind to the Monk in the 5 Spot who plays
> lone chord-bangs on his vast piano
> lost in space and hearing himself
> in the nightclub universe

A few years earlier, after Monk's last set at the club, Ginsberg had
invited Thelonious and the Baroness to join him on an adventure, which
he documented in a couple of photographs for his personal collection.
One shows a shadowy image of Allen and Nica in his Lower East Side
pad, the smoke curling up from her cigarette holder, while in the other,
the bebop pianist and the Beat poet are deep in conversation. Although
we may not know what these icons of the avant-garde discussed, we do
have the cryptic notation Ginsberg scrawled on the back of the photo:
"Thelonious Monk, 1960? After playing at Five Spot (4 am?) & shooting
up / Tompkins Square East w/ The Baroness—a friend of hers, a lady."

By the time Monk's historic Five Spot comeback came to an end,
in December 1957, the pianist's place in the jazz pantheon was secure.
Over the course of his six-month engagement, Monk had not only put
to rest the demeaning caricatures that had plagued him for most of his

professional career but he became an object of veneration for New York's underground avant-garde. Most of all, he was as happy as he'd ever been. "He loved it," Nica later recalled of Monk's time at the scruffy jazz club. "Yeah, [he was] really happy there."

EVEN AS THE BARONESS continued to haunt the Five Spot and the city's other jazz venues, she was being pressured by the Algonquin's managers to curtail her private after-hours jazz salon. And with her ever-expanding hotel tab seriously past due, it became apparent that yet another move was in the offing. "We decided," Nica later recalled, "it was time I should get a house of my own." So just as he had done a few years earlier, when Nica had become persona non grata at the Stanhope, Victor came to the rescue.

Lord Rothschild dispatched a representative to search for a suitable home for his sister, and by the end of 1957 he found a 2,600-square-foot custom-built home perched on a sheer cliff above the Hudson River. Purchased for the not inconsiderable sum of $71,150, the house had not only a spectacular view of the New York skyline but a distinguished provenance. As Nica explained in a 1988 interview, "It was Mr. von Sternberg who owned it," and the reason he was selling the place was that "he was going back to California."

In the late 1940s, Josef von Sternberg, the temperamental auteur, discoverer of Marlene Dietrich, and director of such classic films as *The Blue Angel*, *The Scarlet Empress*, and *Morocco*, had decided to move to the East Coast following a period of failed film projects. Vowing never to return to Hollywood, he sold his modernist house (designed by the then-unheralded architect Richard Neutra) to the novelist Ayn Rand and set off for that hotspot of international celebrity and glamour . . . Weehawken, New Jersey?

While it wasn't exactly Hollywood East, Weehawken was one of a string of sleepy towns just across the Hudson River from New York City that had played an important role in the history of the American film industry, and in von Sternberg's early career. Beginning in the first decade of the twentieth century, fledgling studios, including Fox, Universal, and Goldwyn, had established facilities in places like Fort Lee and Jersey City. Attracted by the visual possibilities of its open fields, dirt roads, woodlands, and rocky outcroppings, filmmakers began using the area as the setting for westerns and popular serials. Among the most successful of these short, action-packed episodic adventures was a series starring the ingénue Pearl White, titled *The Perils of Pauline*. Since Pauline's heart-stopping perils occasionally ended with her precariously suspended at the edge of the Palisades, the riverbank's sheer cliffs, the suspenseful shorts became known as "cliffhangers."

Having gotten his start in the movie business as a teenager, cleaning prints and repairing sprocket holes for some of New Jersey's busy film labs, von Sternberg decided to stage the next act of his life at the edge of the same steep bluffs, in a new Bauhaus-inspired house whose windows framed sweeping views of the Manhattan skyline. In the caption to a photo taken from his living room window (which appears in von Sternberg's endlessly absorbing memoir, *Fun in a Chinese Laundry*), the home's owner declares—no doubt thinking back to his beloved Neutra-designed citadel—"Another ivory tower, built of cement blocks on a rock overlooking the Hudson River, ten minutes from Times Square."

Today Weehawken's location at the western terminus of the Lincoln Tunnel, linking New Jersey to the West Side of Manhattan, has made it one of New York City's most densely populated middle-class bedroom communities. But in 1947, when von Sternberg purchased the property, Weehawken was still a tranquil little town of tidy single-family homes, and the stretch of Kingswood Road he chose was quieter than most. A narrow cul-de-sac winding above the Hudson, the tree-shaded street is lined with a row of traditional homes: there's a mock-Tudor minimansion, a red brick Colonial, a squat craftsman bungalow, and then, on a double lot with a direct line of sight across to the Empire State Building, there's the startling sight of two unpainted cement cubes, stacked slightly off-center, with a small yellow door, sheltered by the overhang of the upper cube, bearing a pair of shiny aluminum numerals, 63.

While a few examples of the director's original modernist decor remained in place when the Baroness moved into von Sternberg's "ivory tower," according to Robin Kelley, "Nica furnished her new home with Thelonious in mind." At least two of the rooms were completely dominated by accoutrements central to his mental and physical well-being. In the top-floor living room, a Steinway grand piano was centered in front of the bank of enormous windows, while downstairs, a spacious dining room was completely given over to a table for ping-pong, a game Monk had mastered as a child at a local community center.

Within weeks, Nica's new house had become "Monk's second home" as well as the permanent venue for her formerly floating jazz salon. Musicians zipped back and forth through the Lincoln Tunnel from New York to Weehawken at all hours of the day and night, and as was her practice, the Baroness continued to record many of their jam sessions, rehearsals, and conversations. Scanning the boxes of tapes that she added to her shelves during this period, we would find entries such as "Typical Day at the Mad Pad with Nellie, Thelonious, Nica: March 1958" and "Thelonious & Sonny Rollins Practice at Mad Pad, Sept. 1958 + Conversation & Records."

The Baroness believed that like the ancestral homes of the British upper classes she had grown up in, her new residence deserved a name. At first she dubbed it the Mad Pad, a hipster moniker intended to reflect the manic atmosphere that prevailed there; but within a couple of years, as a house best known for the jazz cats who prowled the premises was taken over by cats of the four-legged variety, a new name emerged. Shortly after moving in, Nica purchased a pair of purebred Siamese cats named Putterputt and Meow, who were given free run of the house and the freedom to reproduce. Soon there were dozens of offspring nestled in the Steinway and the open instrument cases scattered across the floor. Before long, the official nickname of Nica's home had taken its final form: the Cathouse (pun intended).

One can certainly theorize about the source of Nica's "felinephilia": An outlet for her displaced maternal instinct? The Rothschild propensity for amassing vast collections of flora and fauna? Or simply another instance of her family's deep-seated eccentricity? There is, however, no question about the depth of her fervor, or the toll it took on her family life and her finances. In 1960, her eldest son, Patrick, moved into the Cathouse while he was attending graduate school in New York, but he didn't stay long. While the all-night jam sessions did make sleeping difficult, he bailed out for good when the cats began using the drafts of his term papers as a litter box. As Patrick explained, even with his mother's generous trust fund, she had trouble making ends meet. "She had so many expenses," he noted in an interview with *The National*. "Her cat food and veterinarian bills were astronomical."

Monk wasn't exactly a big fan of the cats either, but once again he made himself at home chez Nica. Not long after the Baroness moved into her new house, he came up with a new composition inspired by the sweeping views of the river just outside her windows. The tune, "Coming on the Hudson," marked a promising start to this new phase of Monk's creative life. Meanwhile, Harry Colomby was happily fielding offers from top-tier jazz clubs and major festivals, and that September, Monk took first place in *DownBeat*'s International Critics Poll. As for Nica, who had never doubted Monk's genius, the pianist's newfound acclaim must have been the ultimate validation for the transformation she had effected in her own life just a few years earlier.

6

Beyond the Five Spot:
Midcentury Modernism
Goes
Mainstream

For the Baroness it was the best of both worlds. She had comfortably settled into her own suburban manse but was only minutes away from her
favorite jazz spots across the river. By the fall of 1958, she was making
frequent late-night jaunts through the Lincoln Tunnel to the Lower East
Side, where Monk had been booked for another multimonth engagement at the Five Spot.

Along with the other dramatic changes that had taken place since
the pianist's debut at the Bowery jazz club, Monk, who was notoriously
fussy about his sidemen, was breaking in a new member of the Thelonious Monk Quartet. Initially fans were doubtful that the tenor saxophonist,
Charlie Rouse, was up to the job, but Nica had been privy to their recent
rehearsals at the Cathouse and knew that Rouse would bring a fresh and
spirited approach to the standard Monk repertoire. Some critics and fans
complained that he wasn't as adventurous or distinctive as his esteemed
predecessors (John Coltrane, Sonny Rollins, and Johnny Griffin), but Thelonious liked what he heard, and Rouse went on to become his longest-
serving sideman and one of his—and Nica's—closest friends.

Monk still had a couple of weeks left on his Five Spot contract, but in mid-October the Terminis gave him time off to take a brief gig at Baltimore's Comedy Club. Since neither Nellie nor Harry Colomby was available to accompany him, Nica offered her services as chauffeur. On the morning of October 15, she picked up Monk and Rouse and hit the road. They had left plenty of time to make the drive (especially with the Baroness at the wheel), but for reasons that would haunt Monk and Nica for years to come, they never made it past the Delaware state line.

Thelonious Monk loved New York. He delighted in the diversity of its neighborhoods and the rhythmic cacophony of its street life. Once, when an interviewer asked where he would reside if he couldn't live there, he dismissed all terrestrial options and succinctly answered, "The moon." On another occasion, when challenged by a reporter to define jazz, he didn't hesitate: "New York, man," he replied. "You can feel it. It's around in the air." And as Nat Hentoff pointed out, "When he does get in trouble, it's almost always on the road."

It was something that was always on Harry Colomby's mind. The racism of America during the 1950s, along with the complications that could result from Monk's periods of mania and psychological withdrawal, haunted his manager. Each time the pianist went out on tour, Colomby held his breath. "My biggest fear in those days," he admitted, "was that he would be shot by a cop."

A few days before Monk was scheduled to leave for Baltimore, Colomby began to sense some subtle changes in the pianist's behavior: "He was acting a little bizarre or [exhibiting] eccentric behavior that usually indicated some mood change." But Colomby kept his concern to himself. "There was no way to get out of [it], and I just couldn't take the responsibility to say, 'Cancel the engagement.'" So he went off to teach his classes at Far Rockaway High School. Nica picked up Monk and Rouse in her new Bentley, headed south, and before long the trio had crossed the bridge into Delaware.

When Nica recounted the story to Max Gordon many years later, she explained that when they reached the outskirts of New Castle, Thelonious began to complain that he was thirsty. Seeing a sign for the Park Plaza Motel and Bar, she pulled into the parking lot. While Nica remained at the wheel and Charlie dozed in the back seat, Thelonious disappeared into the low-slung white building. "When ten minutes passed," Nica told Gordon, "I began to get nervous. As I got out of the car to find out what happened, a jeep drove up, ground to a halt, and two cops dashed up the steps. In a minute they came out with Thelonious between them."

While the accounts vary in minor details, what transpired inside can be pieced together from articles in the New York tabloids, local African-American newspapers, and transcripts of the Superior Court of Delaware, New Castle County. After Monk entered the Park Plaza Motel, he began looking around for the bar. Since there was no one in the office, he made his way to a nearby kitchen where the wife of the motel's owner was washing dishes. According to a story published in the *New York Post*, Mrs. Harold Tonge had suddenly looked up from her task and "found Monk staring at her." She asked him what he wanted "but he gave no answer," and when she asked him to leave, "he just stood there." Mrs. Tonge then called her husband, who also asked Monk to leave the premises. When he maintained his trancelike silence, she called the police.

Nica told Max Gordon that after escorting Monk to her car, one of the cops turned to her and asked, "Who are you? And who is this man? He won't give his name. He won't talk." Although the Baroness had little awareness of Delaware's lingering policy of de facto racial segregation, she later acknowledged that they did make for an unusual aggregation: "I guess we did look pretty suspicious, two black men and a white woman in a foreign car." Nevertheless, when Nica explained that Monk was sick, the officers seemed satisfied. They allowed him to get in the car, and Nica drove off. The police followed them for a few minutes and then—for no apparent reason—pulled the Bentley over and demanded that Monk get out of the car.

As the transcript of the Superior Court of Delaware details, when the trooper ordered the defendant to leave the vehicle, "Monk refused to get out of the car and asked 'why the hell' he should do so, or words to that effect." The police then called for backup, and Monk was forcibly removed from the car and thrown to the ground. "One cop was beating on his hands with a billy club," Nica told Gordon. "I screamed and a crowd gathered." Eventually Monk was subdued, handcuffed, and thrown in the back of the patrol car. Nica and Charlie Rouse were free to leave, but when the police drove away with Monk, they followed close behind. "I feared they would take him off and kill him," Nica told the jazz writer Marc Crawford.

After filing charges against Monk for breach of the peace and assault and battery, the authorities turned their attention to the Baroness, described in the *New York Post* article as a "devotee of the 'cool' sound" often seen in jazz spots "draped in ermine." When the police requested permission to search her Bentley, Nica naively agreed. A search of the car's trunk turned up a small quantity of marijuana ("enough for one stick," she explained to Max Gordon), and a charge of possession of narcotics was immediately filed against Monk, Rouse, and the Baroness.

When the three defendants were brought before Magistrate Samuel J. Hatton, Monk (who was still in handcuffs) tried to attack Trooper Little, the arresting officer, and a second count of assault was added to the list of charges against him. Modest fines were imposed for the breach-of-peace charges, but since the assault and possession penalties were considerably more serious, Judge Hatton set bail at $5,300 for Monk and $5,000 for both Nica and Rouse. Nica made the necessary arrangements to post everyone's bail and they all quickly headed back to New York.

Harry Colomby was in his classroom discussing *Silas Marner* when a monitor came in and told him he had a phone call. He instructed his students to continue their discussion and went to the school's administrative office to take the call. It was one of Nica's lawyers, informing him of the arrests. He says that when he heard the news, "Everything kind of caved in." He walked back to his classroom in a state of shock. "The kids were just continuing, you know, asking questions about *Silas Marner*. I remember saying . . . 'Delaware'—and the kids saying, 'What?' "

For Monk, the consequences were immediate and severe. Without waiting for the outcome of his court case, the New York State Liquor Board stripped the pianist of the cabaret card he had been issued just eighteen months earlier, following a six-year suspension, and once again he was barred from working in any jazz club in New York. At the time,

Colomby experienced it as "a huge defeat." But later, when he looked back on what had taken place in Delaware (and New York City), he expressed a somewhat harsher critique of the incident: "It was shocking, it was immoral, it was unethical, it was criminal."

According to Robin Kelley, the events in Delaware sent Monk "spiraling into a deep depression. For days he couldn't sleep and lost his appetite." On October 21, a week after the incident, he headed to Pennsylvania Station for the train ride down to Delaware for a hearing on the charges, but he never managed to get on board. As the *Amsterdam News* reported the following day, the jazz pianist experienced a breakdown shortly after arriving at the train station and was "taken to Long Island City Hospital for psychiatric treatment." Besides describing the actions that had led up to Monk's arrest ("The baroness drove up to the Park Plaza Motel in New Castle in her $19,000 gray Bentley"), the article reminded readers of the Baroness's previous appearance in the local tabloids ("It was in her home that 'cool' musician Charlie Parker died in March 1955"). Monk remained in the hospital for evaluation as Nica and Rouse headed back to Delaware.

After briefly suspending the hearing to confirm that Monk had indeed been hospitalized, Judge Hatton engaged in a series of increasingly heated clashes with Theophilus Nix, the African-American attorney representing the pair of jazz musicians, over the admissibility of certain evidence, the absence of a court stenographer, and the presence of reporters. Based on the account in the *Baltimore Afro-American*, however, the proceedings against the Baroness—wildly misidentified as the "German Baroness Kathleen Jules Nica deKoenigswarter"—were considerably more serene. The reporter noted, for example, that during the course of the long hearing, the Baroness "posed gracefully for pictures inside and out of the courtroom," and that she "engaged in charcoal tracings throughout the entire trial."

At the end of the day, the case against all three defendants was referred to the Court of Common Pleas for a hearing "at a date to be determined." There was, however, a more immediate consequence for the Baroness: her beloved Bentley was impounded by the police, and as the *Baltimore Afro-American* informed its readers, "If Baroness de Koenigswarter is convicted on the narcotics charge, she faces the loss of the car to the state to be either used by the state or auctioned off."

Monk had long been an enthusiastic consumer of reefer (he had been busted in New York for possession a decade earlier), but the Baroness, whose intoxicant of choice was Chivas Regal, willingly took the rap for the small quantity of marijuana found in the trunk of her Bentley. A few weeks later, therefore, Monk pled guilty solely to the charges of assault and breach of the peace, paid a fine of $123.50, and walked out a free, if severely traumatized, man. He spent most of November 1958 in the hospital undergoing psychiatric evaluation, and another year would pass before he was able to secure the return of his cabaret card.

At the time, it seemed obvious to many that the entire episode had been tainted by racism. As one writer for the *Baltimore Afro-American* put it, "This column believes Monk and the baroness . . . were arrested basically because they were an interracial couple." Monk, however, wasn't willing to jump to such conclusions. At a hearing to reclaim his cabaret card, Harry Colomby questioned him about what had provoked the incident: "Didn't one of those people at the motel call you 'nigger'?" Monk, whose livelihood was on the line, responded, "No, I didn't hear that. But they were acting weird." For Nica, it was just one more example of his unshakable integrity. "Thelonious abhorred liars and never lied himself," she recalled years later. "If being honest meant hurting somebody's feelings, he remained silent."

While the Baroness was relieved that Monk's legal nightmare had come to an end, her own fate remained very much in doubt. She hired a team of high-priced lawyers and went through a series of trials that had the potential to end in prison or deportation. In the spring of 1960, she was tried without a jury in the Delaware Court of Common Pleas and found guilty of illegal possession of narcotics. According to the account in the *New York Times,* she was "sentenced to three years in prison" (and fined $3,000) for "having $10 worth of marijuana in her car when she was arrested with Thelonius [*sic*] Monk, Negro pianist, and another musician." The article indicated that "the 46-year-old mother of five," who had "served five years with the Free French forces in Africa, Italy and France," had been released on $10,000 bail and would appeal the conviction.

Whenever Nica was asked about this episode, she shrugged it off with a blasé indifference. "Well, I'm not going to talk about that," she declared in a 1988 interview, "because that is a bore!" But in a private journal entry written on the day her verdict was due, she was considerably less sanguine. "Today is the day upon which my entire future may well depend," she began. "At this very moment it may be being decided . . . Release—miraculous escape . . . a chance to start afresh, with a clean slate . . . or the onset of inevitable catastrophe . . . the beginning of the end . . ." In three closely written pages she poured out her anxiety and wondered if even the few people with whom she did share her fears, including her daughter Janka, Mary Lou Williams, and Sonny Rollins, truly understood the seriousness of her situation.

Nica's greatest concern, however, was for Monk and Nellie. "And as for Thelonious," she wrote, "his protection is the root of the whole business . . . I have *never* discussed it with him . . . I do not believe he is really aware of it . . . I do not want him to be . . . He and Nellie have enough worries as it is." Finally, she took some comfort in the spiritual faith of her friend Mary Lou Williams, who had been a devout Christian for a decade. "She promised to go to Mass for me . . . and I know she will not fail me."

Whether it was due to the power of prayer or the skill of her attorneys, Nica's appeal to the Superior Court of Delaware, New Castle County, which was finally decided on January 19, 1962, turned out to be a slam-dunk. In a direct rebuke to the police and lower courts, the judge in the case declared that the meager evidence of narcotics discovered in the search of Nica's car was obtained "without due process," "the search was not made pursuant to a legal arrest," "there was no search warrant issued," and "[the defendant] was not informed of her constitutional rights." As to the state's contention that Nica had freely given permission for her car to be searched, the judge held that in fact such permission had been provided under duress after she had "seen her companion twice beaten in the presence of several police officers for passively resisting arrest in connection with a minor charge." Case dismissed!

Years later, when the Baroness rehashed the episode with Max Gordon ("Darling, I never dreamed that Delaware could be such a mean, uptight little state"), she reserved her greatest scorn for the state's leading family. "The Du Ponts, had they wanted to, could have prevented the whole sorry mess," she told Gordon. "The Du Ponts have known the Rothschilds for generations. But would the Du Ponts lift a finger? No, of course not."

SHORTLY BEFORE Thelonious and Nica set off on their fateful trip to Delaware, Harry Colomby had received a telegram that offered a reprieve from his latest anxieties: "INTERESTED IN THELONIOUS MONK MUSIC. STOP. FOR MOVIE." Although the startling offer was signed "Marcel Romano," Colomby soon determined that Romano was writing on behalf of the French filmmaker Roger Vadim, who had recently directed the international sensation *And God Created Woman*, starring his soon-to-be-former wife, Brigitte Bardot. Vadim was beginning work on his next feature, a contemporary adaptation of the eighteenth-century novel *Les Liaisons Dangereuses*, and he wanted Monk to compose the music.

When a copy of the completed film was brought to New York in January 1959, Harry, Nica, and the entire Monk family attended a private screening, followed by a visit to the Cathouse for refreshments and conversation. Thelonious had recovered from his post–New Castle breakdown, but he remained in a fragile state. Ultimately he was unable to create any new compositions to accompany the classic story of seduction and deceit, so Vadim (and Romano, his music producer) selected some of Monk's warhorses and skillfully wove them into the narrative. For the most part, Monk's music serves to underscore, or provide a counterpoint to, the chilling sexual chess match that propels the plot of the film. But in one extended party sequence set in the protagonist's sleek modernist duplex, an onscreen jazz band composed of a couple of prominent African-American musicians perform an original tune credited to Art Blakey; titled "Weehawken Mad Pad," in honor of Nica's anarchic abode, it provides the perfect accompaniment to the frantic amorality and casual cruelties of the Parisian jet set.

In fact, over the previous few years, filmmakers on both sides of the Atlantic had been using jazz as a convenient signifier of the decadence of the urban netherworld. On closer inspection, however, midcentury cinema's jazz elements often conveyed a more complicated message. Take *The Man with the Golden Arm*, Otto Preminger's 1955 adaptation of Nelson Algren's novel about small-time grifters and gamblers, starring Frank Sinatra as Frankie Machine, a professional card dealer and aspiring jazz drummer with "a forty-pound monkey on his back." Here Elmer Bernstein's brassy, jazz-inflected score (which received an Academy Award nomination) serves to enhance both the movie's noirish milieu and the moral corruption of its characters. Yet in the film's pivotal scene, Frankie auditions for a gig that, ironically, provides his last best hope of finding refuge from the lowlife—in the jazz world.

Two years later, another of Bernstein's jazz scores made an even more potent contribution to Alexander Mackendrick's classic New York noir, *Sweet Smell of Success*, starring Burt Lancaster as J. J. Hunsecker, a power-obsessed gossip columnist modeled on Walter Winchell (Nica's old nemesis), and Tony Curtis as the oily and ambitious publicist Sidney Falco. Once again the film reflects the era's ambivalence about jazz. While Bernstein's dissonant score evokes the seamy reality lurking behind the glittery façade of the urban nightscape, it is the character Steve Dallas, a hip young jazz guitarist and bandleader (played by Martin Milner), who emerges as the embodiment of personal integrity, and who serves as a foil for the depravity and materialism of Hunsecker and company.

Throughout the late 1950s, other Hollywood movies—from major studio releases like Otto Preminger's 1959 courtroom drama, *Anatomy of a Murder* (with a score and onscreen appearance by Duke Ellington), to low-budget noirs like Orson Welles's 1958 masterpiece, *Touch of Evil* (music by Henry Mancini)—made effective use of jazz-based scores.

While the narratives of these films link the music to the murky under-belly of contemporary society, just as often jazz functions as a metaphor for moral rectitude and urban sophistication. Either way, the music had clearly secured a central role in midcentury American popular culture. Outside the Hollywood mainstream, however, there were filmmakers for whom jazz was not just a vehicle to enhance a story's ambiance but an inspiration for their art.

In 1957, when the young New York actor and teacher John Cassavetes got the idea to spin off one of the exercises he had developed with his students into a film project, he was directly inspired by the improvisations of jazz artists he was hearing at the Five Spot and other clubs. The film's narrative focused on the issues of race played out among three apparently biracial siblings and was set within the city's bohemian subculture; but as Cassavetes acknowledged, he "began shooting without having the slightest idea what had to be done or what the film would be like." Instead, each scene would be shaped around the actors' improvisations and filmed guerrilla-style on the streets of New York.

Although jazz has a marginal role in the film's plot, its aesthetic—or a distorted stereotype of the same—was central to its method. "The jazz musician doesn't deal with structured life," Cassavetes contended in an issue of the journal *Sight and Sound*. "He just wants *that night* like a kid . . . Jazz musicians don't want success. They want a good time and millions of memories to share of nights locked in." When it came time to commission a score for his fast-paced 16mm black-and-white movie, he turned to one of the era's most creative jazz musicians and composers, the bassist Charles Mingus. The novice director put together a rough cut and scheduled a recording session for Mingus's ensemble with the expectation that, as the band watched the film, they would simply do what jazz musicians did: improvise. But Cassavetes was in for a surprise. "No, man—can't do it! Can't do it!" Mingus responded. "We're artists. It's got to be written. Man, I got to work six more months. It's going to take me a long time, you know. I went to Juilliard."

Finally the desperate director (who had already booked three hours of studio time) managed to persuade Mingus to riff on a couple of the musical themes he had already sketched out, but the disconnect between the compositionally oriented jazz musician and the improvisationally inclined filmmaker was never entirely resolved. A year later, when Cassavetes's film—bearing the evocative title *Shadows*—was shown for the first time, the very last thing up on the screen was a mission statement from its director: "The film you have just seen was an improvisation." It was yet another example of the various ironies that played out during the era, as artists sought to infuse their work with the spontaneity and emotional honesty of a musical style (and a culture) they often misunderstood.

After a screening of *Shadows* at New York's Paris Theater to a select audience of "underground film" fans, Cassavetes got funding to reshoot the film based on a carefully crafted screenplay. When he couldn't track down Mingus to provide additional music for the reconfigured film, he hired one of his sidemen, the saxophonist Shafi Hadi, who, for a payment of one hundred dollars, went into the studio and, as Cassavetes pantomimed a series of emotional vignettes, concocted a series of highly charged solos. Inspired by Hadi's spur-of-the-moment inventiveness (and unwilling to acknowledge the compromises to his experiment in pure cinematic spontaneity), the director simply appended the very same declaration of his artistic credo—"The film you have just seen was an improvisation"—to the end of the *scripted* version of his film.

The second version of *Shadows* premiered on November 11, 1959, as part of a program titled "The Cinema of Improvisation." It was preceded by *Pull My Daisy*, a half-hour film produced over the preceding couple of months by a contingent of Five Spot regulars who had been inspired by the original version of Cassavetes's film, which they had seen at its Paris Theater premiere. The film's plot, adapted from an unpublished play by Jack Kerouac, was based on an event from the life of Neal Cassady, the model for Dean Moriarty, the manic hero of *On the Road*. According to David Amram, Kerouac's play was about "a guy who worked for the railroad and brought his friends home for a party. After their goofing around, his wife got mad and threw them all out." The plan (such as it was) would be for the painter Alfred Leslie to direct and Robert Frank (who had just published his classic book of photographs, *The Americans*) to serve as cinematographer. But beyond that, Alfred Leslie insisted, "Everything will be improvised."

Leslie was true to his word. "The day we began filming," Amram wrote in his memoir, *Vibrations*, "was a prelude to weeks of chaotic, fun-filled madhouse clowning." In an effort to keep things from getting completely out of control, Kerouac was banned from the set, but the other participants—including Allen Ginsberg and his partner, Peter Orlovsky, Gregory Corso, David Amram, Larry Rivers, Alice Neel, the gallery owner Richard Bellamy, and the classically trained French actress Delphine Seyrig (who spoke little English)—more than made up for his absence.

When Robert Frank finished shooting, he edited the thirty hours of film into a half-hour slice-of-Beat-life drama whose soulful ambiance and textured black-and-white cinematography transposed Italian neorealism to the Lower East Side. Now all the silent film needed was a soundtrack. Kerouac was called in to improvise a narration as he watched the film unspool for the first time. "His words were like a great jazz solo, soaring above and weaving through the structure of the film," Amram recalled. The saxophonist Sahib Shihab dubbed in the scenes of Larry Rivers playing the sax ("I never sounded *that* good," Rivers admitted when he heard the results), and the hip jazz vocalist Anita Ellis performed the film's playfully erotic title song (with lyrics by Ginsberg, Cassady, and Kerouac; music by Amram):

> *Pull my daisy*
> *tip my cup*
> *all my doors are open . . .*

For many film historians, the double bill that screened that November night in 1959 represents nothing less than the birth of American independent cinema. But having contributed $40,000 of his own money to the creation of this enterprise, Cassavetes was broke. So when the offer of a starring role in a new TV series came along, the actor and aspiring auteur couldn't refuse.

Essentially a clone of *Peter Gunn*, a popular detective show with its own jazz-inflected Henry Mancini theme song, *Johnny Staccato* featured Cassavetes as a jazz pianist turned private eye—or, as Staccato put it in one of his hard-boiled voiceovers, though his "heart was still on the bandstand, he'd pay for the groceries away from the piano." As for Waldo's, the fictional Greenwich Village jazz club where Staccato often sat in with a band of real-life West Coast musicians, it came off like a Hollywood version of the Five Spot, with its genial Italian-American proprietor, diverse audience, and abstract expressionist paintings hanging on its brick walls. Unfortunately, Cassavetes continually locked horns with the show's producers, and before the first season was over, so was the show.

MEANWHILE, BACK AT the actual Five Spot, the various components of New York's avant-garde were coming together to form exciting new collaborations that fused jazz with poetry (initiated by Kerouac and Amram), theater (particularly the Living Theatre's production of Jack Gelber's *The Connection*), and experimental film (as in the abstract handmade shorts by Harry Smith). An ad in an issue of the poetry magazine *Zazen* seemed to say it all: "The Five Spot: Home of Thelonious Monk—Home of Jazz-Poetry—Home of America's Leading Painters, Sculptors, Composers, Actors, Poets, PEOPLE."

By the end of the 1950s, the unprepossessing nightclub had become not only the headquarters of New York's downtown bohemia but a racial and sexual "free zone," liberated from the constraints of Eisenhower-era America. On at least one occasion, the Five Spot even managed to free itself from the tyranny of the city's cabaret-card regime. It was an unforgettable night for the eighty or so people packed into the club; and since one of them documented the event in his best-known (and most anthologized) poem, the occasion has achieved a permanent place in American cultural history.

Billie Holiday only went to the club that night because her piano player, Mal Waldron, was accompanying Kenneth Koch in one of the Five Spot's weekly jazz-poetry performances. Joe Termini was hanging out at the bar with an off-duty cop who often frequented the joint, and when he noticed Holiday sitting in the audience, he asked Joe if she might be persuaded to sing. When Termini explained that she didn't have a cabaret card, he was told that "it wouldn't be a problem." Reassured, he walked over to Holiday's table. "Hey, Lady," Joe began, "you gonna sing for us tonight?" She looked around the room. "No way," she told him. "Too many fuzz around here." "But Lady," Joe responded, "that's who wants to hear you sing."

Kenneth Koch recalled, "It was very close to the end of her life, with her voice almost gone, just like a whisper, just like the taste of very old wine, but full of spirit. She sang these songs and it was very moving." The place was packed, but among those who had squeezed into the club was Koch's friend and fellow New York School poet Frank O'Hara, who had found a little standing room near the bathroom door.

On June 17, 1959, a few months after her impromptu set, Holiday died in a New York hospital where she had been under house arrest for drug possession. O'Hara learned of her death when he saw the headline on a copy of the *New York Post* upon leaving the Museum of Modern Art, where he worked as a curator. Within a few hours he had completed his celebrated poem "The Day Lady Died." In the final verse of his elegy, O'Hara recalls both her recent performance at the Bowery jazz club and the intensity of his own response to the beauty embodied in her ravaged voice:

> *And I am sweating a lot by now and thinking of*
> *leaning on the john door in the 5 SPOT*
> *while she whispered a song along the keyboard*
> *to Mal Waldron and everyone and I stopped breathing*

Unfortunately, there was one Five Spot regular and ardent Lady Day admirer who had missed that memorable night; in fact, from the fall of 1958 to the summer of 1960, the person most conspicuously absent from a club that proclaimed itself "the Home of Thelonious Monk" was Thelonious Monk. But as the pianist waited once again for his cabaret

1. New York's 52nd Street in its late-1940s heyday, a time when swing-era stalwarts were giving way to a corps of young jazz modernists. *William Gottlieb Collection. Music Division, Library of Congress*

TRING PARK.

2. The manor house at Tring Park, where Nica spent many of her formative years. The grazing emus, a familiar presence on the four-thousand-acre estate, were part of Walter Rothschild's zoo and museum of natural history, the largest private collection in the world. *Photograph by Samuel Glendenning Payne. Courtesy of Chris Reynolds; www .hertfordshire-geneology.co.uk*

3. Nica's father, Nathaniel Charles Rothschild, hitches a ride on one of his brother Walter's giant tortoises, as Walter looks on approvingly. © *Natural History Museum, London*

4. Jules de Koenigswarter: banker, war hero, and diplomat. After twenty years of marriage and five children, Jules sued Nica for divorce after Walter Winchell broadcast the news of Charlie Parker's death in his wife's apartment. *Courtesy of Musée de l'Ordre de la Libération*

5. This 1947 photo by William Gottlieb captures (from left) Thelonious Monk, Howard McGhee, Roy Eldridge, and Teddy Hill in full bebop regalia at Minton's Playhouse, the birthplace of modern jazz. *William Gottlieb Collection. Music Division, Library of Congress*

6. News of Bird's death in Nica's Stanhope Hotel suite devastated the jazz world, while the ensuing scandal made Nica a target of suspicion and resentment. New York *Daily Mirror*, March 15, 1955.

Bop King Dies in Heiress' Flat

By RICHARD KENNY and DAN MAHONEY

Jazzdom's "Bop" king, Charlie "The Bird" Parker, 53-year-old saxophonist, died Saturday night in the swank Fifth Ave. apartment of wealthy Baroness Nica Rothschild de Koenigswarter, and has lain unclaimed in Bellevue Hospital morgue ever since, it was learned Monday night.

DR. MILTON HELPERN, New York County Medical Examiner, said an autopsy completed Sunday on the famed jazzband leader showed he had died of lobar pneumonia.

The Baroness—a member of the English wing of the internationally famous House of Rothschild banking family—became Mrs. de Koenigswarter when she married a French diplomat.

Monday night she explained that Parker, "a friend of mine," had been taken ill while visiting her in her suite at the Stanhope Hotel, 995 Fifth Ave. en route to a Boston engagement, and had been treated by the hotel physician.

DR. ROBERT FREYMAN, of 9 E. 79th St., the hotel doctor, said he was summoned to the apartment "last Wednesday or Thursday" from an ulcer and other complications. He said Parker died of an acute heart attack at 8:45 p.m. Saturday.

The Baroness, who described herself as an "avid music lover and jazzophile," said she was born in England and that her brother, Lord Rothschild, was also known as a jazzophile and amateur pianist. She said she has five children, ranging from 3 to 18.

SHE SAID she had known Parker for many years and that he stopped off at her apartment last Wednesday to discuss a charity concert before going on to Boston for an engagement at Storeyville, a jazz spot.

Parker was suddenly taken ill while they were talking, she said, and, though the doctor advised hospitalization, the musician refused. She said he was watching a TV show Saturday night when he suddenly keeled over and "died in a few minutes."

Parker's wife, Chan Richardson Parker, a lovely fair-skinned brunette...

Jazz idol, Charlie "Yardbird" Parker, died Saturday of pneumonia in the Fifth Ave. suite of Baroness de Koenigswarter.
(Mirror Photos)

GOP to Keep Rent Curbs In City, 7 Other Areas

ALBANY, March 14 (AP).—Republican Senators agreed Monday night to drop rent controls for 17 Upstate counties and retain them for seven others and the New York City metropolitan area for two years, ending June 30, 1957.

The proposal was accepted unanimously by a conference of the GOP Senate majority. It was to be submitted later Monday night to members of the Republican majority in the Assembly.

WALTER J. MAHONEY, Senate majority leader, indicated the bill would be passed and sent to Gov. Harriman on a take-it-or-leave-it basis. Harriman has called for statewide controls.

"If he vetoes it (the Republican bill), there is no rent control," Mahoney told a news conference.

The present Rent Control Law expires June 30 unless a measure extending it is enacted.

be permitted to pass along increased operating expenses in the form of rent boosts.

Rent controls would be continued as is in Albany, Clinton, Jefferson, Monroe, Oneida, Onondaga and Rensselaer counties.

SIMILARLY affected would be New York City and Nassau, and Westchester counties, with some tightening provisions for New York City. Mahoney said the tightening would apply mostly to rooming and boarding houses.

One- and two-family owner-occupied houses would remain fully controlled in New York...

7. Lee Friedlander's photograph
of a 1957 Riverside recording
session shows the Baroness and
an unidentified listener absorbed
in the music of Thelonious Monk.
In May of that year, the label
released *Brilliant Corners*, the
album that featured his homage
to the Baroness, "Pannonica,"
as well as his ode to her Central
Park West apartment, "Ba-lue
Bolivar Ba-lues-are." © *Lee
Friedlander; courtesy Fraenkel
Gallery, San Francisco*

8. In the spring of 1957,
Esquire ran a photo-essay by
Burt Glinn about the new
home of New York bohemia.
The magazine's original
caption read, "In a corner of
the Five Spot (left to right)
are sculptor David Smith;
Frank O'Hara, a poet; Larry
Rivers and Grace Hartigan,
both artists; an economist,
Sidney Rolfe; dancer Anita
Huffington; and Bill Hunter,
a neurosurgeon. Bar jumps till
four a.m." (Omitted from this
impressive list was the woman
holding a glass with her back to
the viewer, the painter Helen
Frankenthaler.) *Photo by Burt
Glinn, courtesy Magnum Photos*

Park Plaza Motel AAA

U.S. Route 13 & 40
Miles South of Delaware Memorial Bridge
NEW CASTLE, DELAWARE

MOTEL

AAA
PARK PLAZA
MOTEL
TELEVISION
VACANCY

10

9. In 1958, while driving Monk to a gig in Baltimore, Nica stopped at the Park Plaza Motel and Bar so that Thelonious could get a cold drink. After being refused service, the pianist —along with Nica and the saxophonist Charlie Rouse— were arrested, initiating a series of trials and appeals that dragged on for four years. *Author's collection*

10. Allen Ginsberg, who lived just a few blocks from the Five Spot, was a regular at Monk's performances. One night, following the pianist's last set, the two midcentury modernists had an opportunity to bond (circa 1960). *Courtesy of Allen Ginsberg Collection*

11. After a night of music and conversation, the sunrise transformed a baroness and a Beat poet into shadowy silhouettes. *Courtesy of Allen Ginsberg Collection*

12. In 1958, after being kicked out of some of New York's most exclusive hotels, Nica retreated to a Bauhaus aerie atop the Palisades in Weehawken, New Jersey, built for the director Josef von Sternberg. *Author's collection*

12

13. Monk and the Baroness at the Five Spot Café (circa 1967) during one of his final engagements at the legendary jazz club. © *Raymond Ross Archives / CTSIMAGES.COM*

14. Nica and the great tenor saxophonist Coleman Hawkins share a laugh backstage at the Village Vanguard. © *Raymond Ross Archives / CTSIMAGES .COM*

14

THE CATHOUSE.

18 April '76

Darling Mary Lou,
I didn't come backstage after the concert because I know what a crowd there would be!... (also had to get home to give Thelonious his dinner!!) and, since then, have tried unsuccessfully to reach you on the phone to tell you how **ABSOLUTELY SUPERB** I thought you were...!!! Though it may make you angry, I **HAVE** to tell you the impression I got, because it was so extraordinarily vivid!! Rather than an "embrace", it seemed to me like a **CONFRONTATION**! Between Heaven & Hell !!! — with you (Heaven!) emerging **GLORIOUSLY TRIUMPHANT** !!! I **KNOW** it wasn't meant to be that way! — but that **IS** the way it **SEEMED** !! (Berit & Kari, who were with me, thought so too...) I also know what a sweet cat C.T. is, and what beautiful things he writes (in **WORDS**, that is...), but the funny part is that he **LOOKS** just like the Devil when he plays!! — as well as sounding like it, as far as I am concerned...!!! (**SHEETS** of

NOTHINGNESS"!? ... apparently seductive to some...???) Anyway, I **LOVED** Mickey Roker & Bob Cranshaw for seeming like Guardian Angels, coming to your defence !!? (particularly **MICKEY ROKER** !)... and it was worth it all to hear you **BRING IT BACK TO MUSIC** !!! (However wrong you may say I am, that crowd in Carnegie Hall made it clear that they felt the same way !!)

LOVE you !

Nica.

15. When Mary Lou Williams gave a duo piano concert at Carnegie Hall with the free-jazz pioneer Cecil Taylor, Nica not only attended the performance with two of her daughters but the letter she wrote Mary the following day may also have been the most incisive—and vivid—review of the high-profile event. *Mary Lou Williams Collection, Institute of Jazz Studies, Rutgers University*

16. In the 1980s, Nica met the young pianist Joel Forrester at the West Boondock, a Chelsea jazz club. She then invited him to her home to play his arresting compositions for Thelonious Monk, who had taken shelter there a few years earlier. Although Monk never engaged directly with Forrester, Nica and Joel maintained a close friendship until her death in 1988. *Courtesy of Ariel Warner*

card to be restored, a new performer stepped into the void and shook up the jazz world in a way no one had for a long time.

Ornette Coleman, a Texas-born alto saxophonist, arrived in New York from Los Angeles in the fall of 1959 to begin a two-week engagement at the Five Spot. But those who had already heard him out on the West Coast wondered if he would even make it past opening night. One New York musician who had already checked out the new arrival at L.A.'s Hillcrest Club recalled that a few minutes into the saxophonist's set, "The audience en masse got up, leaving their drinks on the table and on the bar, and headed for the door." As it turned out, Coleman not only completed his gig at the Five Spot, but the Terminis held him over for another two months. And the following spring they brought him back for four months more.

Ironically, what had turned off Ornette Coleman's Hillcrest audience—his shrill, keening sound (overlaid with honks and squeals), the raucous collective improvisation of his quartet (seemingly devoid of all coherence), his wild hair, full beard, and exotic dress—turned out to be exactly what appealed to many of the Five Spot's resident modernists. Not everyone was thrilled, but week after week curious jazz fans made the pilgrimage to 5 Cooper Square to hear what the fuss was about. "Every night the club would be jammed," Coleman remembered, "with some people hating what I was doing and calling me a charlatan, and other people loving it and calling me a genius."

While the members of the Five Spot's artistic avant-garde embraced the likeminded newcomer, the response of New York's jazz musicians to what he was playing—initially dubbed "the new thing" and later "free jazz"—mostly ranged from skepticism to outright fear and loathing. The great swing-era trumpeter Roy Eldridge staked out one point of view: "I think he's jiving, baby. He's putting everybody on." Miles Davis offered his own diagnosis: "If you're talking psychologically, the man is all screwed up inside." The legendary bebop drummer Max Roach didn't say anything at all; instead he "followed Coleman into the Five Spot kitchen between sets, and punched him in the mouth."

On the other hand, many of the jazz critics who gathered at the Five

Spot heralded Coleman's "new thing" as a giant leap in the consecration of modern jazz as high art. One *DownBeat* reviewer labeled his music "astonishing" and predicted, "Coleman may be the next great influence." Leonard Bernstein not only showed up at the club several times but he enthusiastically joined the band onstage on at least one occasion (and officially declared what he heard "the greatest thing that has ever happened to jazz!"). Monk was more circumspect in his judgment. "Hell, I did that twenty-five years ago," he told Charles Mingus after a brief foray down to the Five Spot, "but I didn't do it on each tune." The Baroness, like many dedicated jazz fans, was simply confused.

In the spring of 1960, not long after Ornette Coleman's New York debut, Nat Hentoff went to Nica's Weehawken home to interview her for an *Esquire* profile. But he quickly discovered that she had other things on her mind. As Hentoff recounted it, "The Baroness was uneasy at not having been able to understand Coleman's work," and she wanted the noted jazz writer to help her make sense of it.

Hentoff listened as Nica and Nellie Monk "discussed the problem" they confronted while listening to one of Coleman's latest recordings. But before he could offer his own analysis, Thelonious emerged from the bedroom to settle the matter. "There's nothing beautiful in what he's playing," he declared, as Nica "vigorously nodded [in] agreement." As Monk continued his assessment, "the Baroness nodded again." Finally, in an effort to prove a point about the saxophonist's debt to his own innovations (something Coleman readily acknowledged), the pianist dug out one of his old recordings and put it on Nica's hi-fi. Satisfied that he had established his bona fides, Thelonious rested his case with a typically generous flourish: "I think he's got a gang of potentiality though."

Over the course of the long evening, as Nat's wife sat in Nica's bedroom with Thelonious—who never uttered a single word—the Baroness entertained the jazz critic with stories of her Rothschild childhood, her wartime adventures, her marital woes, and her whole-hearted immersion in what Nat referred to as "the Jazz Life." A few days later she sent him a long handwritten addendum to their conversation, providing new details and clarifications so that he could present a more complete and accurate account of her life and times.

Although Hentoff catalogued the conflicting perspectives of Nica within the jazz community and touched gingerly on the tabloid scandals over Bird's death and her arrest in Delaware, on balance his article offered a vivid and sympathetic portrait of the Jazz Baroness (whom he memorably described as "an aging child who hasn't quite given up the hope that the Pied Piper may yet return"). It would be the last time she would subject herself to such unfettered scrutiny, however. When the jazz writer Gary Giddins sought—and was denied—an interview with the Baroness for his book *Celebrating Bird: The Triumph of Charlie Parker*, he learned that Nica had come to consider Hentoff's article (as Giddins put it) "wildly slanderous."

AMONG THE MORE surprising details in Hentoff's *Esquire* profile was his revelation that, in addition to serving as patron, cheerleader, and confidante to the jazz community, the Baroness had occasionally assumed the onerous job of manager for some of her closest jazz comrades. In doing so, Hentoff suggested somewhat waggishly, Nica was exhibiting the kind of "courage [she had] demonstrated during the war years." But according to Nica, she was only doing her part to shield sensitive and creative artists from the unseemly demands of the marketplace. "A musician," she insisted, "should never have to sit around a booking agent's office and try to sell himself."

Though Hentoff's list of the Baroness's "clients" included the pianist Sir Charles Thompson and the tenor saxophonist Hank Mobley, he pointedly noted that "her first charges were Art Blakey's initial Jazz Messengers." While he didn't pursue the subject in his profile, Nica's involvement with Blakey has been the subject of rumor and innuendo for decades. One of the music's greatest drummers, and nominal leader of one of the most respected and enduring small bands in jazz history, Art Blakey was a brilliant musician and a controversial and complex human being: a hard-core junkie during bebop's drug-ravaged heyday, a devout convert to Islam and a pioneer in exploring the African roots of jazz, a loyal friend of Monk during the pianist's most desperate years, and an inveterate womanizer and occasional bigamist.

Although Nica's early support for Blakey's band may have been simply a manifestation of her advocacy for any great jazz artist, she didn't go around buying every musician a pair of brand-new luxury cars. In his account of Blakey's relationship with the Baroness, Art's lawyer, Bruce Wright, boasted that "the drummer could have anything he wanted from her—that is, anything money could buy. There was no need to ask; she gave voluntarily and generously." And since Blakey needed a large car to transport the band and his drum kit, she surprised him one day with a roomy Rolls-Royce. Blakey's reaction was not what Nica had hoped for. According to Wright, "Art rejected the expensive gift with some anger, lashing out at her, saying, 'God damn it, you know I wanted a Cadillac!'" And, as Wright recalls, "he got one."

So just what was Nica's relationship with Art Blakey? As with so many intimate details of the Baroness's life, one confronts the frustrating reality that for the most part, those who say don't know, and those who know won't say. Even Bruce Wright, who takes note of the "many rumors and gossip that nagged her reputation," is quick to acknowledge that based on his own encounters with the Baroness, she was nothing more (or less) than "a gracious European woman who loved jazz and those who played it." Yet when Monk's son, Toot, was asked about the persistent rumors of a romantic relationship between Nica and Thelonious, he volunteered that when the Baroness and his father first met, "Nica was Blakey's girlfriend."

When pressed, those in the Baroness's inner circle respond to queries on the subject with blank stares or equivocation, Jon Hendricks's reply being typical: "I don't know anything about that." Though there's no evidence that Art Blakey ever addressed the question directly, his responses to Nica's request for his "three wishes" (collected in her posthumously published book, *Three Wishes: An Intimate Look at Jazz Greats*) are more than a little suggestive. While Art's first wish was for his son's well-being, the others were directed to the Baroness herself: one, "That *you* loved me"; the other, "That I get a divorce and we get married."

By most accounts, however, Nica's relationships with jazz musicians weren't rooted in matters of the heart, or the bottom line. So while Hentoff acknowledges that Nica might have occasionally "sat around a few booking agents' offices" in support of one or another of her jazz favorites, he suggests that the free-spirited Baroness was perhaps "less effective in handling her artists' business affairs than in supplying them with encouragement and a sympathetic ear." It's also clear that musicians relied on Nica's ear for more than her empathetic attentiveness. As Robin Kelley tells it, "She knew the music very well," and "her ear was respected" by many musicians.

Yet not everyone was so ready to accept the Baroness's participation in the often hardnosed—and male-dominated—jazz business. In the early 1960s, for example, Nica began to champion a pianist named Barry Harris who had recently come to New York from Detroit, where he had established a reputation as a creative teacher and loyal keeper of the bebop flame. When one of Harris's early recordings was being readied for release by Riverside Records, the Baroness paid a visit to the label's offices in the heart of Times Square to make sure everything was in order. At the time, Chris Albertson was a new member of the Riverside staff. An Icelandic immigrant who would go on to become a respected record producer and author of the definitive biography of Bessie Smith, Albertson recalls looking out the window one day and seeing Nica drive up to the curb, hop out of her Bentley (leaving the door open and the keys in the ignition), and blithely make her way into the building. She soon swept into the office, sipping from a silver flask. "She was very nice," Albertson recalls, "very smartly dressed and very pleasant." Announcing that she had come to "approve" the cover of Harris's new LP, she was, as Alberston put it, "humored," but "no one took her very seriously." She came back a couple of other times under similar circumstances, eliciting a similar response of bemused forbearance from the Riverside staff. In retrospect, Albertson sees Nica as a "Jewish mother" whose protectiveness of her jazz cohorts "sometimes made her intrusive," but who on balance "meant well."

FROM THE MOMENT the Baroness immersed herself in the New York jazz scene seven years earlier, she was accompanied every step of the way by her eldest daughter, Janka. Nica's account of Bird's final days, for example, describes how her daughter helped nurse the saxophonist after he collapsed on her Stanhope doorstep, how Janka took him pitchers of water to quench his insatiable thirst, played peggity with him to pass the time, sat beside him as they watched a TV juggler do his tricks, and comforted her mother when he passed away.

As her other children reached adulthood, Nica reestablished a maternal bond with each of them (just as they developed a familial attachment to Thelonious), but it was Janka who made the most profound connection to jazz. "She used to go to all these nightclubs with me, always," Nica recalled, "and she was so good on the music." When the Baroness and her daughter were in Iceland at a jazz event, there was a radio contest in which listeners from around the world were asked to identify the performers on a series of recordings. "Janka and I won out of hundreds of countries," Nica boasted, "because Janka knew the sidemen on every record!"

Although Janka makes brief appearances in a couple of jazz-world memoirs, for the most part she is depicted only in passing as a shy young woman fading demurely into the background. According to Toot the limp that some members of Nica's inner circle mention when they describe her was the result of a mild case of clubfoot, whose effects were so subtle that most observers noted only a slight irregularity in her gait. Taken together, however, these recollections can make Janka sound like the hip younger sister of the Tennessee Williams character Laura Wingfield, tending a menagerie of inbred cats instead of glass figurines and graciously entertaining a house full of gentlemen callers who just happened to be America's greatest jazz musicians.

One person who did manage to establish a connection with Janka during this period was Thelonious's niece, Jackie Smith, who was also a jazz-crazed teenager. "It was great," Jackie recalls, "a great friendship. We would go hear the music, and we exchanged phone numbers and would talk together all the time—I mean *all* the time! Nica ran a tight ship," Jackie explains, "but I must have passed muster." So when Janka sought out her mother's permission to head out for one of their girls' nights out on the town, Nica would demand, "Who are you going with?" And when she would respond, "Jackie," Nica's only response: "Have a good time."

Janka soon took her own plunge into the deep end of the jazz life. In the early 1960s, an exciting young African-American drummer named Clifford Jarvis came to New York, fell into Nica's orbit, and began a romantic relationship with her daughter. In 1965, the twenty-six-year-old Janka gave birth to their son, Steven, but Jarvis, a brilliant if volatile musician, wasn't ready to settle down. For the next decade, Janka and Nica raised Steven together at the Cathouse; he attended a local school, developed a personal attachment to his "Uncle Thelonious," and eventually became one of the pianist's favorite ping-pong partners. It's also not clear just how much Janka (or her mother) knew about Clifford Jarvis's early life, or when they learned the story of his father's connection to one of the civil rights movement's legendary heroes.

Having grown up on the mean streets of Boston's Roxbury neighborhood, Clifford's father, Malcolm, was about sixteen years old when he met a recent arrival in town who shared the same first name. Although Malcolm (Shorty) Jarvis had already joined the musicians' union and was playing trumpet in a couple of local big bands, before long he was spending more time hanging out with his new friend, hustling and committing petty crimes. A few years later, the teenagers were arrested following a string of burglaries, and it was during their incarceration that Jarvis's running buddy, Malcolm Little, began his conversion to Islam and adopted the name Malcolm X. On this basis, Shorty (who has taken credit for shepherding the future Nation of Islam minister on his spiritual path) took his place as a footnote in black history and became known as "the Other Malcolm."

After Jarvis served his time, he secured a steady day job and resumed playing trumpet in local gigs. Eventually, his son Clifford, followed in his father's musical footsteps. He studied drums at the prestigious Berklee College of Music in Boston and then worked professionally with the likes of Jackie McLean, Barry Harris, and Sun Ra, all good friends of the Baroness. Shorty's memoir—a combination of autobiography, spiritual reflection, and score-settling (especially with Spike Lee, who portrayed Shorty as a buffoon in a Technicolor zoot suit in his biopic, *Malcolm X*)— doesn't go into detail about his relationship with his son. But by the time his grandson was born, father and son had been estranged for years. After Clifford moved to England following Steven's birth, his father became an occasional visitor to the Cathouse. One photo in Malcolm's memoir shows him holding a beaming two-year-old boy on his lap above the caption: "Shorty with his grandson, Steven de Koenigswarter (Clifford and Janka's child—and the famous Baroness's grandson)."

Thelonious's niece Jackie recalls that following the birth of Janka's son, there was a dramatic change in the relationship of the former best friends. "After the baby," Jackie recalled, "Janka really closed off—you didn't see her at the clubs, you didn't see her at all." In the late 1970s, Janka and Steven abruptly left Weehawken for England, but the move wasn't an attempt to reunite with Steven's father; instead, Janka had crossed the Atlantic to enroll their son in a venerable British private school. According to a friend of Steven's, life as a fatherless biracial Jew in suburban New Jersey hadn't been a bed of roses (he once told her how he had been beaten by a gang of white students). Not that the idyllic British academy offered a respite from his teenage angst. But rather than retreating to the consolations of home, Janka and her son set off to start a new life in Israel.

The Rothschilds' Jewish identity has always been a double-edged sword. Throughout the generations, the family has been alternately celebrated as exemplars of Jewish achievement and philanthropy and vilified as venal conspirators in a Zionist plot for world domination. In reality, Nica and her siblings had been raised by a pair of socialist-leaning secular humanists. As her brother, Victor, described it in a memoir of his early life, "My father and mother were, I suppose, atheists or agnostics. At any rate there was no religious indoctrination at home." So perhaps no one was more surprised than the Baroness when her eldest daughter rediscovered her cultural roots and took up residence in the Jewish homeland ("She is fanatical," Nica told an acquaintance, with more than a little ambivalence). Although Steven returned to England when he reached adulthood, Janka, a talented painter, remained in Jerusalem, where she lives to this day.

EVEN WITHOUT MONK, the Five Spot was thriving, both creatively and financially. So when the Terminis heard that a large, loftlike space was available a few blocks away, the brothers took over the room; they spruced it up with an assortment of concert posters, art exhibit fliers, and modernist paintings, and dubbed the joint the Jazz Gallery. The Terminis had hoped to book Monk for their new club's grand opening, in December 1959, but the pianist hadn't been able to secure his cabaret card.

Thelonious and Nellie continued to make themselves at home at the Cathouse. On any given day, old friends would drop by to hang out and musicians would gather to jam, as dozens of cats (the four-footed ones) prowled the property. It's true there were no longer any hotel managers knocking on Nica's door, but her neighbors weren't exactly thrilled about the carnival she had brought to their quiet cul-de-sac. She often joked that it was easy to find her house, because it was the only one on the block without a "For Sale" sign in its front yard.

By the summer of 1960, Harry Colomby was finally able to reclaim Monk's card, and the Terminis took out ads in the local papers announcing the Thelonious Monk Quartet's Jazz Gallery debut. It had been a year and a half since Monk had performed at a nightclub in his hometown, and by 8:00 an excited crowd had begun assembling outside the club. According to Robin Kelley, "It was as if they were waiting for the resurrection." Monk arrived at about 10:15, accompanied by Nellie and Nica, and immediately bounded onstage as if eager to reclaim his rightful place as the era's foremost modern jazz pianist.

Monk made a number of return appearances to the Jazz Gallery, then took off on an extended tour of Europe (the first since his 1954 concert at the Salle Pleyel, at which he had been introduced to Nica), and added yet another *DownBeat* "Best Pianist" award to his rapidly expanding résumé. In some quarters, however, there was a growing sense that Monk, whose style hadn't changed much since he had emerged from his Minton's apprenticeship, was being overtaken by a coterie of free-jazz firebrands like Ornette Coleman and Cecil Taylor. But don't try telling that to the Baroness.

The issue came to a head in the summer of 1962, when Monk and his quartet were back at the Jazz Gallery and Cecil Taylor's band was holding forth at the Five Spot, just a few blocks away. According to Taylor's bass player, Buell Neidlinger, "Norman Mailer came in one night while we were playing and he'd had a lot to drink." For a while he sat quietly digging the music when "all of a sudden he jumped up and said, 'I've just come from the Jazz Gallery listening to Monk, and this guy, Cecil Taylor, is much better than Monk.'" Unfortunately for Taylor, it seems that Nica also happened to be at the club at the time, and she was not amused by Mailer's boozy proclamation. At the end of the evening, Iggy Termini came up to the band and delivered the bad news: they could finish out the week, but then they were through. Initially, the firing was blamed only on "a powerful friend of Thelonious Monk's," but Neidlinger later revealed that it had been the Baroness's doing.

Mailer wasn't the only Monk acolyte to shift his allegiance to the new generation of jazz modernists. By the early 1960s, abstract expressionism's unfettered freedom, once linked to bebop's raucous harmonies and headlong tempos, now seemed more aligned with the aesthetic principles of Cecil Taylor and Ornette Coleman. After all, they didn't call it "free jazz" for nothing; in 1961, when Coleman released a new recording titled *Free Jazz*, the cover of the double-wide-gatefold album featured a reproduction of the Jackson Pollock painting *White Light* as a way of highlighting these affinities. Nat Hentoff also noted that having "become friendly with several of the abstract expressionist painters who have made the Five Spot a clubhouse, Coleman is now intensely interested in painting." As a result, he reported, "the saxophonist can often be found exploring local museums like the Guggenheim, Metropolitan, and the Museum of Modern Art."

While Monk's gigs at the Five Spot had always attracted their fair share of New York's artistic avant-garde, there are no reports of any interactions between the pianist and the throng of adventurous painters who frequented the club. But as Nica pointed out, Monk also enjoyed visiting the Guggenheim—at least in his own unique way. "Thelonious was a great admirer of Frank Lloyd Wright," she explained, "and he loved going to the Guggenheim." In particular, she recalled their visit to "an exhibition of extremely avant-garde art." At one point, she noticed Thelonious standing in an obscure alcove of the museum, "gazing at something— backing away from it and peering at it" with such intensity that a crowd had gathered around him. Nica soon caught up with her companion and discovered the object of his scrutiny. "It turned out to be the museum's air cooling system." She remembered that "Monk was delighted" by his childlike prank, and he "danced backwards the whole way down the circular ramp."

AT THE SAME TIME that Nica was making regular visits to the offices of Riverside Records on behalf of Barry Harris, Harry Colomby was plotting Monk's departure from the same company. Eventually Colomby put together a deal that added his client's name to the roster of the country's most prestigious popular music label, Columbia Records. In addition to a stable of best-selling pop vocalists such as Tony Bennett, Johnny Mathis, and Barbra Streisand, Columbia had recently become home to two of the jazz world's biggest stars, Miles Davis and Dave Brubeck. Thelonious Monk had finally made it into the big time.

In the fall of 1962, Monk walked into Columbia's 30th Street Studio, sat down at one of its pristine Steinway grand pianos, and began to record his first major-label album. Under the supervision of the company's premier jazz producer, Teo Macero, he emerged from the sessions with a strong collection of original compositions (including an homage to the Terminis titled "Five Spot Blues") along with inventive improvisations on a couple of his favorite popular songs, "Body and Soul" and "Just a Gigolo."

While no one could have been happier than Nica to see Monk getting the attention and financial rewards he deserved, the Baroness was also somewhat perturbed that when it came time to commission the liner notes for his Columbia debut (appropriately titled *Monk's Dream*), Macero declined her offer to write an ode to her hero in favor of the enthusiastic testimony of some of the country's most prominent jazz critics. Still, Nica was desperate to have a hand in this exciting new stage in Monk's career, if only she could manage to keep her appointment with his producer.

A letter she wrote to Macero (now in the collection of the Library for the Performing Arts at Lincoln Center) highlights both Nica's eagerness and the difficulties she had functioning within the constraints of the business world—even the jazz business. Using a sheet of her new personal stationery, embossed at the top with a tasteful blue crown above her Weehawken address, she implored Macero to at least consider using one of her paintings for the cover of Monk's next album ("I'm really keen to do an album-cover for him!"). She explained that doing so would "more than make up for the disappointment of having had one of my paintings chosen by Charlie Parker" for an album "he, unfortunately, never made." But when the producer set up an appointment with the Baroness to look over some of her paintings, she didn't show ("I arrived five minutes after you all left," she lamented). Nica concluded the letter by entreating Macero to give her one more chance. "I promise that, if you give me [another] appointment, I will see to it that I make it on time, for once!"

As part of her campaign to write the liner notes for Monk's next LP, Nica sent Macero the draft of a long, laudatory essay in which the extravagance of her accolades is matched by their over-the-top presentation. A handwritten work of art in its own right, her letter combined multicolor Magic Marker text and various collage elements to extol the glory of Thelonious Monk. Along the way, she suggested a title for the album—*The Living Legend*—and testified about the profound impact Monk had had on her own life and values. "I suspect that the majority of musicians never DO give forth with all they have inside them," she declared. "One of the things Thelonious seems to do for anyone who works with him"—speaking perhaps of herself—"is to give them the courage and confidence *they* need to do this . . . I think he makes them dig it would be shaming not to . . . !"

In a two-page appendage to her proposed liner notes titled "Some thoughts about Thelonious (for what they are worth . . .)," Nica revels in her privileged place in the life of the seminal pianist and composer: "[Too many] spend their lives lamenting the gods who have gone . . . Well, I can't help being gassed by the thought of future generations, to whom Thelonious will be ONE OF THE LEGENDS OF ALL TIME . . . and here I am living right in the middle of it!"

Worn down by Nica's persistence, and perhaps wary of alienating the patron of the newest addition to Columbia's jazz lineup, Macero placed a highly edited version of Nica's unsolicited manuscript on the back cover of Monk's next album, *Criss Cross*. After toning down her purple prose and tacking on his own brief descriptions of a couple of specific tunes, Macero ran the Baroness's essay above the prominent byline "Nica de Koenigswarter." But listeners in the know would have been aware of her disembodied presence on the album just from a glance at its track list, for among the compositions included on the follow-up to Monk's Columbia debut were those he had dedicated to the two most significant women in his life: "Crepuscule with Nellie" and "Pannonica."

Thelonious Monk's new status as a "Columbia Recording artist" was a harbinger of things to come. Over the next few years, the once obscure pianist would be both heralded by the house organ of the middlebrow establishment as the preeminent symbol of modern jazz and enshrined by the era's black intelligentsia as one of the icons of African-American culture. Yet as Nica entered middle age, she not only suffered once again the reductive distortions of the mainstream media, but also faced the ire of a newly empowered radical fringe. The "misty legend" of the Jazz Baroness was about to expand well beyond the insular subculture of New York, but there were going to be some serious challenges ahead—for the Baroness, for Monk, and for jazz itself.

7

The Sixties:
The Best of Times,
the Worst of Times

In the opening lines of his poem "Annus Mirabilis," the British poet Philip Larkin identifies the year 1963 as a watershed in the history of sexual relations in his homeland—"Sexual intercourse began / In nineteen sixty-three / (which was rather late for me)"—and frames the new era of erotic awakening with a pair of symbolic cultural markers—"Between the end of the *Chatterley* ban / And the Beatles' first LP," separated by just three years. It's no wonder that for those of Larkin's generation (he was born in 1922), this sudden explosion of sexual freedom made 1963, as the title of his poem put it, "a year of wonders."

Across the Atlantic, however, shouts of "Freedom Now!" were identified less with sexual liberation than with a potent movement for civil rights inspired by a young black preacher and a charismatic new president committed (if more reluctantly than myth suggests) to fulfilling the long-deferred dream of racial equality. Here as well, a sudden cultural transformation was bookended by a pair of emblematic events that were separated by just a few months.

In August 1963, hundreds of thousands of Americans, black and white, joined together in a historic March on Washington, where they listened to the protest songs of Bob Dylan and heard Martin Luther King's call for a time when people would no longer be "judged by the color of their skin but by the content of their character." By December, however, the assassination of President Kennedy had cast a deep pall over the summer's outpouring of optimism.

In the jazz world, performers had been addressing America's escalating racial turmoil for a few years. In 1958, for example, Sonny Rollins released an album whose nineteen-minute title track, "Freedom Suite," featured a roiling interplay between Sonny's tenor saxophone and the drums of Max Roach that perfectly illustrated the sentiments Rollins expressed in his liner notes. "America is deeply rooted in Negro culture: its colloquialism, its humor, its music," he wrote. "How ironic that the Negro, who more than any other people can claim America's culture as his own, is being persecuted and repressed, that the Negro, who has exemplified the humanities in his very existence, is being rewarded with inhumanity."

A year later, Charles Mingus responded to the violent confrontations taking place in the South with his composition "Fables of Faubus," a sardonic indictment of the Arkansas governor, Orval Faubus, who had mobilized the National Guard to prevent the integration of Little Rock Central High School. A year after that, Max Roach produced a highly charged recording, *We Insist! Max Roach's Freedom Now Suite*, containing lyrics written by Oscar Brown, Jr. (sung by Roach's wife, Abbey Lincoln), that reflected the deepening political consciousness of many African-American jazz musicians. Then, in 1963, after hearing the news that four young black girls had been killed in the bombing of a Birmingham church, John Coltrane recorded an elegy, alternately searing and solemn, titled simply "Alabama."

Meanwhile, a small but vocal faction of musicians and critics had become engaged in a campaign to claim jazz as an exclusively black art. Some of the more extreme proponents of musical separatism even began pressuring African-American bandleaders to hire only black sidemen. Dubbed "Crow Jim" by its opponents, a group largely composed of lib-

eral white jazz critics, the phenomenon inspired heated debate that fragmented the jazz community.

During this volatile period, Thelonious Monk, who had a complex and at times contradictory perspective on racial issues, became
an emblem both for proponents of Afrocentric identity politics and for
mainstream apologists for the status quo. For the Baroness, who over the
previous decade had turned her back on a life of white privilege to ally
herself with a generation of young, politically assertive black jazz musicians, things were about to become considerably more complicated.

Perhaps the best way to characterize Thelonious Monk's attitude
toward his African-American identity is with a term that during his formative years carried powerful connotations of pride and self-respect: he was
a "race man." In numerous interviews given over the course of his career,
Monk revealed himself to be both acutely aware of contemporary racial
dynamics and knowledgeable about black history and its heroes. But
while he often spoke passionately—and from personal experience—about
issues of prejudice and police brutality, he also resisted all attempts to
adhere to anyone's ethnocentric orthodoxy. On one occasion he declared,
"My music is not a social commentary on discrimination or poverty or the
like. I would have written the same way even if I had not been a Negro."
Yet a few years later, when he was confronted with the quote, he insisted
he had never said it. Challenged by the strident demands for racial purity
during the "Crow Jim" era, he continued to go his own way. "A lot of guys
are telling me I should have a black manager," he once confided to Harry
Colomby, "but I don't believe in that bullshit."

Although Monk frequently contributed his talents to fundraisers for
national civil rights groups like CORE and SNCC, as well as to community organizations in New York's black neighborhoods, he never joined
other African-American artists and celebrities at the high-profile dem-
onstrations taking place during these years. Colomby recalls a visit to
Monk's West 63rd Street apartment on August 28, 1963, the day of the
massive rally for jobs and freedom in the nation's capital: "I remember
sitting with him in his room and watching the March on Washington,
and, you know, [Harry] Belafonte and Lena Horne . . . were in front

walking with Dr. King. And Thelonious said, 'I think I'm contributing as much with my music as these people who are marching.'"

ALL THESE ISSUES were very much in the air during the summer of 1963, when the editors at *Time* magazine decided to schedule a major jazz-related feature story. After eliminating other prospective candidates for the cover, including Ray Charles (heroin bust) and Miles Davis (who hung up on them), they gave the nod to Thelonious Monk. Although Colomby was concerned that the article might be derailed by one of Monk's "episodes," he was thrilled that a magazine representing the voice of the establishment was going to be a vehicle for "the validation of Thelonious Monk, of what he has worked for, and what he has contributed, and the importance of the man."

After hanging out with Monk at home and on the job and conducting thirty interviews with his family, sidemen, and jazz insiders, Barry Farrell, the *Time* writer who had lobbied for the assignment, produced a dutiful five-thousand-word profile of the pianist; the artist Boris Chaliapin painted a moody, expressionistic portrait for the cover; and the editors scheduled the story for the week of November 29, 1963. A week before the issue was due to hit the newsstands, the printers began running off the Monk cover story, and Harry Colomby finally began to breathe easily.

On the afternoon of November 22, Colomby was in his classroom when the PA system came on. "I thought it was something about the astronauts," he recalls, "and then they announced Kennedy was shot." Although other feelings soon overtook him, he admits his "first reaction, candidly, was, there goes our cover." So a week later, when Harry picked up a copy of the magazine, he was hardly surprised to see the image of the new president, Lyndon Baines Johnson. *Time* held on to the Monk story, however, and a few months later, on February 28, 1964, Monk joined a select circle of jazz musicians (including Louis Armstrong, Duke Ellington, and Dave Brubeck) who had graced the magazine's cover during its forty-year history.

Titled "The Loneliest Monk," the article was a somewhat muddled affair. While there were still a few smirking references to the pianist's "mystical utterances," and an off-hand depiction of him as a "perfectly normal neurotic," Farrell celebrated Monk's unique artistry and highlighted the ecumenical spirit of his politics (in the context of the jazz world's recent racial upheavals). But the Baroness, featured prominently in the article's text and photos, was still shadowed by the lurid and superficial stereotypes of the past.

Depicted as Monk's "mascot," an "honest-to-God baroness" who arrives at the Five Spot "in her Bentley" each night "with a purse crammed with Chivas Regal," Nica comes off as a kooky sidekick who drops Monk off at his apartment as day dawns, then disappears back "home to Weehawken where she lives in a luxurious bedroom oasis, surrounded by the reeking squalor of her 32 cats." Even as Monk was inducted into the *Time*-sanctioned cultural pantheon, the Baroness was reduced to a caricature or dismissed as just another of the pianist's exotic accoutrements, like one of his stylish hats.

For the most part jazz fans were thrilled by the overdue acknowledgment of one of the music's masters, and African-Americans celebrated the honor bestowed by the mainstream culture on one of their cultural heroes. However, this feel-good consensus proved to be short-lived. The radical black journal the *Liberator* soon published a scathing deconstruction of the *Time* cover story titled "The American Way," which analyzed the Monk profile from a Marxist perspective. As its author, Theodore H. Pontifelt, expressed it, "Behind the façade of the genius recognized," the *Time* article intentionally obscured a more fundamental socioeconomic reality: "Thelonious Monk is earning a living with his talent, but is also being cruelly exploited." While *Time* and Columbia Records were taken to task for "fatten[ing] their pockets" at Monk's expense, the Baroness bore the brunt of Pontifelt's critique. Like other African-American entertainers, he asserted, Monk was at the mercy of "the ruthless demands handed down by money-hungry agents, cabaret owners, recording companies, and women like the Baroness Pannonica de Koenigswarter." In *Time*'s depiction of Nica as Monk's steadfast patron, he discovered yet another example of the emasculation of the African-American male. "She serves as a bitter insinuation to both black and white Americans alike," he declared, "that a rich white woman is the black man's salvation."

Finally, Pontifelt raised the still-potent specter of miscegenation. "*Time* magazine's message is very clear," he explained. "It warns white America that in these days of talking integration . . . they should remember that it could mean more of their daughters will be bringing home an occasional black genius." For Pontifelt, the moral of *Time*'s story was a simple one: the pianist's success was little more than a devil's bargain in which "Monk and Nellie remain as pure as honey" and the presence of the Baroness is the inevitable price that must be paid, "the bitter part of the sweet."

So it was that a decade after the death of Charlie Parker, the Baroness had metamorphosed from the "luscious, slinky, black-haired" sexual seductress who lured Bird to her deadly lair into a castrating surrogate mother without whom Monk "is made to seem helpless." Although she had just turned fifty, the dramatic shift in Nica's persona had less to do with her own transition to middle age than with the rapid transformation of America's racial politics. But while Pontifelt's critique offered an ironic echo of the reactionary innuendoes that had initially dominated the accounts of the Baroness, in other respects Nica's image had come a long way in just a few years.

BY THE MID-1960S, the gossip columnists who had once assailed Nica in the New York tabloids were treating her with a bemused affection. While they may still have had some difficulty defining her role in Monk's life—mascot, muse, or mother?—she had gradually become just another boldfaced name in their survey of goings-on about town. Take the following item from a 1963 column by Charles McHarry in the *Daily News*:

Baroness Nica de Rothschild, hearing jazzman Thelonious Monk was interested in buying her Bentley coupe, offered to sell it to him at cost. "How much?" he asked. "$19,000" was the reply. "Nineteen thousand," screamed Monk, "for $19,000 I can buy a home with four bedrooms, living room, kitchen and garage." "Of course you can," replied the baroness, "but where will it take you?"

Nica continued to be a familiar sight at clubs across the city; she organized benefits for fallen jazzmen like the bebop pianist Sonny Clark; she made her home available for jam sessions and regularly took in down-on-their-luck musicians for short-term respites, and even some extended residencies. But as the demands of Monk's burgeoning career began impacting his physical and emotional well-being, the Baroness focused the bulk of her energy on his health and welfare. Along the way, she became an honorary member of the extended Monk/Smith clan, a status that was acknowledged when in 1959 Nellie's sister, Evelyn (a.k.a. Skippy), gave birth to a girl on December 10, Nica's birthday. In honor of the coincidence—and in recognition of the Baroness's unique role in their lives—the baby's parents named their daughter Pannonica and informally dubbed her "Little Nica."

During this period, the Cathouse became a clubhouse for Monk family gatherings. On weekends and holidays, everyone would gather to share food, conversation, and music with Monk, Nellie, Nica, and whatever jazz musicians happened to be around at the time. According to Toot's somewhat hyperbolic description, "There'd be a whole bunch of them," with his father always at the center of the chaos. "He'd be forcing everybody to play ping pong all night and stuff like that, and Nica's taking a hundred million pictures of everybody and three thousand cats running everyplace all day and all night!"

When she did manage to find some quiet time for herself, Nica started to work on a new project, which paired her archive of intimate and revealing Polaroid photos with the collection of "three wishes" she had elicited over the years from some three hundred jazz musicians (from Louis Armstrong to Joe Zawinul). By the time she was finished, the Baroness had filled two Hermès leather journals with her collaged entries, creating a family album of her jazz *mishbocho*. On the first page she pasted a sketch of Thelonious Monk (from one of his Columbia LPs) and typed in an intriguing, if plainspoken, title: *The Jazz Musi-*

cians & Their 3 Wishes . . . as told to Baroness Nica de Koenigswarter. She
shopped the manuscript around to a number of publishers, but none of
them could see a viable market for the book. Disappointed by the lack of
interest, Nica filed the project away.

DESPITE THE ENORMOUS publicity generated by the *Time* cover story,
it wasn't long before the executives at Columbia Records began expressing concern about Monk's profitability. His ongoing episodes of emotional disequilibrium, combined with a hectic schedule of national and
international concerts, had already slowed his recording schedule. And
when the label did manage to pull together enough material for a new
LP, sales proved disappointing. Not ready to give up on his commercial
prospects, Columbia producers proposed a variety of marketing strategies, including an album of original Monk tunes set to lyrics by his old
friend and Columbia label mate Jon Hendricks.

In the late 1950s, Hendricks had formed a pioneering trio special-
izing in the contemporary art of "vocalese," a technique that set original lyrics, along with sections of improvised scat singing, to famous jazz
instrumental recordings. Lambert, Hendricks and Ross were undisputed
masters of the form, and over the next couple of decades, their casually hip Columbia LPs would become the inspiration for a variety of
singers from the worlds of jazz (Al Jarreau and Kurt Elling) and rock
(Joni Mitchell and Van Morrison), as well as a model for such second-
generation vocalese groups as Manhattan Transfer. In 1964, when Monk
was in San Francisco playing a weeklong club date, the pianist and the
lyricist got together to see what they could come up with.

At the time, Hendricks and his wife, Judith, were living on a house-
boat in Sausalito, so Jon made the half-hour drive into the city to pick up
Thelonious at his hotel. Although they hadn't discussed the specifics of
their collaboration, as soon as they got on board the boat, Thelonious sat
down at the piano and launched into "Pannonica." The soulful melody
filled the air, and Jon began sketching a set of lyrics. After a couple of

choruses, he put down his pencil and asked Thelonious to take it from the top. As he played, Jon crooned an affectionate ode to the Baroness that ended with an image inspired by her exotic name:

Delicate things,
such as butterfly wings,
poets can't describe, 'tho they try.
Love played a tune
when she stepped from her cocoon.
Pannonica my lovely, lovely, little butterfly.

Suddenly, Hendricks recalls, Monk jumped up from the piano bench and began pacing furiously, muttering under his breath: "No, muthafucka! No, muthafucka! No, you can't do that!" Distressed at his reaction, Hendricks asked him why he was so upset. "No, muthafucka, you can't do that," the pianist vented. "You can't write a lyric that quick! It took me six months to write that melody!"

Hendricks was famous for his ability to turn out inspired lyrics at astonishing speed, but Monk wanted a second opinion. He insisted they go back into the city to pick up his wife. But when they pulled up at Monk's hotel, Hendricks was surprised to find that Nellie wasn't alone. Standing beside her, smiling broadly, was Pannonica in the flesh. Nica had decided to fly in to attend Monk's performances, so the two women hopped in and Hendricks headed back to Sausalito. After some tea and homemade scones (courtesy of Jon's wife), they all moved to the piano and Hendricks sang his freshly minted lyrics. Before the last chord had faded away, Monk turned to the women. "What do you think?" he asked. "I think it's beautiful," Nellie replied. "I think it's just marvelous," Nica added enthusiastically. "Kiss my ass!" was Monk's frustrated response.

Recalling these events years later, Hendricks was characteristically modest. As he tells it, he had learned from the Austrian-born jazz pianist Joe Zawinul (now best known for having cofounded the jazz-fusion band Weather Report) that Nica's name was derived from a species of butterfly native to his homeland. "As soon as I found out what it meant," Hendricks explains, "the song wrote itself."

Hendricks's lyrics may have been an effort to capture Thelonious Monk's affection for Nica, but the lyricist was also speaking for himself. "I knew what she had done with her own life," he explains, "and it was unprecedented. I mean, she was royalty and she had come into the West and had embraced the art form of America's most despised people. For her to do that showed a very large heart and a huge concept of what is real and what is not. And when you arrive at that, you show a great awareness of the truly important things of life and you dismiss all the racism that stuffs the ears and warps the mind."

AFTER A DECADE of tabloid scandal-mongering, mass-market magazine profiles, and jazz-world word of mouth, the Baroness had become a renowned figure in the international jazz community. So in 1964, when the French jazz aficionado Francis Paudras picked up the phone in the New York hotel room he was sharing with the great bebop pianist Bud Powell, the woman who introduced herself—"in French, with a charming little English accent"—really needed no introduction. As Paudras recalled in his memoir, "Of course I had heard of Nica, the Baroness de Koenigswarter, whose reputation as a patron of the arts and friend of musicians was legendary."

Later that day, Nica arrived to pick up Powell and Paudras at their hotel. Hoping to beat the rush-hour traffic, she immediately headed over to the Lincoln Tunnel for the short trip to Weehawken. "Nica maneuvered her Bentley with the skill of a racing driver," Paudras noted. "A cigarette holder between her teeth, she took the turns at breakneck speed without batting an eyelash." Along the way she brought them up to date on the latest jazz gossip, and "as if by magic, before I knew it we had crossed the Hudson River to New Jersey and were pulling into Nica's driveway."

Once inside, the Baroness and her guests made their way upstairs into the airy living room, dominated by her Steinway baby grand and the wall of glass framing the expansive view of the Hudson River and the New York skyline. "The minute I saw the room," Paudras recalled, "I was overcome with emotion. It had the serenity of a chapel and the open piano was like a living presence. On that piano Monk had composed his greatest songs, along with Bud and Sonny Clark." Nica had the whole evening carefully planned. Later they would return to the city for a quiet dinner, and then head over to the Five Spot, where she had reserved a table for Charles Mingus's late set. "In the days that followed," Paudras gushed, "each time [Bud and I] saw Nica was a veritable delight. Nothing was too good for us. Every gesture was made with utter discretion, as if it was perfectly natural. Once and for all I was certain that she was the great lady of jazz."

Born into a musical family in 1924, Earl (Bud) Powell had been a child prodigy. By the time he was eight years old, he had worked his way through a sizable portion of the classical repertoire and was beginning to turn his attention to the world of jazz. As a teenager living in Harlem, he found his way to the jam sessions at Minton's and began absorbing the new musical ideas of Dizzy Gillespie, Charlie Parker, Kenny Clarke, and Thelonious Monk. Recognizing the younger pianist's potential, Monk took him under his wing.

Before long, Powell's technical prowess and unbounded musical imagination were dazzling even the most celebrated jazz musicians of the era. According to one anecdote, the teenaged Powell was at Minton's piano when the widely admired virtuoso (and composer of "Misty") Erroll Garner walked in. After listening for a while, someone turned to him and asked, "Hey, Erroll. You gonna play a set?" Garner just looked at the guy and said, "Not after that motherfucker, I ain't!"

Monk shared his deep harmonic knowledge with Powell, and took special pride in his young protégé's rapidly expanding reputation. They soon became inseparable, and Bud became the younger brother Thelonious never had. For his part, Powell not only developed tremendous personal affection for his mentor, but in 1944, when he was playing piano with the trumpeter Cootie Williams, the nineteen-year-old novice convinced his boss to add "'Round Midnight" to their recording session. It marked the debut of Monk's masterpiece on disk and was the first Monk composition available on recording.

In 1945, the friends faced the first in a series of events that would have devastating effects on both their lives. While accounts of the first incident vary, there's no debate about its calamitous consequences. The version that appears in Paudras's memoir sets the scene in a "smoke-filled bar on the outskirts of Philadelphia," while an early biography of Monk claims it took place at Harlem's Savoy Ballroom. But they both agree that when the police stormed into the joint and were in the process of arresting Monk, Powell rushed in to intervene. "Stop that, man!" Powell demanded. "You don't know what you're doing! The guy you're pushing around happens to be the world's greatest pianist!" At this point, one of the cops wheeled around and began raining blows on Powell's head with his nightstick. Monk and Powell were soon back out on the street, but Powell began to be plagued by excruciating headaches, which spiraled into bouts of mental instability. As Bud was being cared for by his family, Monk expressed his gratitude by writing a swinging bebop homage to his bosom buddy, titled "In Walked Bud," which continues to be one of Monk's best-loved compositions.

Meanwhile, Powell began drinking heavily, and by the early fifties, he had also become addicted to heroin. It wasn't surprising, therefore, that when Bud and a friend drove over to Monk's apartment one night in August 1951, he was holding. But when the police walked up to the parked car where the friends were hanging out, Monk was somehow left holding the bag. Perhaps it was just an example of his brotherly protectiveness, or yet another payback for Powell's costly efforts on his behalf a few years earlier, but Monk took the rap for possession, spent the next few months in jail, and spent the next six years without a cabaret card.

Critics still debate the effect of these traumas on Bud Powell's creative efforts, but the brilliance of some of his later work is beyond dispute. Take Powell's 1951 recording of his composition "Un Poco Loco," a joyful four-minute, forty-two-second Afro-Cuban symphony. While its title may have contained more than a touch of self-conscious irony, his performance has long been considered a jazz masterpiece. In the late

1980s, the renowned literary and cultural critic Harold Bloom included "Un Poco Loco" in a list of the most "sublime" works of twentieth-century American art, alongside Faulkner's *As I Lay Dying*, the poetry of Hart Crane, and the ending of the Marx Brothers' *Duck Soup*.

Throughout the 1950s, however, there were more drug arrests and hospitalizations, debilitating drinking binges and electroshock therapy. By the time the difficult decade came to an end, Powell had fallen into a childlike dependency, and he was whisked off to Paris in the clutches of an old childhood friend, Altevia Edwards (known as Buttercup), who took complete control of his life and finances.

After settling in Paris, Powell began performing in local jazz clubs with top-shelf French musicians and American expats. French fans were thrilled to have one of their heroes in their homeland, but none more so than the young commercial artist and amateur pianist Francis Paudras. When he befriended Powell, Paudras became aware of the pianist's dysfunctional circumstances, and he struggled to free him of his dependency on alcohol—and on Altevia Edwards. A fictionalized version of how Paudras "rescued" Powell, nursed him back to health, and arranged for his triumphant return to America eventually became the basis for Bertrand Tavernier's acclaimed 1986 film, *'Round Midnight*.

In 1964, however, when Powell and Paudras arrived in New York for Powell's Birdland comeback, they were virtually broke, and after a few nights in a cheap midtown hotel they were forced to take refuge in Ornette Coleman's unheated basement flat. It was winter, and Paudras quickly realized that Powell, who had been recuperating from a bout of tuberculosis, needed more help than the free-jazz pioneer was able to provide. So, as Paudras wrote in his memoir, "Ornette suggested we ask Nica to put us up for the rest of our stay. Naturally, she said we could come at once."

The Baroness was already putting up one penurious pianist in the person of Barry Harris, who a few years earlier had moved into a small upstairs bedroom during a bout of pneumonia and had never left. But Nica took pains to make Bud and Francis as comfortable as she could. The expanded household soon fell into a pleasant routine. Barry would cook up a little something for dinner, and then they'd all gather round the piano as Bud, Barry, and Francis would take turns at the keyboard. "Often," Paudras later recalled, "we'd watch the sun rise over Manhattan through the huge window, a fascinating spectacle." Occasionally, however, their amiable evening musicale would be shattered by the howls of one of Nica's cats stuck in a tree outside the house. According to Paudras, "Nica would get up and go to infinite pains to rescue the poor animal. I never met anyone who loved cats as much as she did." Unfortunately, the same couldn't be said for Bud.

For Bud, who had something of a feline phobia, the Cathouse proved to be a challenging environment. One night, perhaps seeking a respite from the mewling horde, he found his way down to the basement, where the Baroness stored the cases of Mouton Rothschild she received each year from the family vineyards. After a late-night binge, Powell—whose delicate equilibrium was upended by the consumption of even modest amounts of alcohol—disappeared. The next morning, when Nica and Francis discovered that he was missing, they tore off in the Bentley on a frantic search of New York's jazz clubs that led from the depths of Brooklyn to Harlem's most obscure after-hours in-spots. "Never in my life did I visit so many clubs and musicians' haunts in so short a time," Paudras recounted in his memoir. "Nica spent a fortune that night. She knew everyone, and often, before leaving a place, she would leave a little money for someone in trouble."

Finally, four days after Powell disappeared, a call came from a New York City policeman who had found him collapsed in a Greenwich Village doorway. Paudras thanked the policeman by slipping him some cash Nica had provided for just such a purpose and together they whisked Bud back to Weehawken, where he fell asleep for two days. Meanwhile, Paudras soaked up Nica's seemingly endless store of jazz anecdotes. "She remembered names and dates and places with astonishing accuracy and a wealth of detail," he wrote in his memoir. "Her memory is a veritable treasure house and with her critical eye, her infallible ear, and unfailing wit, she painted for me a unique and utterly memorable fresco of the music world."

The night before their departure, Powell left Nica's to spend some time with members of his family. Although he assured Paudras that he would be at the airport early the next morning, he never made the flight. Over the next few months there were other episodes of dysfunction, and in 1965, Powell's highly anticipated concert at Carnegie Hall proved yet another failure. A year later, the man who is generally recognized as the definitive jazz pianist of the modern era died, at the age of forty-one.

Forty years later, a photograph taken at the Cathouse during Powell's brief residence appeared in *Three Wishes,* Nica's long-abandoned and posthumously published Polaroid scrapbook. It shows a pensive Nica, casually elegant in an azure Japanese dressing gown over a little black dress set off by a pearl choker, sitting at the piano next to Powell, whose rumpled figure and wide-eyed stare seemed to contain both the tragic awareness of some ancient seer and the helplessness of a lost and frightened eight-year-old.

THELONIOUS MONK was still headlining international jazz festivals and winning *DownBeat* jazz polls, but as his output of new compositions petered out, frustrated Columbia executives began exchanging nervous memos about his future at the label. By 1967, however, the company, like the rest of the recording industry, was coping with a serious identity crisis, as the so-called rock revolution, kicked off by that "Beatles' first LP," fundamentally transformed the pop music landscape and raised doubts about the very future of jazz.

Over the course of its long history (it was founded in 1888), Columbia Records had come to consider itself—much like CBS, its television counterpart—the Tiffany label. At this point, Columbia had a prestigious classical music division (Vladimir Horowitz, Glenn Gould, Leonard Bernstein), an enviable stable of pop vocalists (Tony Bennett, Johnny Mathis, Barbra Streisand), and a roster of progressive jazz stars (Dave Brubeck, Miles Davis, Charles Mingus). While it had left the dynamic music of America's regional subcultures (from country to rhythm and blues) to less venerable independent labels, early in the decade the sounds of the burgeoning "folk revival" had caught the discerning ear of the company's famous producer John Hammond (who had already played a key role in the careers of Count Basie, Benny Goodman, and Billie Holiday).

Hammond began signing some of the young urban folksingers who had been attracting a growing audience to the summer festivals at Newport and the dank basement clubs in Greenwich Village. Though he had missed out on the reigning queen of the folkies, Joan Baez, he persuaded the higher-ups at the label to sign a scruffy twenty-year-old college dropout who had arrived in the Village a few months earlier, looking for Woody Guthrie. In the spring of 1962, Bob Dylan's eponymous debut album of old blues and ballads—produced by Hammond for a total cost of $402—was released without much fanfare and even less in the way of sales. Around the water cooler in Columbia's executive offices, Dylan was quickly dubbed "Hammond's Folly." But it was Hammond who had the last laugh (as he would again after signing Aretha Franklin, Leonard Cohen, Stevie Ray Vaughan, and Bruce Springsteen to the label).

Hammond was never part of Nica's inner circle, but their paths often crossed, and long-time members of New York's music scene have testified to their enduring, if casual, friendship and mutual respect. Three years her senior, John Henry Hammond was a scion of the Vanderbilt fortune who grew up in the hushed grandeur of one of the great upper Fifth Avenue mansions. Much like Nica, Hammond became captivated at an early age by the sounds of jazz, and while he followed his father's footsteps to Yale in 1928, he dropped out three years later in order to pursue a life in the world of African-American music. Though both Hammond and Nica had rebelled against the conventions of society and their own social class to embrace the music of a demeaned subculture (and used their social status to challenge the prevailing racial prejudices of the period), their individual musical preferences were often at odds. While they were both unabashed enthusiasts, Hammond's most strongly held musical prejudice (he never got Ellington) and stylistic blind spot (he was never won over by bebop) provided Nica with two of her greatest passions.

When Nat Hentoff asked Teddy Wilson to assess Nica's role in the jazz community for his *Esquire* profile, the pianist drew a clear distinction between Hammond, the consummate professional, and Nica, the ultimate fan. Wilson acknowledged that Nica "tries to help young musicians," but he admitted that she "often doesn't know how to go about it." While Hammond "puts people on records and interests booking agents in them," Nica's contribution was, as Wilson diplomatically phrased it, "usually much more diffuse." Yet the great swing-era pianist was also quick to note that in courageously wielding her prestige to combat the decade's harsh racial climate, the Baroness had often paid a high price. "When I went to tour England in 1953," Wilson explained, "she met me at the airport, and that fact alone made headlines in the scandal sheets."

Hammond remained closely involved with Columbia's jazz divison, but increasingly his commitment to social justice found an outlet in the progressive agenda of the folk revival. In 1963 he produced *The Freewheelin' Bob Dylan*, an album of original "protest songs," including "Blowin' in the Wind," that captured the urgency of the era. A year later, Dylan issued a decade-defining album, *The Times They Are a-Changin'*, whose title directly addressed the racial dramas being enacted on the streets of the South. But it was a proclamation that could just as easily be applied to the complacent pop music industry.

By the mid-sixties, homegrown rock bands had finally rallied to defend America's indigenous music against the advances of the British Invasion, and Columbia Records found itself in the middle of the fray. Inspired by Bob Dylan's new style of jukebox poetry, the Byrds, an L.A.-based band recently signed to Columbia, took an as-yet-unrecorded Dylan tune, "Mr. Tambourine Man," added an infectious twelve-string electric guitar riff, and in June 1965, took their new hybrid (appropriately dubbed "folk rock") to the top of the pop charts. A month later, at the Newport Folk Festival, Dylan "went electric," causing consternation among hard-core folkies while catapulting him to pop stardom. That September, Dylan's new producer, Tom Wilson, took a dreamy acoustic folksong called "Sounds of Silence," added a rockish backbeat, and conjured up Simon and Garfunkel's first number-one single.

In 1967, Columbia's ambitious president, Clive Davis, a former staff lawyer who a few years earlier had negotiated Thelonious Monk's Columbia contract (for a $10,000 advance), attended the nation's first major rock festival, in Monterey, California, and by the end of the weekend he had taken steps to sign three of the event's most promising acts to the label: a moody, soul-inflected singer-songwriter (Laura Nyro), a dynamic Latin-tinged Bay-area rock band (Santana), and a volatile female blues-rock belter (Janis Joplin) and her backup band—for $200,000. Around this same time, Davis also signed Chicago, a horn-heavy act from the Windy City, and Blood, Sweat and Tears, an eclectic New York–based band whose drummer happened to be Harry Colomby's younger brother, Bobby.

As rock's hegemony over the pop music market expanded, the jazz scene imploded. Already weakened by the harsh dissonances, confrontational attitudes, and racial posturing of the genre's avant-garde, jazz entered a deep depression; jazz clubs closed by the dozens (including, in 1967, the hallowed Five Spot); bands lost their record contracts as labels began to promote their rock rosters, and some of the genre's most successful musicians scuffled for anonymous session work or gigs in Broadway pit bands. Meanwhile, various arbiters of cultural significance, including former Five Spot habitués Leonard Bernstein and Allen Ginsberg, began shifting their allegiance from jazz modernists like Thelonious Monk and Ornette Coleman to Bob Dylan and the Beatles.

Now that its rock-dominated pop music division was generating the lion's share of Columbia's profits, the company's jazz artists came under intense pressure to tap into the new youth market. In their desperation, producers floated increasingly bizarre schemes to help Monk "cross over" as Miles Davis had recently done with his jazz-rock fusion, *Bitches Brew*. How about pairing the pianist with the label's funky blues singer, Taj Mahal? one wondered. Or what about a Monk collaboration with Columbia's hot new rock band, Blood, Sweat and Tears? Someone even proposed that Monk cut an album of Beatles covers, and took the liberty of sending a sheet-music demonstrator to Monk's apartment to deliver a Fab Four songbook and play the tunes for him, just in case the brilliant composer didn't read music!

Monk never made any official pronouncement on the musical taste of the Woodstock generation, but after examining his quotes on the subject, Robin Kelley concluded that he "tolerated rock and roll but was never a fan." An anecdote in Francis Paudras's memoir paints a somewhat different picture, however. And it all began with a missing Beatles record.

"One afternoon," Paudras recalled, "Thelonious showed up at Nica's in a state of excitement unusual for such a calm man. His eyes were shooting daggers and he couldn't sit still." Finally he calmed down enough to explain the cause of his distress. "He said he'd just heard that one of his children had brought a Beatles recording into the house." Monk had made a thorough search of the apartment, but had been unable to find the offending album, and that had "only made him madder." Although Paudras was horrified that the home of a jazz hero had been defiled by the shallow commercialism of rock and roll, he confessed, with some chagrin, that "Nica later told me that at the children's request, she had hidden the record at her house."

In any event, when Columbia finally did get the pianist into the studio again, what emerged was 100 percent unadulterated Monk, backed by his regular sidemen and supplemented only by a vocalese version of "In Walked Bud" by Jon Hendricks. Since the record made no concessions to the musical taste of the baby boom demographic, the company saved its promotional hype for the album cover. In a clumsy effort to co-opt the spirit of the times—it was 1968, and revolution (or at least its rhetoric) was in the air—the label titled the LP *Underground,* and designed an elaborately staged scene re-creating a French Resistance hideout replete with a captive Nazi officer, a table littered with grenades (and baguettes), and a photo of General de Gaulle on the wall below the scrawled graffiti "Vive la France," as Monk sat at a beat-up upright, a rifle slung across his shoulder and a cigarette dangling from his lips. As for that dark-haired, beret-wearing young woman holding a machine gun in the background, she's a dead ringer for Nica, circa 1944.

In another scheme to sell Monk to the rock audience, Columbia booked him into such hippie meccas as San Francisco's Carousel Ballroom and New York's Fillmore East. But as always, Monk maintained his musical integrity, and the closest he ever came to psychedelia was when a young fan slipped him some acid after a gig in Minneapolis, causing the pianist to traipse down the block on the top of a row of parked cars. "He had delusions and hallucinations," Harry Colomby told Kelley. "Had to be bedridden for weeks."

For over a decade, Colomby had served as Monk's advocate and aide-de-camp. Although his loyalty to Monk remained as strong as ever, Harry had begun to get restless. He had recently started managing a young comic named John Byner, whose career was taking off, so Colomby quit his teaching job, arranged for his brother Jules (a longtime jazz producer) to take over as Monk's manager, and headed off to Hollywood, where he eventually got into the movie business.

Ironically, just as Monk seemed in danger of being permanently eclipsed by the rock revolution, the pianist was being lionized as one of the icons of contemporary black culture. In 1967, for example, a community group on Chicago's South Side appropriated the façade of a brick tenement building to create what came to be known as the Wall of Respect, a boldly painted mural of African-American heroes including Harriet Tubman, Malcolm X, Billie Holiday, Marcus Garvey, Nat Turner, LeRoi Jones, and Thelonious Monk. Meanwhile, poets (black and white), captivated by Monk's singular musical style as well as by his enigmatic persona, ecstatic dances, and exotic hats, made him one of their favorite subjects. One recent study of the era's jazz-oriented poetry found that "Monk had more poems written in his honor during his lifetime than any other jazz musician in history. He has also, of course, been the subject of numerous posthumous tributes."

BY THE LATE 1960S, Monk's acute spells of dissociation and manic depression had become both more frequent and more acute. While the exact nature of his psychological condition had proven elusive, for about a decade he had been taking massive doses of Thorazine, whose debilitating side effects he countered with frequent doses of Dr. Freymann's feel-good remedies. Weed remained his recreational drug of choice, but he rarely turned down a good bourbon or a cold beer, or something with a little more kick if it happened to come his way.

In January 1969, Nica accompanied Monk to Chicago for a club date, but before the week was out, he had a severe breakdown that required immediate hospitalization. After a few days, doctors believed they had gotten a clearer perspective on his muddled mental (and pharmaceutical) landscape, and they issued a new diagnosis of his condition: "biochemical imbalance." On the basis of these findings, Nica—and Nellie, who had immediately flown to Chicago when she received word of her husband's situation—initiated a decade-long effort to unearth the most effective treatment for his ills.

Nica bore her anxieties about Monk's health stoically, but occasionally she did seek support from certain members of the jazz community, among them the influential critic Dan Morgenstern, who had recently taken over as the editor of *DownBeat* magazine. A voracious reader of the jazz press, Nica had known and respected Morgenstern for years, and she would periodically reach out to him when she needed counsel or consolation.

Morgenstern is still touched that Nica called him to unburden herself. "She really unloaded on me with all her worries," he mused. "I just wish I could have given her some help. But what could I do, except to tell her she was doing whatever anybody possibly could do?" Nor, Morgenstern pointed out, was Monk the only jazz musician whose medical difficulties had become a focus of Nica's intense personal engagement. A few years earlier, he recalled, Nica had sought his assistance when rumors of Coleman Hawkins's imminent death set off a furor across the jazz world.

In the summer of 1967, the sixty-three-year-old tenor saxophone legend had collapsed onstage during a Jazz at the Philharmonic concert in Oakland, California. Hawkins had been subsisting for most of the grueling multicity tour on a diet of brandy, so perhaps it shouldn't have come as a shock when he suddenly clutched the microphone stand for support and had to be helped offstage. After a good night's rest, however, he resumed the tour at the Hollywood Bowl, and by most accounts, he performed brilliantly. The incident would have been just an obscure footnote in Hawkins's remarkable career if not for the fact that the syndicated jazz critic Ralph J. Gleason, having heard a rather overstated account of Bean's transitory infirmity, produced a column that amounted to a premature obituary of the saxophonist, set within a scathing indictment of American racism. According to Bean's biographer, "the story was picked up by an international news agency and telexed around the world. It was as though Hawkins had played his last note."

As the editor of the country's premier jazz journal, Dan Morgenstern felt obligated to weigh in on the growing controversy. In his next *Down-Beat* column, he took Gleason to task for his assertion that Hawkins was "a prime example of the injustices suffered by the Negro artist in a hostile society" and for his contention that as a consequence, the jazz great had become "possessed of a 'death wish.' " After declaring Gleason's article "a new low in irresponsible journalism," Morgenstern explained that while he "had intended to say a great deal more" on the subject, *DownBeat* had "received an open letter which says it far better than we could have." The 450-word diatribe that followed was signed "Baroness Nica de Koenigswarter."

After opening with a seemingly incongruous rhetorical question— "Have you ever had the privilege of hearing the great Coleman Hawkins laugh?"—Nica offered a celebratory evocation of the same: "There is no laugh like it in the world! It comes from wa-a-ay down . . . and is as gigantic and all-encompassing as the sound of his horn! Not a trace of a 'death wish' in it, Mr. Gleason!" She went on to reveal that on the very day that Gleason's "quasi-obituary appeared in the New York *Post*," she was having dinner with Hawkins at a Greenwich Village jazz club. Nica explained that when he read the news of his impending demise, "the Coleman Hawkins roar of laughter rang out, and almost stopped the show!"

The Baroness also challenged Gleason's erroneous and demeaning attempt to cast Hawkins as an object of pity. Instead, she painted a portrait of a heroic figure enjoying the material blessings of his artistic genius: "Driving around the town in his brand-new Chrysler Imperial, or relaxing in his beautiful penthouse overlooking Central Park, Coleman Hawkins shows no signs of suffering from frustration or from a hostile society." Nor was there any need to bemoan Bean's declining musical prowess, since, as she declared in her rousing conclusion, "He is still blowing everyone off the scene!"

While this episode offers yet another example of her unwavering loyalty, it soon became apparent that Nica had presented a somewhat rosy picture of the saxophonist's physical condition. Not long after the publication of her *DownBeat* letter, Hawkins was diagnosed with bronchial pneumonia. When his doctors indicated that the end was near, Nica and Monk rushed to his bedside. As usual in such situations, Monk was thrown into a state of intense emotional turmoil, and he paced the hospital corridor tightly clutching a stack of Hawkins's recordings that the saxophonist had given him as a parting gift. The following morning, May 19, 1969, Hawkins passed away, and Monk returned home. According to one of his nieces, he "didn't sleep, he hardly talked . . . But he played those albums Bean had given him for three days." For the next few months, Monk remained mired in depression.

Nica coped with Bean's passing better than Thelonious, but a decade after his death, she would once again feel impelled to come to Hawkins's defense. In 1980, Max Gordon published *Live at the Village Vanguard*, an intimate memoir of his fifty-year career in the nightclub business. Along with a lifetime's worth of insider anecdotes about his famed basement "joint," Gordon devoted a chapter to the Baroness. Though his warm, if somewhat bemused, recollection of her seemed innocuous enough, Nica felt deeply betrayed by Gordon's portrait. And her most vociferous objection concerned his depiction of her relationship with Coleman Hawkins.

As Gordon recounts it, one night about ten years earlier, Nica had spontaneously launched into a rambling monologue about her life and legend that included a reverie about "the Hawk" that (uncharacteristically) focused on her own selfless acts of philanthropy. Gordon described how the Baroness regularly filled Hawkins's refrigerator with milk, fruit, and egg rolls and how she had arranged to have a couple of phone lines installed in his Central Park West apartment. Finally, Gordon claimed that Nica had revealed a secret she had kept even from the saxophonist's closest friends: "Coleman Hawkins was an epileptic."

It all seemed harmless enough, but the Baroness was not amused. The first indication of her displeasure came in a personal letter to the writer and critic Seymour Krim, who had reviewed Gordon's memoir in the *Village Voice*. Krim's lengthy article celebrated the "benign leprechaun-elf-Yiddish Santa Claus" who for half a century had overseen one the most significant nightclubs in jazz history. Along the way he praised Gordon for his golden "ears," his "Zen"-like equanimity, and the deftness of his thumbnail sketches of such Vanguard luminaries as the "mystic Sonny Rollins," the "heroic Rahsaan Roland Kirk," and the "misunderstood Baroness." Although Krim also chided Gordon for the unaccountable "puritanism" that prevented him from appreciating "the two most brilliant wordmen ever to play the Vanguard—Lenny Bruce and Jack Kerouac," he declared the book "a pleasure and a tasty gas," and ended his review with a resounding "Mazeltov!"

About a week after the *Voice* review hit the stands, Krim received a handwritten letter of congratulations from Nica for his "MAGNIFICENT" article—"I enjoyed it more than I can say!" But, she continued, "I must tell you, that the chapter in which I am involved 'rang' COMPLETELY UNtrue, UNclear and UNfunny to ME, and to everyone who knows me well!!" The Baroness ended her note by calling Krim's attention to a letter to the editor she had written on the subject for an upcoming issue of *Jazz Spotlight News*.

Nica's letter to *JSN* detailed a litany of complaints about Gordon's memoir, most of which attempted to deflect any suggestion that she was Bean's savior—or any implication that he needed one. "Bean (whom I never referred to as 'the Hawk') was positively not epileptic! Nor did he have any need of me to install telephone extensions in his apartment." "I not only loved Bean," she declared in closing, "I revered him and could never have spoken about him the way Max has it down." Nica knew how to hold a grudge, and the fallout from Gordon's book caused a serious breach in their long and amiable relationship.

In truth, Gordon's portrait of the Baroness was a far cry from the tabloid smears and gossip-column innuendoes that had plagued her since her arrival in New York; but as time went on, Nica seemed to have become sensitive to even the most innocent utterances about her in the press—or behind her back.

One of the few people she felt comfortable opening up to unreservedly was Mary Lou Williams. It's unclear what specific incident prompted Nica to unburden herself to Williams, but Mary's response, written in December 1965, suggests that a decade after Bird's death, the Baroness still felt herself under siege from hostile forces. After apologizing to Nica for some less-than-charitable remark she had made about a mutual friend, Mary explains how her own spiritual journey had helped her transcend the slings and arrows of the unenlightened. "Often I was suspicious of people," she tells Nica. "This is condemning to a soul . . . Father [Woods] often sat with me saying: 'Stop being suspicious of everyone . . . watch without being suspicious.'" Mary goes on to offer a message of acceptance with grace: "Nica, whenever a scandal or anything happens to anyone . . . people will say unpleasant things through jealousy etc., but you must remember that a star is made and everyone wants to meet you as much as they do Duke Ellington or Monk . . . so what are you gonna' do about it? You cannot change it . . . so learn to live with it and laugh, the way you do." She also points out that Nica's legendary heritage made her especially vulnerable to such sniping: "You are one of the Rothschilds, this makes you a target. The Duponts, fords [sic], Rocks . . . smile and all the greedy rich folks are at each other['s] necks to keep all the loot in their pockets. You may seem notorious to them but look at them they are murders [sic] of men's souls. You are very kind to those you love. You can imagine the horrors in their closets . . . ?"

Dan Morgenstern was also aware of the unwarranted suspicion Nica endured, and he recognized the vulnerability behind her intrepid façade. "A lot of people really didn't understand Nica," he insists. "They immediately assumed that if a white woman gets involved with black musicians, that it had to do with sex or drugs." According to Morgenstern, there were a lot of people, "including musicians who didn't know her," who kept alive the salacious rumors about the Baroness long after Bird's demise. "But generally speaking, musicians who knew her at all were very fond of her; that's why you get 'Nica's Dream' and all the other things that were dedicated to her." Ultimately, Morgenstern suggests, it was Nica's unwavering love of jazz that enabled her to transcend any of the lingering aspersions that were directed against her. "She was deeply involved in the music," he explains. "That was the main thing in her life." Nor does he believe that by giving herself over to the jazz life in this way she had turned her back on her children. "I'm sure she was a good mother," Morgenstern contends—"of course, in her own fashion."

Nica's children have never publicly discussed their relationship with her, but occasionally one or another of them has provided brief written responses to specific questions, as when her son Shaun replied to queries from Barry Singer for his 2009 *New York Times* feature about the publication of Nica's photo scrapbook, *Three Wishes*. Asked about his mother's immersion in the world of jazz, Shaun acknowledged, "Not all members of her family were enthused about the life she chose to lead (especially our father!), but most recognized the fact that she was an exceptionally determined and strong-willed person and respected her right to live her life as she saw fit." He also explained that as attitudes about race and class evolved, a fundamental transformation did take place within the Rothschild–de Koenigswarter clan. "Over the years, many of those who had initially disapproved, particularly in the light of the many viciously biased and racist press reports about her, came to understand and appreciate what she was all about."

As Shaun saw it, there was no dark mystery about Nica's motivation: "She devoted more than 35 years of her life to Jazz and Jazz musicians simply because she loved their music and was in a position to offer help, assistance and encouragement to those musicians in need, as well as to assist in promoting and publicizing the merits of this unique and, at the time, still underappreciated American art form." Finally, Shaun proposed that his mother's unconventional lifestyle could best be understood in the context of her Rothschild heritage. "It should be noted," he wrote, "that her family had produced over the generations, and almost always ended up appreciating, many highly original or eccentric personalities among its members."

Nica gradually reestablished a bond with each of her five grown children (despite the inconvenient fact that they were scattered around the globe), and she reveled in their rapprochement. During the difficult months that followed Coleman Hawkins's death, a Christmas reunion with her children became an occasion for both private solace and maternal pride. "Happy happy *HAPPY* New Year!" she wrote in a 1968 letter to Mary Lou Williams. "Have ALL my kids, bar Patrick, here . . . craziest Christmas *EVER*!!! My youngest son [Shaun] has to return to Paris tomorrow, unfortunately, but Berit & Kari would love to see you again." She concludes by describing "the transformation" of the Cathouse that she had completed "in their honour": "The studio has been turned into a dormitory—with a door, to keep the cats out!!—and painted white and yellow!"

The Christmas reunions became an annual tradition, and a decade later, in another letter to Mary, Nica again joyfully described the gathering of her far-flung tribe (including her grandson, Steven): "All the family was here for Christmas (except for Patrick, who is still in the Phillippines [*sic*]!); Janka, Steven (nearly 15!) & Kari from London; and Shaun from Paris . . . (Berit is the only one still in New York!)." Nica took particular pride in the fact that all of her children had come to embrace the music that she had made her raison d'être. When Nica was asked late in her life how she had explained her relationship to Thelonious Monk to them, she was slightly nonplussed. "You know, they have been playing Thelonious from their earliest childhood. They are hip. They don't need to be told anything," she said, laughing. "They all are, all my children . . . they are all very hip to jazz."

For his part, Thelonious never left any doubt about the value he placed on his relationship with their mother. In 1969, he was prompted to share some of his feelings about the Baroness with the bassist Walter Booker, who had recently joined his band. As he had with many of his young sidemen, Thelonious became both a musical mentor to Booker and a father figure as well, offering advice about how to conduct oneself amid the temptations of the jazz world. "One night he saw me hitting on some girl at the club or something," Booker told Robin Kelley. "He said to me, 'Be sure you want to have her for a girl or have her for a friend, because if you make love to a girl, she ain't gonna be your friend. Because you can have a friend, like Nica's my friend, and I wouldn't touch her. She's the best friend I ever had."

8

Chez Nica:
The Cathouse
Years

One night early in 1973, Nica was driving with Thelonious back to Weehawken. As her Bentley climbed the hill to her house high above the Hudson River, he turned to her and uttered five simple words: "I am really seriously ill." Monk's sudden announcement set the stage for a distressing period in both their lives that only ended a decade later, with Monk's death. "I was so shocked," Nica recalled. "He was the most uncomplaining person you ever heard. It knocked me out because it was unlike him; that is when I started looking for doctors and trying to get the thing worked out, because he never said this again. He knew . . ."

The previous couple of years had been difficult ones for Monk. In 1970, after two years of not setting foot in the recording studio, Columbia Records released him from his contract. Again he spiraled into an extended period of depression, and often he seemed either confused or uncharacteristically hostile. After an onstage altercation, the saxophonist Charlie Rouse, his close friend and loyal sideman for over a decade, abruptly quit the band. Extended hospitalizations on both coasts yielded conflicting diagnoses—bipolar disorder, schizophrenia, biochemical imbalance—and a series of interventions, including electroshock treatments, often did more harm than good. Monk had even been subjected to traditional psychotherapy, with mixed results. "It was ridiculous," Nica explained. "All that happened was the psychiatrist had to go to their psychiatrist." Judging by a story that appears in Robin Kelley's biography of Monk, Nica's description may have been an understatement.

In the fall of 1970, near the end of a two-week club date at San Francisco's Jazz Workshop, Monk experienced a severe manic episode that landed him in Langley Porter Psychiatric Institute. One of the doctors on staff at the time happened to be a young jazz trumpeter named Eddie Henderson, who was daylighting as a licensed psychiatrist. "No one knew who he was," Henderson told Kelley. "I said, 'Wow, that's Monk!'" From then on, he made himself an unofficial liaison between the pianist and the rest of the hospital staff. So when a colleague decided to administer the Thematic Apperception Test to the new patient, Henderson was there to observe.

The doctor showed Monk illustrations of various ambiguous scenes and asked him to explain what he thought was taking place. After looking at one picture of an obviously distressed young boy sitting in a chair as his parents loomed above him, Monk cast a sidelong glance at Henderson and said, "Is this motherfucker crazy? I don't see nothing. It's just a picture." When the doctor pressed Monk for an interpretation, the pianist responded with deadpan seriousness, "'Okay, the little boy is really drugged . . . Because his mother won't give him no more pussy.'" Henderson fell out laughing, but his colleague dropped his clipboard in shock and abruptly terminated the interview. "That was his sense of humor," Henderson explained, "but the staff thought he was nuts. Besides being sarcastic, he just didn't want to relate on that stupid level." Two months later, Monk walked out of the hospital with yet another diagnosis—schizophrenia, unclassifiable type—and a prescription upping his daily intake of Thorazine to 2,500 milligrams (50 milligrams being the average recommended dosage).

As always, the Baroness joined Nellie at Monk's bedside. "I have been in more nuthouses than you would believe," she told an acquaintance many years later. But Nica never complained, and as Monk's economic situation worsened, she unobtrusively assumed the financial burden of his complex and costly medical treatments. In the meantime, Nellie began to take a more hands-on role in her husband's health care. Frustrated by her own experience with the medical establishment and inspired by the latest theories of nutrition and holistic health, Nellie bought a couple of heavy-duty Norwalk juicers and began formulating her own organic fruit and vegetable concoctions. After personally experiencing the benefits of her detoxification program, Nellie prescribed a similar regimen for her husband's physical and psychological infirmities. Then she turned her attention to Nica.

In the spring of 1970, Nica's predilection for late-night hot-rodding finally caught up with her. The accident resulted in a few cracked ribs, a seriously damaged Bentley, and a new patient for Dr. Nellie. For a while, at least, the Baroness followed the strict dietary program formulated to help her heal—not only from the crash but from a bout of hepatitis (she blamed one of Dr. Freymann's "vitamin" shots) and a flare-up of cirrhosis (caused by her long years of devotion to Chivas Regal). Although Nellie remained an advocate for a holistic approach to better health, both Nica and Monk soon fell off the juice wagon. Before long, Nica was again sipping scotch—and slipping Monk junk food behind Nellie's back.

Over the next few years, Nellie garnered a growing reputation within the New Age underground, attracting an impressive jazz-world clientele to her ad hoc clinic. According to the saxophonist Mario Escalera, "Nellie made preparations for people to detox, and for people who were ill. She was kind of famous for that. She would detox a lot of the great musicians, and she had a great measure of success. She also schooled a lot of people behind her, including my old lady." Escalera recalls accompanying his girlfriend up to the Monks' new apartment (they had recently moved to a high-rise on West End Avenue), where Nellie had installed her powerful juicers and an industrial-size refrigerator. "I don't think people know the scope of what she did," Escalera continued, "but I was awed. And she was doing this long, long before most people."

In 1972, despite Nellie's best efforts, Monk once again fell into a catatonic state. This time, however, the Baroness took the initiative. Paul Jeffrey, the new saxophonist in Monk's band, recalls that Nica "had Monk in the best hospital, Gracie Square—which was like a country club—and she was paying." At the time, Gracie Square, a small private hospital on the Upper East Side, was doing pioneering work in orthomolecular psychiatry, an approach that focused on vitamins, diet, and the use of lithium salts to address the chemical imbalances that were associated with mental disorders like manic depression. It took a few weeks, but the new course of treatment, combining a strictly controlled diet and lithium, began to have a positive effect on the pianist's condition. By the summer, he was able to complete a successful gig at the Village Vanguard and sign on to a world tour that extended well into the fall.

Monk returned home tired but in decent emotional shape, until the deafening roar of Nellie's high-powered juicers and the hordes of health-seekers began disrupting his fragile equilibrium. But as Robin Kelley suggests, it wasn't simply peace and quiet he craved: "Monk had become so dependent on Nellie that now he felt neglected." One bitterly cold night in January 1973, Nica drove him home from the Vanguard, but when she pulled up in front of his building, he refused to get out. Paul Jeffrey, who had also hitched a ride with Nica, remembers that the two of them spent hours trying to cajole Monk into going up to his apartment. Finally, as daylight began to filter across the skyline, an exhausted Nica convinced Monk to go upstairs. But Monk had finally had enough. The next day he issued an ultimatum: either the juicers went or he would.

Later that afternoon, Monk phoned Nica and asked her to pick him up. His niece Jackie happened to be at the apartment that day, and she still recalls Nellie watching in silence as the Baroness stood at the door, her arm reaching out to Monk. "She said, 'Come on, Thelonious. Let's get the fuck out of here,' in her clipped British accent . . . They got on the elevator and that was it. He moved in with Nica and never came back."

Following a series of Monk family conferences, it was decided that it was probably best, at least for the present, for Monk to remain in Weehawken, where he would be well cared for by Nica and find refuge from the noise of the juicers and the demands of well-meaning musicians and fans. When Toot was asked about the circumstances that led to his father's decision, he explained that "living out in New Jersey was ideal—because I can tell you I was living in the apartment in New York and everybody and their mother would be at the door, at any day, at any hour . . . So, yeah, he withdrew from all that, but he didn't withdraw from me, and he didn't withdraw from his daughter or his wife."

WEEHAWKEN WAS ONLY a half-hour bus ride from the Monks' Upper West Side apartment, and once Nellie had come to terms with the new arrangement, she began making daily trips across the river loaded down with freshly blended concoctions and home-cooked meals. Typically, when she got to the Cathouse, Nellie would find Thelonious in bed, dressed in a suit and tie, his door shut against the feline incursions. "He used to lie on the bed with cats all over him," Nica recalled. "He loved them, and named them and everything. But when he was ill, he didn't want them in his room."

The other thing he now seemed intent on avoiding was the gleaming Steinway that was located just outside his door. There are different theories about why Monk turned his back on the instrument through which he had spoken most eloquently for most of his life. Robin Kelley believes that it might have had something to do with the side effects of the lithium he had been taking over the previous couple of months, since the drug (especially in high doses) can cause "a fine tremor of the hands" as well as "indifference, malaise [and] passivity." Monk's son offered a simpler rationale for his father's unofficial retirement from the keyboard. "He was just very uncomfortable as a result of prostate surgery that he had," Toot explained. "He was just physically unable to perform comfortably." Nica concurred. "When he stopped playing, it was because it was a physical impossibility for him," she insisted. "Nothing else could ever have stopped him."

Not that the Baroness was about to give up on her dream that with the right doctor, treatment, therapy—or perhaps divine intervention—

Monk would once again hold forth at the piano and give birth to new works of genius. Over the next few years, she retained a retinue of nutritionists, acupressurists, physical therapists, and assorted New Age healers. A letter to Mary Lou Williams describes her efforts to secure the help of one renowned specialist. "I have a line on a new doctor for T. . . . he is just about the greatest expert there is on biochemical imbalances (which is precisely what T. is suffering from . . .) & I am trying to get his help . . . I am not telling ANYONE (including T.) about this, at the moment, but I want YOU to Please say a prayer for us that he Will be able to help." Through it all, Nica served triple duty as head nurse, chief coordinator of medical services, and de facto morale officer. After she delineated her daily duties to an acquaintance, his only question was, "Where did you get the energy?"

At first, Nellie rarely missed a day at her husband's side ("She used to come over and cook for him, the things he liked," Nica recalled). But gradually the visits began to peter out. A couple of years later, when Mary Lou Williams requested an autographed photo of Thelonious, Nica apologized for not having something suitable, explaining, "When I see Nellie again (she has no telephone) I will try & get her to rout some out; but her visits are few and far between." Other members of the extended Monk/Smith clan, who had once turned the Cathouse into the site of joyful family gatherings, also gradually fell by the wayside.

Among those who experienced the loss of this familial bond most keenly was Thelonious's niece (and Janka's girlhood chum) Jackie Bonneau Smith. From the time she was a young girl, Jackie had forged a special bond with her uncle, a connection Monk acknowledged in one of his most frequently performed compositions, "Jackie-ing," written in 1959, as his niece sat beside him on the piano bench. "Things changed drastically once he got sick and he was 'over there,'" Jackie remembers. "No one saw him—musicians, family members—we didn't even go 'over there.' Before, it was like day and night—we never gave it a second thought." Now everything was "put on hold, never knowing if it would ever start up again."

But while other relatives commiserated with each other about the dissolution of the Cathouse's glory days, Jackie refused to abandon her relationship with Thelonious. Besides, she now had a ten-year-old daughter, Elisa, and Jackie was determined that she would get to know her famous uncle. Along with her husband ("Nica really liked him; he was a mechanic and she would ask him all kinds of questions about her car") and her young daughter, Jackie made the trip from Brooklyn to Weehawken as often as she could. "My mother loved him so much," Elisa explained many years later, "so she wanted me to experience who this jazz giant really was."

Elisa still recalls her Uncle Thelonious wandering through the Baroness's living room, occasionally stopping to smile down at her in recognition— "Oh, you're Jackie's daughter." And for a while her mother was still able to break through his deepening disengagement. "As his world was starting to close more and more," Elisa recalls, "Nica was still trying to make his world more open, social, and loving." When he eventually did retreat into permanent isolation, rarely emerging from his room, Nica entertained the family with her customary warmth and hospitality.

For Jackie's young daughter, the trips to the Cathouse were unencumbered by bittersweet memories of the past or echoes of long-ago jam sessions. Nor was the little girl from Brooklyn much impressed by the exalted provenance of Nica's midcentury modernist manse (or its million-dollar view)—not when there was an army of adorable pussy-cats. "Everywhere you turned, there was a cat," she recalls. "I think there must have been at least a hundred cats." At one point, Elisa shyly approached Nica with the obvious question, "Why do you have so many cats?" Nica explained how she had first brought in one and then another, and then they had families, and "I couldn't let them go." But after observing the devotion with which she cared for them, Elisa came to believe that the cats were simply another outlet for Nica's seemingly inexhaustible need to nurture; and like so many others, Elisa would make the punning connection between the two species of cats Nica provided for so unstintingly.

"Nica supported you unconditionally," Elisa asserted. "She was that type of lady. She loved jazz and she loved the people she was supporting, unconditionally. She just took you for the whole package, for better or worse. That's rare and it's brave." Elisa came to realize that Nica's unconditional acceptance also transcended issues of race. "She was colorblind. She just loved you for you." When asked what she remembers most about Nica, however, Elisa responded without hesitation: "Everything she did, she did with intensity and passion. That's what I learned from Nica."

NOT LONG AFTER MONK moved into the Cathouse, the Baroness celebrated her sixtieth birthday. In photographs from this period, however, we see not only the expected depredations of time—the black hair now streaked with gray, the laugh lines and the extra pounds—but also the undiminished ardor of her smile and her aura of optimism. Those who encountered Nica at the handful of jazz-related events she was able to attend during these years recall only her charisma and her effortless elegance.

One event Nica wouldn't dream of missing was organized by her old friend Mary Lou Williams. The 1979 Carnegie Hall concert, titled "Embraced," was conceived as a meeting of the minds between Williams, the embodiment of the jazz piano tradition, and Cecil Taylor, the pioneering free-jazz iconoclast. Unfortunately, however, it turned out not to be the highly anticipated embrace of its billing but, in the words of a *New York Times* reviewer, a "tug of war." Nica attended the performance with her daughters Berit and Kari, and the next day she wrote a letter to Mary that left little doubt about who she thought had triumphed in the battle of musical wills. According to Williams's biographer, Linda Dahl, Nica's two-page letter also happened to be "perhaps the best review" of the high-profile concert.

"Though it may make you angry," Nica wrote to the spiritually inclined Williams, "I HAVE to tell you the impression I got, because it was so *extraordinarily* vivid!! Rather than an 'embrace,' it seemed to me like a CONFRONTATION—between Heaven & Hell—with *you* (Heaven) emerging GLORIOUSLY TRIUMPHANT!!!" Although she went on to acknowledge "what a *sweet cat* C.T. is," she insisted that, at least from her Manichean perspective of the proceedings, Taylor "LOOKS just like the Devil when he plays!!—as *well* as *sounding* like it, as far as I am concerned . . . !!! (SHEETS of NOTHINGNESS!!?) . . . apparently seductive to some." The Baroness concluded by assuring Mary that she was hardly alone in her judgment. "However wrong you may say I am, that crowd in Carnegie Hall made it clear that *they felt the same way!!*"

On this and the other rare occasions when Nica treated herself to a night out on the town, she did so—in sharp contrast to her freewheeling prime—with one eye on the clock. For example, it was during this same period that Jean Bach, a longtime member of New York's culturati and director of the 1994 Academy Award–nominated jazz documentary, *A Great Day in Harlem*, spotted Nica's Bentley parked outside the popular Greenwich Village piano bar Bradley's. "Since I had a leg of lamb roasting slowly in the oven," recalled Bach (who had met Nica when she arrived from Mexico), "I popped in to see if she'd care to join me and a couple of friends for dinner." After Nica elicited a detailed account of the menu, "which appeared to meet her approval," the two women headed off to Bach's house, located in a picturesque Village mews. Suddenly Nica stopped short. "Good heavens, what *time* is it?" she asked. With that, she hastily offered her apologies and rushed back to her car. "Turns out she was already late for Thelonious Monk's night-time tray."

The curious image of the Rothschild baroness toting a midnight snack to the pampered jazz pianist stayed with Bach. When she next encountered Barry Harris, who was living at the Cathouse during these years, Bach asked him, "Does someone—usually Nica—always deliver the tray?" Harris confirmed the story, adding somewhat defensively, "And they better not ask *me* to bring one." But the truth is, Barry idolized Monk, and for many months he had been doing what he could to draw his hero back to the keyboard, from reminiscing about the good old days to feigning confusion about the correct chords for one of Monk's classic compositions (to no avail).

In 1974, Harris became a key figure in a larger effort to reawaken his housemate's musical appetite when the producer George Wein hired him to perform at a Carnegie Hall tribute to Monk. The band, led by

Paul Jeffrey, included Thelonious's old cohort Charlie Rouse on tenor sax and his son, Toot, on drums, so there was considerable consternation when Monk stubbornly refused to leave his room to attend the concert. When Harris left the Cathouse for Carnegie Hall, he was convinced that the night's guest of honor wouldn't be there.

At the last minute, however, Nica cajoled Monk into her car, and they arrived just as the show was scheduled to begin. As the pair made their way through the throng of well-wishers and old friends, something remarkable took place. The trumpeter Jimmy Owens, who was seated in the hall, described the scene to Robin Kelley. "Barry was out on stage getting ready to play. Paul Jeffrey was about to count the song off, and who should walk out of the door but Monk. Everybody just went crazy. Monk sat down at the piano and just started to play." A stunned Barry Harris watched from the wings. "I got paid," he remarked, "and didn't have to play at all." Over the next two years, Monk performed only four more times, including a brief impromptu set at Bradley's on July 4, 1976, when he got up from the table he had been sharing with Nica, took over the keyboard from Harris, and played in public for the last time. He was fifty-eight years old.

After that, Monk returned to Weehawken and again took to bed. He would get up each morning, dress himself in a suit and tie, and just lie there for hours. "It was like he wasn't here, when he was here," Nica once explained. "Imagine somebody lying in the bed like that. That is something that really used to get to me. When I would take in his food, you know, get him to take his pills or something, it would be almost like he wasn't there. I could usually get some reaction from him, but almost nobody else could."

Not that those who loved and respected Monk gave up trying. In 1978, Paul Jeffrey, who had started teaching at Rutgers University, not far from Nica's New Jersey residence, knew Thelonious could no longer be tempted back to the piano, but he wanted to bring a little music back into his life. "Monk was more or less staying in his room all the time," Jeffrey recalled. "And I thought it would be a good idea if we would just play his music outside his window."

Nica described the scene in a letter to Mary Lou Williams a few months later. "Did you hear about Paul Jeffreys bringing over 20 or 30 of his students last November to play T's music to him under his window??? It truly was a BEAUTIFUL idea!!! Unfortunately, it was freezing cold, so they had to come in and play in the studio, instead . . . (T. bore up pretty well under the strain . . . !!!!)" Although Monk never did come out of his room (or even open his door), Jeffrey was satisfied to know that he had heard their gesture of love and respect, and as always, the Baroness proved to be a gracious hostess, serving hot coffee to the numb-fingered young musicians.

Resigned to the fact that Monk's performing days were over, Nica had one other plan up her sleeve, which she hoped might inspire him at least to resume composing: she organized an effort to secure Thelonious a Guggenheim Fellowship. She recruited several distinguished figures from the jazz establishment to write letters of recommendation on his behalf, with the hope that such recognition might inspire him to continue his life's work. Among the testimonials included in the application was one from the noted critic Martin Williams, an early admirer who had once hailed Monk as "the first major composer in jazz since Duke Ellington." Now Williams declared him not only "the greatest living jazz composer" but "one of the great American composers of whatever category." In 1976, the name Thelonious Monk appeared on a list of the year's Guggenheim Fellows, but it didn't have the effect Nica had hoped for. Monk maintained his silence until the end.

ON ONE OF NICA'S infrequent New York outings, she befriended a pianist named Joel Forrester, who had arrived in the city a few years earlier from San Francisco. It was about four in the afternoon, and the thirty-year-old Forrester was sitting in the West Boondock, a Chelsea restaurant that featured "Boss Soul Food and Fine Drinks"—along with an array of top-tier jazz pianists—when he noticed an attractive woman of a certain age sitting alone at the bar. "I knew who she was," Forrester remembers. "I'd been coming to New York to hear Monk at places like the Vanguard and the Half Note since the mid-sixties and sometimes she would be there." So he walked over and addressed her with what he hoped was a suitable degree of formality: "Baroness Pannonica de Koenigswarter . . ."

After correcting the pronunciation of her first name (emphasizing its long *o*), she invited him to sit down, and they wound up talking for the better part of two hours. Along the way, Nica explained that having completed some errands she had come in for a drink before heading back to Weehawken. When she asked Forrester what he was doing there, he told her, "Well, Nica, I'm here for an audition. I'm trying to get a gig here." Without missing a beat, she confidently assured him, "You will." For his audition piece he played Monk's "Pannonica," and whether it was fate or the quiet word Nica had with the club's booker, Forrester got the job. He went on to perform regularly at the restaurant for the next decade.

Then, as if living up to her legend, Nica took out her hip flask, knocked back a quick slug, and offered to drive Forrester home. Cigarette holder clenched firmly in her teeth, she propelled the Bentley into the stream of traffic. "If she could get away with actually not using the brake," he recalls, "she didn't." After dropping him off, she extended an invitation to visit the Cathouse to play for Monk. Before long, he had commenced what would become a curious two-year ritual. Forrester, who later cofounded the Microscopic Septet and composed the theme song for NPR's *Fresh Air* (in addition to about 1,200 other compositions), would head out to the Cathouse every few weeks, take his place at the Steinway grand parked just outside Monk's bedroom, and begin to play.

"In a sense," he later admitted to Leslie Gourse, the author of a 1998 biography of Monk, "I was in on the level of the witch doctors, massage artists, and others who the baroness brought in, in a vain attempt to figure out whether Monk might respond to some invitation to live in a fuller way." Although Monk never ventured out of his room during these impromptu recitals, if he heard something he liked, he would slowly open the door. "The things he couldn't tolerate," Forrester remembers, "were not only repetition of ideas but anything glib, or where I attempted to show off." Then the door would abruptly close again.

Like so many other young musicians before him who had been the beneficiaries of Thelonious's tutelage—Bud Powell, Sonny Rollins, David Amram—Forrester explains that Monk's enduring influence transcended such practicalities as harmonic theory or instrumental technique. "Monk got my head straight," Forrester declares. "He deepened my sense of concentration and set me on the road to finding my own music." Yet he notes that in her own way, the Baroness had just as profound an effect on his creative evolution. "Nica's influence was simply as strong. With her, it came in the context of maintaining a sense of personal integrity." In fact, he believes that this shared credo was at the heart of the bond between Thelonious and Nica. "In the presence of either one of them, you had to fall back on yourself—so sustained regular exposure to those two helped me really find my way to the music and the bands I'm involved with now."

Nor is it a coincidence, Forrester contends, that an uncompromising commitment to one's personal truth also happens to be the essential element of jazz: "What we're talking about is being wrenched radically into the moment. That's what we want when we improvise, we want to be 'in the moment' to play. Nica's presence—not only because of who she was, but because of her refusal to accept the self-image of the person in front of her, wanting only the real person—could take you to a place where you could freely improvise. So she was a force for freedom among musicians. She wanted the real person playing from his real heart. I see her as a liberating force in a music that demanded that."

As their friendship deepened, the Baroness's support for Forrester's music took another familiar form: she subsidized one of his early recording projects. In appreciation for both her patronage and her inspiration, Forrester responded as had so many who preceded him: he wrote a composition in her honor. The immediate motivation for his tribute, however, was another of her spontaneous acts of generosity. Aware that Forrester and his wife had two cats, the Baroness arrived at their loft one day with a custom-made catbox shaped like a house (similar to ones she had strategically placed around her own home). Though she was touched by Forrester's musical homage—appropriately titled "Nica's Gift"—after he played it for her, she quipped, "When the grad students ask you for the genesis of the tune, you needn't mention the catbox."

Occasionally the Baroness would steal a few hours away from Monk's care to attend one of Forrester's gigs, and he became aware of just how potent her mere presence could be. "There's an undeniable strain in the jazz tradition that has to do with a kind of sympathetic magic and the use of touchstones," he explains, "which could even be humans who in their presence allow you to forget about the picture of yourself and let you express who you are in a deeper way. Her presence could provoke that." One night when Nica showed up at a performance of his new band, for example, she immediately shifted the consciousness of everyone onstage to a deeper level. "She was sitting by the bandstand when the Microscopic Septet was playing," he remembers, "and it was remarkable to see these self-involved, posturing musicians suddenly spring to attention— to desire to play something that would catch her ear."

Nica's insistence on authenticity was something she also sought to manifest in her own life. According to Forrester, "People who wanted to make her into an adornment on their own self-image would never get away with that for very long. She would get right past that and force you to confront her as who she was." Nor did she have any patience for those expecting her to conform to their preconceived notions. During one conversation, when Forrester casually prefaced a remark by invoking her title ("Well, Baroness . . ."), she interrupted him, insisting, "The name is Nica." The chastened composer later made amends by using her alliterative disclaimer as the title of a second tune he wrote in her honor.

Paradoxically, Forrester also claims that despite her oft-stated disavowals of her depictions in the media, Nica had consciously appropriated elements from the Myth of the Jazz Baroness into her persona. "Nica was a living character," he explains. "She had already made that integration between drama and life. I can always hear Nica's voice in my head when I want to, I can even hear her saying things she never said, as if she were an actress, because she was able to fuse two things that are generally set apart—which on one hand is the theatrical, and on the other, ordinary, daily life."

During this period Forrester came across a copy of "The Pursuer" ("El perseguidor"), Julio Cortázar's short story à clef set in New York's 1950s jazz underground. But when he rushed to tell her about his discovery of the fictional account of the brilliant, if dysfunctional, alto saxophonist Johnny Carter and the heedless, sexually charged heiress Tica (a.k.a. "the marquesa"), it turned out that not only was she familiar with the story, but she embraced Cortázar's depiction of her youthful persona. "When I started to talk with her about her life during that time," Forrester recalls, "she referred me to that story. Several times she mentioned that the story gives an accurate portrait of what she was like."

IN 1980, FAMILY commitments required Nica to visit England and Israel. It had been over a decade since she had traveled so extensively on her own, and the first time since Monk had taken up residence in her home that she would be so far away from him for so long. "I'm not a crier," she recalled years later. "That day, when I left here, I started to cry. When I went to say goodbye to Thelonious . . . I could not stop. I remember [him] saying, 'It's all right, I will be here when you come back. I'm not going anywhere, I will be here.'"

As Nica streaked across the Atlantic, the tears wouldn't stop. "I wrote to him on the Concorde and the letter was all stained. It was almost like I said my farewells to him then." But Monk was true to his word. When she returned from her trip, she found him pretty much as she had left him, and so he remained for the next two years. But on February 5, 1982, Barry Harris discovered Thelonious lying unconscious in his room. An ambulance took him to a nearby hospital, where it was determined that he had experienced a cerebral hemorrhage. Monk lay in a coma for twelve days. Then, on February 17, he quietly passed away, with Nellie sitting at his side.

According to his son, Toot, "If there was anything appropriate for him to be looking at when he moved to the next life, it was Nellie, and she was there. She was always there. That's one of the reasons I say that, on balance, Thelonious, he did all right. It could have been a lot worse."

Meanwhile, having already cried herself out in anticipation of his passing, Nica had no tears left. "I didn't cry when Thelonious died," she told an acquaintance, "and I haven't cried since."

Ten days later, a memorial service for Thelonious Monk was held in the modernist sanctuary of St. Peter's Lutheran Church on Lexington Avenue, just a short walk from 52nd Street, where almost four decades earlier Monk and Co. had brought the sound of bebop to midtown. Among the approximately one thousand mourners were scores of Monk's former sidemen, collaborators, and disciples, as well as hundreds of loyal fans. Appropriately, Monk's music took center stage at the ceremony, with moving performances of his classics by Charlie Rouse, Tommy Flanagan, Marian McPartland, Gerry Mulligan, Barry Harris, and Max Roach.

The Baroness put her stamp on the proceedings by selecting the epigram that appeared on the first page of the memorial program. In a letter to the jazz critic Marc Crawford, written only a few days earlier, she described the source of the passage and her rationale for choosing it. "I once came across something in a study of Kahlil Gibran," she explained to Crawford, "which seems to me to apply perfectly to Thelonious." In part, the quote (which appears in the preface to a study of Gibran's *The Prophet*) reads: "There is a race of strangers, of wayfarers, that exist upon the earth. They dwell with us a while, calling us brothers, but we come to be aware that they are of an immortal stuff . . . and only insomuch as we receive and comprehend their utterance . . . may we partake in brief and finite measure of their communion."

A snippet from a film of the service made for a documentary about Monk's life released in 1989—shows the pianist's casket being carried to its place of honor at the apron of the church's temporary stage. And as the camera pans across the assembled throng, it provides a brief glimpse of Nellie (elegantly shrouded in black, her face shielded by enormous dark glasses) and Nica (looking haggard and distraught, her hair streaked with gray), sitting side by side in a front pew. Although the documentary cuts away at this point, the three-hour ceremony—which also featured a series of eulogies (by turns waggish and reverential) from jazz critics and old cohorts—was a fitting memorial to Monk. As it turned out, the day's only discordant note was struck behind the scenes.

Following the service at St. Peter's, a caravan of mourners, led by a limousine bearing the immediate family, lined up to begin a tour of local Monk landmarks, including a stretch of 52nd Street (where he had first performed as sideman with Coleman Hawkins), the West 63rd Street apartment (where he had lived most of his life), and Minton's Playhouse (where he'd helped forge the sound of modern jazz), before beginning the twenty-five-mile drive to Ferncliff Cemetery in Hartsdale, New York, for his interment. At least that was the plan, until the emotionally distraught Baroness learned that her Bentley wasn't going to be first in line behind the hearse bearing Monk's earthly remains, as she had envisioned. After trying to reason with her, members of Monk's family finally acquiesced: Nellie, Toot, and Boo Boo climbed out of the limo and joined Nica. The Baroness pulled up behind the hearse, and the slow procession made its way through the streets of New York and onto the highway.

They were only about mile from the cemetery when, without warning, Nica's vintage Bentley broke down and slowly came to a stop as the other cars passed them by. As Robin Kelley recounts the episode, it was Nellie who broke the strained silence. "Considering the prospects of divine intervention, she asked, 'What does it mean?'" Without missing a beat, Kelley recounts, her daughter Boo Boo replied, "with a trace of her father's legendary wit, 'It means that everyone in the front get to the back, everyone in the back go to the front!'" Although the tension was broken and the family quickly squeezed into other vehicles, Nica was left alone on the side of the road to wait for assistance. Whatever the cosmic significance of these events, as the day wore on, a larger question began to emerge for the Baroness: now what?

BEFORE CONFRONTING her new reality of life without Monk, Nica joined with his family to secure Thelonious's legacy. This quest was spearheaded by Boo Boo, a talented singer and dancer, who had recently joined her brother Toot's new band as a featured vocalist. Only a few months earlier, the group had scored a dance-funk hit with an original composition, "Bon Bon Vie," but now Boo Boo turned her creative energy toward a series of projects dedicated to preserving her father's place in the history of jazz—and in the city he loved.

After lobbying the New York Landmarks Preservation Commission to declare the Phipps Houses (the complex in which Monk's apartment was located) a New York landmark, Boo Boo initiated plans to establish an arts program in Monk's memory at a local public high school and won approval to officially rename a cul-de-sac on West 63rd Street in his honor. The dedication ceremony for Thelonious Sphere Monk Circle featured speakers such as the jazz impresario George Wein and performances by the late pianist's friends and collaborators Max Roach and Barry Harris. The Baroness hired a videographer to document the event and later helped edit the footage for an hour-long documentary that aired on French television.

Tragically, only seven months later, Monk's twenty-nine-year-old daughter died of breast cancer. While the family mourned, they consoled themselves that Thelonious, a sensitive and doting father, had been spared what would have been an insupportable loss. A few months later, Toot took over his sister's mission; a few years after that, their efforts culminated in the founding of the Thelonious Monk Institute of Jazz, a national organization devoted to expanding the music's role in American culture.

Meanwhile, Nica kept a close eye on what quickly became a tidal wave of albums honoring the late pianist. The first of these, a collaboration between two Monk alums, Charlie Rouse and Ben Riley (along with the pianist Kenny Barron and the bassist Buster Williams), was recorded on February 17, 1982, the very day Thelonious died. Ironically, the project had originated as yet another attempt to revive Monk's dormant creative energy. "What happened," Charlie Rouse explained, "was we wanted to dedicate a whole album to Thelonious. My intention was if he heard it, it might get him inspired to come out and play, because actually nobody can play a Thelonious composition the way he plays it." It was only when Rouse got home from the recording session and turned on the radio that he learned of Monk's passing, and the album, *Four in One*, was transformed into a memorial.

Soon other performers jumped on the bandwagon with their own Monk tribute albums. Before the year was up, the veteran vibraphonist Milt Jackson, who had played on a couple of Thelonious's earliest Blue Note records, released his LP, *Memories of Thelonious Sphere Monk*, while an album by the pianist Tommy Flanagan contained not only an assortment of Monk compositions (including "Pannonica") but an original tune whose cut-and-past title, "Thelonica," paid joint homage to Monk and the Baroness. Making Flanagan's record even more of a family affair was the fact that Nica's daughter Berit did the soulful sketch of Monk that appeared on the cover. Meanwhile, Columbia, which had jettisoned Thelonious from its roster a decade earlier, began churning out compilations of previously unreleased Monk material from its vaults.

Two years later, however, another album established that Monk's compositions could hold their own in any context. In fact, it was the narrow focus of all the tribute recordings and memorial concerts following Monk's death that prompted the twenty-eight-year-old producer Hal Willner, whose eclectic taste ranged from the film scores of Nino Rota to the most obscure niches of musical Americana, to initiate his own genre-busting tribute to Thelonious. Titled *That's the Way I Feel Now*, the project evolved into a two-record extravaganza that brought together (among others) an arena-rock superstar (Peter Frampton), a New Orleans R&B piano guru (Dr. John), a jazz-rock hipster (Steely Dan's Donald Fagen), a rootsy proto-jam band (NRBQ), a progressive rock experimentalist (Todd Rundgren), and a representative of New York's downtown avant-garde (John Zorn), along with a lineup of musicians like Charlie Rouse, Randy Weston, Gil Evans, Carla Bley, Steve Lacy, and Elvin Jones, spanning the entire contemporary jazz spectrum. To close out the album, Willner persuaded Barry Harris to record a solo version of "Pannonica."

On the final day of the recording sessions, a silver Bentley pulled up in front of the studio on 57th Street, and after Harris exited from the passenger seat, Willner watched in astonishment as Nica emerged from behind the wheel. The young producer was familiar with the Baroness

("I knew about her legend from the time I read my first jazz bio"), but he acknowledges, "I never thought she was someone I'd actually meet! It was like Jane Austen walking into the room—or Fellini! And Nica was even more so," he explains, still somewhat nonplussed a quarter century later, "because she was so mysterious. I didn't know what she looked like; there were never any interviews with her. She was just this *muse*."

Once they settled into the recording studio, however, Willner found Nica to be unpretentious and direct. He set Harris up at a tack piano— an instrument tricked out to produce a distinctively tinny, old-timey sound—that happened to be in the studio. "She loved the tack piano because it was a Monk thing," Willner observed. Then he took his seat beside her as Harris reeled off a couple of takes. "She was just so cool and confident," he recalls. "We sat up front. She needed to hear the song—it was about her!" After checking that Barry and the Baroness were both pleased with what they heard, he ushered them out to her car and watched as it smoothly glided away. "It was just a storybook way to end the album," Willner says of the experience.

Among the hundreds of other anonymous musicians and fans who had crammed into St. Peter's Church for Thelonious's memorial was a young Harvard-educated pianist and longtime Monk devotee named Robert Kraft. For years, Kraft had been sending birthday cards and Christmas greetings to Thelonious care of the Baroness's Weehawken address, and following the service, he was moved to create his own musical tribute. As he walked through Central Park, Kraft began shaping a melody in celebration of Monk's imperishable spirit. A year later, the completed song, "The Night That Monk Returned to Heaven," appeared on a best-selling album by the jazz-pop vocal ensemble Manhattan Transfer.

Kraft would soon move to L.A., but he was still in New York, a few weeks after Monk's funeral, when a letter showed up at his apartment with a Weehawken return address. "I received a letter out of the blue, from the Baroness," he recalls, "saying, 'Dear Robert Kraft, I wanted to let you know that while cleaning out Thelonious's room, behind his headboard, I found your cards and letters.'"

Nica's thoughtful note might have served as the basis for an entertaining anecdote, but it turned out to be the prelude to a warm (if largely epistolary) friendship that lasted until her death. Kraft would write to her about his latest album, or his marriage, or the birth of his sons, and as he describes it, Nica "responded as a kind of doting grandmother." For example, after sending a letter with the exciting news that he had just completed his first feature film score (for the Francis Ford Coppola–produced movie *Seven Minutes in Heaven*), she responded with her congratulations ("You certainly ARE into the Big Time!!!"), and assured him, "I and my 51 cats are in fine form." Today, her colorful letters, written on a variety of personalized "Cathouse" stationery, hang in the hallway of his Los Angeles home.

Kraft continued to compose, earning an Academy Award nomination for his song "Beautiful Maria of My Soul" for the 1992 film *Mambo Kings*, and to contribute music for dozens of other movies and TV shows. Gradually, however, he made the transition from the recording studio to the executive suite, and in 1998 he was appointed president of Fox Music Inc. But he never stopped thinking about Nica. So when asked about her role in America's jazz culture, he immediately launched into a brief history of European patronage that linked the Jazz Baroness and the legendary sponsors of the Florentine Renaissance. "Here a hand reached down from the clouds to say, 'Come up to the penthouse with me . . . I'll treat you like a king, like the court of the Medici,'" he intoned somewhat grandly, yet with absolute sincerity. "There's something really magical, and maybe fabulously traditional, about a rich patroness, a traditional role from another era, that was hard to fit into a forties mentality."

Yet in assuming this perhaps anachronistic role, he suggested, Nica was being neither self-aggrandizing nor entirely selfless. "She made an unbelievable connection to the music," Kraft asserted. "It inspired her. She had, under the thin disguise of a cynical, jaded, sophisticated Eurotrash baroness, a great charitable spirit, an understanding artistic spirit that connected to the music and the artists and just said, 'This makes my life worthwhile.'"

. . .

THE ROYAL ROOST ... Café Bohemia ... Jimmy Ryan's ... Bird-land ... the Hickory House ... Minton's Playhouse ... Bop City ... the Paradise Club ... the Three Deuces ... Basin Street East ... the Famous Door ... the Half Note ... Kelly's Stable ... Café Continental ... the Open Door ... the Jazz Gallery ... the Five Spot—and those are just a few of the jazz clubs that were flourishing in every corner of New York City during the early years of Nica's residence there. Over the intervening decades, however, they had all been shuttered, surviving only in the nostalgic reminiscences of an increasingly small circle of aging musicians and fans. By the early 1980s, even the handful of rough-and-tumble outposts for live jazz that had taken root on New York's as yet ungentrified margins during the dark days of disco and corporate arena rock had already come and gone—some with a whimper, like the roster of artist-run "loft jazz" venues, and some with a bang, like the notorious East Village hard-bop-centric club Slug's, shut down in 1972 after the trumpeter Lee Morgan was shot to death onstage by his common-law wife.

Monk's death marked the end of an era, not only in jazz history but in Nica's life as well. After a decade of selfless devotion to a reclusive genius, the Baroness gradually resumed her regular forays into the city, where she found sustenance in the music and companionship of jazz-world comrades old and new. Though the options for live music were now considerably reduced, jazz hadn't entirely disappeared from the New York scene. Along with the venerable Village Vanguard and the reliable piano bar Bradley's, one of Nica's favorite nightspots during this period was an Upper West Side cafeteria that had been a favorite hangout for Jack Kerouac and Allen Ginsberg when they were still Columbia University undergrads.

Located at Broadway and 113th Street, the West End Café had begun featuring jazz in the mid-seventies, when the disk jockey, jazz raconteur, and Charlie Parker scholar Phil Schaap began organizing live performances at the well-worn venue. A few years later, when he was asked to describe the club's music policy, Schaap explained succinctly, "We present the 52nd Street sound." It was more than a little ironic, therefore, that thirty years after her arrival in the Big Apple, Nica was able to find refuge among the swing-era survivors and aging bebop pioneers she had befriended shortly after arriving in the city.

Nica became a West End regular, dropping by on as many as one hundred occasions, often with one of her daughters in tow, to listen to the music of (and reminisce with) veteran Basieites and Ellington alums like Jo Jones, Russell Procope, and Big Nick Nicholas, as well as first-generation beboppers like Lee Konitz, Allen Eager, and Dizzy Gillespie. "She was genuinely liked by all those great musicians," Schaap recalls. "She had a sense that led her to the greats, and [they] trusted her implicitly." And while she rigorously maintained what Schaap describes as her "creed of taste and connoisseurship," he also recalls how gracefully she would "disarm and put at ease" anyone who might be intimidated by her title or her legend.

The Baroness was also an occasional visitor to the studios of WKCR, the Columbia University radio station where Schaap hosted *Birdflight*, a long-running, five-morning-a-week program devoted exclusively to the music of Charlie Parker. Although she never yielded to Schaap's periodic entreaties to go on the air, she did readily engage, off-mic, in long, candid conversations about her exploits in the jazz world, and she was even willing, Schaap recalls, to "rehash the old Stanhope business" for the Bird-obsessed DJ. But as she did with other interlocutors, whenever he brought up Monk, Nica would abruptly end the conversation. Not that she resented his interest. "She knew I was pro Monk," Schaap explains, "and that made her pro me."

But of all the New York nightspots that struggled to keep the jazz flame alive during the Baroness's final years, the one that was closest to her heart was a dingy storefront on a bleak stretch of Eighth Avenue in midtown Manhattan called the Jazz Cultural Theater. An education and performance space that had opened its doors just a few months after Monk's death, the JCT was cofounded by Nica's close friend and longtime Cathouse tenant Barry Harris, along with the veteran bass player Larry Ridley and the jazz promoters Jim and Cornelia Harrison and Frank Fuentes. For five years, Nica made the scrappy neighborhood music school cabaret a home away from home and used her waning financial resources to keep it afloat.

Today the block where the Jazz Cultural Theater once stood marks the gentrified northern edge of Chelsea, but back in the early 1980s the theater's nearest neighbor was a seedy five-dollar-a-night SRO hotel, while on its shadowy sidewalks hookers and drug dealers plied their trade. Though the place may not have been much to look at—peeling paint plastered over with jazz posters and a motley assortment of mismatched chairs and tables—its prevailing spirit of community and inclusiveness made the place an oasis of creativity. And a banner bearing a defiant motto—"Jazz Is Alive and Well in New York City"—was hung above its entrance.

For Barry Harris, the Jazz Cultural Theater was all about "passing down the tradition," something he had been doing ever since his childhood in Detroit. "I think I've been a teacher all my life," Harris explained on the occasion of the JCT's first anniversary. "It started when I was a kid," he told a reporter for the *Times*. "Maybe I was a little bit ahead of the next cat, so I taught him something." After arriving in New York, where he quickly carved out a successful performing career, Harris had a hand in the musical education of a number of prominent jazz performers, including Yusef Lateef, Charles McPherson, and the Israeli guitarist Roni Ben-Hur.

Ben-Hur heard about the JCT from a bass player who had recently returned home after his own studies with Harris. So in 1985, when he landed at JFK Airport on his first visit to New York, he headed straight there. "Right away, Barry made you feel you were part of the family," Ben-Hur recalls. "He had a wonderful spirit you could sense as soon as you walked in." Before long Ben-Hur had become a fixture at the center and one of Harris's prize students. Naturally, he soon became acquainted with the Baroness. "She would come on weekends and hang out, with her long cigarette holder and that beautiful English accent." And while Ben-Hur soon became aware of the crucial financial support Nica provided for the enterprise, he also noted that "she never asked for any kind of recognition—there was no 'sponsored by' or anything."

On weekends, the Jazz Cultural Theater's teaching area was transformed into a cozy cabaret, and though Nica tried to blend discreetly into the nondescript audience of jazz students, out-of-work musicians, and members of the local Chelsea community, the aging Baroness (who turned seventy not long after the JCT opened its doors) radiated an aura of charisma. One young woman who encountered her during this period was Ariel Warner, a member of the New Wave pop group the Waitresses, whose infectious single, "I Know What Boys Like" had made them one of the one-hit wonders of the 1980s. Two decades later, Warner still recalled Nica's vitality, casual elegance, and powerful presence. "I used to hang around with Joel Forrester and Nica," Warner explained, "and even in her seventies, she had the sexiest walk you ever could witness on any human being. She glided down the street and *arrived*, rather than walked, into a room. She was beyond poise, and at the time, I wanted to be just like her."

ANOTHER YOUNG WOMAN whose life would be transformed by her encounter with the Baroness traveled all the way from London to meet her. Not long after she learned of Nica's existence, Hannah Rothschild, the twenty-two-year-old granddaughter of Nica's brother, Victor, made her first visit to New York, accompanied by her father, Jacob (a.k.a. Lord Rothschild). Hannah remembers how she "cold-called" the Cathouse, bursting with youthful enthusiasm: "Hi, I'm your great-niece." From the other end of the phone line came what Hannah describes as "a most un-great-aunt-like response—'Wild!' "—and an invitation to meet at 1:00 A.M. at a jazz joint in what she recalls as a "not a particularly salubrious area" on Manhattan's West Side. When Hannah expressed concern that she might have difficulty locating the obscure nightspot in the unfamiliar city, Nica told her, "Just look for the Bentley."

Sure enough, when she arrived at Eighth Avenue and 28th Street, Hannah glimpsed a silver Bentley convertible haphazardly parked in front of the Jazz Cultural Theater, just as Nica had described. She also couldn't help noticing the two shabby locals sitting in the car's red leather seats, drinking from a bottle wrapped in a brown paper bag. Inside the JCT, Hannah introduced herself to her long-lost great-aunt and mentioned the unsavory characters who had made themselves at home in the gleaming convertible. "Oh, that's good," Nica said, laughing hoarsely. "Now no one will steal it!"

Once they were seated at a table not far from where Barry Harris was playing the piano, the Baroness filled Hannah's cup from the teapot that stood at her elbow. Suddenly the young woman's polite expression of thanks was interrupted by a fit of coughing, as an unexpected jolt of whiskey hit the back of her throat. After another burst of laughter, Nica put her fingers to her lips. "Shush," she instructed. "Just listen to the music, Hannah, just listen." The evening soon drew to a close, and Hannah returned to her hotel. Although she would get to see her great-aunt only one more time before Nica's death, when Hannah returned to London, she began receiving warm letters from her, along with record albums geared toward furthering her jazz education.

Hannah completed her studies at Oxford, and after graduation she began working for the BBC on a series of documentaries about artists, writers, and filmmakers (including Picasso, Sergei Eisenstein, and R. B. Kitaj). Gradually, she also began researching the details of Nica's extraordinary life and videotaping interviews about her with reluctant family members (most notably Nica's sister Miriam), jazz critics (like Gary Giddins and Stanley Crouch), and the musicians with whom the Baroness had established close and enduring friendships. Although Nica's five children all refused to participate in her project, Hannah pushed on, and in 2009 she completed *The Jazz Baroness*, a documentary about her great-aunt's life, which played the international festival circuit and was broadcast on the BBC and HBO.

Hannah was not the only member of Nica's extended family to journey across the Atlantic—and across the generations—to make her acquaintance during her last years. Nadine de Koenigswarter was still in her teens when she flew in from Paris and headed to the Jazz Cultural Theater. Nadine's father, Louis de Koenigswarter (Jules's son from his first marriage), was three years old when Jules married Nica at New York's City Hall. Following their divorce, Louis moved to Paris to complete his education and begin a long career at the investment bank Lazard Frères. But he remained close to his younger stepsiblings, and over the years, as Jules's diplomatic postings took him to Peru and Indonesia, they would often stay with Louis for extended periods. In 1986, having grown up hearing their stories about the colorful Baroness, Nadine flew to New York to meet her in person.

Nadine's memories are a mosaic of now-familiar elements: the vintage Bentley, late-night visits to out-of-the-way jazz clubs, an ever-present cigarette holder, and an uncountable collection of cats. Although they shared only a few evenings together, Nica left a powerful impression on her young relative, and twenty years later, Nadine, an artist living in Paris, remembered the seventy-two-year-old Jazz Baroness as someone who "had a gift for life" and was "full of fantasy." She also witnessed first-hand the easy rapport Nica continued to maintain with the musicians they encountered on their nights out on the town. "As soon as the musicians heard her nonchalant, British-accented voice," Nadine recalled, "we in the audience felt a wave of joy and friendship sweep from the stage toward her. The musicians would call out to her, " 'Nica, my lady!' or 'There's the Baroness!' and go over to embrace her or kiss her hand."

When Nadine returned to Paris, Nica reclaimed her regular table at the Jazz Cultural Theater and settled back into the warm embrace of her surrogate family. Unfortunately, the cozy community arts center was about to become another victim of New York's waning jazz culture. Despite Barry Harris's heroic efforts, by 1987, skyrocketing rents in the rapidly gentrifying neighborhood, along with the JCT's "pay-what-you-can" fees and no-alcohol policy, made it impossible to keep the place afloat.

Nica lost yet another of her favorite jazz hangouts, but a couple of exciting new ventures were emerging to fill the void. On the West Coast, Clint Eastwood was finally completing preproduction on his feature film *Bird*, a Charlie Parker biopic that had long been a labor of love for the jazz-obsessed actor and director. On the East Coast, Bruce Ricker, a lawyer and neophyte filmmaker who had directed a well-received documentary about Kansas City's jazz heyday, *Last of the Blue Devils*, was already several years into the production of a documentary about Thelonious Monk. Soon the two films, which had been advancing on separate, if parallel, tracks, converged, and the Baroness became a linchpin in the evolution of both.

IN THE SUMMER of 1987, David Valdes, a producer working with Clint Eastwood, came across Ricker's colorful evocation of Kansas City's 1930s jazz scene while researching Bird's early years in that midwestern capital of sin and swing. After passing along his boss's kudos, Valdes set up a phone call between the two directors, and it was during their free-wheeling conversation that Eastwood—who had been seeking an interview with the Baroness about Bird's last days—learned about Ricker's latest project and the friendship he had established with Nica during its protracted development.

Five years had already slipped by since Ricker first encountered the filmmaker Christian Blackwood on the streets of New York and heard about an obscure Monk documentary he and his brother, Michael, had produced for German television in the late 1960s. Ricker's *Last of the Blue Devils* had just opened at a local art theater to strong reviews, so when the ambitious director (and ardent Monk fan) learned that fourteen hours of raw black-and-white footage of Monk was, as he put it later, "just sitting there like the Dead Sea Scrolls" in the Blackwoods' storeroom, Ricker knew what his next film would be. He made a deal with Christian and Michael for rights to the material and recruited the cinema verité veteran Charlotte Zwerin (who had previously worked with the Maysles brothers on their groundbreaking fly-on-the-wall films *Salesman* and *Gimme Shelter*) to direct. Almost immediately, however, the project became mired in delays over copyrights and capital. Realizing that his fortuitous connection to one of Hollywood's box-office powerhouses could unlock the funding he needed to complete his project, Ricker phoned Charlotte Zwerin with a wager: "I'll give you odds I can get Eastwood to put up the money for the Monk film." Zwerin just started laughing, but Ricker assembled a short presentation reel and sent it to Eastwood. Twenty-four hours later, he had a deal to complete the film.

A few months later, filming on Eastwood's *Bird* biopic had wrapped, but for various reasons the director had yet to meet the Baroness. Meanwhile, Ricker and Zwerin had assembled footage from their Monk documentary, and they were eager to share it with their Hollywood backer. So when Eastwood arrived in New York, following an appearance at the Cannes Film Festival, Ricker set up a screening of the documentary and planned a get-together with Nica. After receiving her official blessing for his project, Eastwood returned to California and thoughtfully sent Nica a headshot of the actress who was playing her in the film.

In a subsequent letter to a friend, Nica shared her impressions of both the director ("Clint Eastwood seems to be REMARKABLY cool") and of her cinematic alter ego ("He sent me a picture of the actress, & I thought she looked like a constipated horse!!!"). She attended the film's Museum of Modern Art premiere, but since the "Baroness Nica" (as she's referred to in the film) appears only briefly in the two-and-a-half-hour biopic—first, when she's introduced to Bird in a shadowy 52nd Street jazz club, and later as part of a dramatic re-creation of his death in a Hollywood version of her Stanhope Hotel suite—there wasn't much to complain about.

Meanwhile, Ricker and Zwerin had run into their own difficulties with the Baroness. After canceling a series of appointments to do the interview she had promised, Nica suggested that they provide her with a tape recorder so she could pour out her spontaneous reflections in private. While they waited, Zwerin finished piecing together footage from the Blackwoods' film, rare archival clips of Monk at the Five Spot, and new performances of his tunes by Barry Harris and Tommy Flanagan. But after conducting a series of on-camera interviews with Harry Colomby, Charlie Rouse, and Toot (who talked candidly about his father's psychological issues), they were still waiting; weeks went by, but the spools on Nica's tape recorder remained blank. Then one day the Baroness called Zwerin to report that she'd had "a revelation," requesting that she come to the Cathouse the following evening with Bruce Ricker and a bottle of scotch.

When they arrived, Nica explained that the previous night, Thelonious had appeared to her in a dream. He told her that since she was no longer drinking herself, Ricker should do it for her, and thus, vicariously put at ease by the intoxicated ambiance, she would be freed to answer the filmmakers' questions about her three decades in the jazz life.

As the lights of New York City spread out across the night sky, Ricker turned on the tape recorder and began pouring himself shots of Johnnie Walker Red. Haltingly at first, then more spontaneously—as Ricker worked his way through the entire bottle—Nica provided a revealing and emotional account of her misadventures with Monk, along with anecdotes about her Rothschild relatives, marital conflicts, feuds, and scandals. Perhaps most startling, however, was the offhand revelation that the Baroness had written an autobiography. "Well, I started a book, ten years ago," she suddenly announced, "and it is really quite a gas, if you can imagine such a thing. There is only one bit about jazz in it . . . a lot of other things happened besides jazz."

Finally, as dawn broke over the Hudson, Ricker asked if she had any regrets. After a moment's hesitation, the only thing that came to mind was that she "didn't find the right doctor for Thelonious . . . that is my only regret." Later, however, Nica took back even this understandable (if unwarranted) expression of self-reproach. "It's a stupid thing for me to have said," she admitted, "for the simple reason that I don't believe the 'right doctor' exists. What I really meant was that I wish he could have got well, or not been ill . . . more than anything else."

Although Nica did see a rough cut of the documentary ("the Thelonious film will be BEAUTIFUL," she wrote to a friend, "because it's HIM!—taken in his lifetime"), she didn't live to view the finished film, titled *Thelonious Monk: Straight, No Chaser*—or to attend its U.S. premiere at the 1989 New York Film Festival. But she would surely have been pleased to read the reviews that confirmed her confident prediction.

The Legend Lives On

By the late 1980s, Nica's late-night excursions through the Lincoln Tunnel had become fewer and farther between. Periodically, however, Joel Forrester would get a call from her and they would head out to a concert by one of her old favorites. On one occasion, Nica invited Joel to join her at a recital Barry Harris had organized in a New York church.

Forrester found the program, which included a choir made up of Harris's vocal students, rather sentimental ("It was like those early attempts to make jazz a lady," he explains), but he noticed that the music seemed to provide a genuine spiritual experience for audience members in the pews around him. At this point, Forrester recalled, "Nica turned to me and asked, rather wickedly, 'Well, what do you think of this, Joel? Do you think it's good?'" Caught off-guard, he struggled to formulate a response that would express his conflicted feelings. "Well, in a way, Nica—" But before he could complete his thought, Nica cut him off: "Yes, and it is in that way that the music should be appreciated!" Her clever riposte suggested that the Baroness was unwilling to suspend her critical faculties even for one of her favorites ("She realized that this wasn't the real stuff," Forrester noted), but it also attested to her generosity of spirit and her willingness to accept all music on its own terms.

While her wit may have remained as acute as ever, Forrester gradually realized that Nica's hearing had begun to fail. Yet here again she found a way to put her infirmity in the service of her discriminating taste.

"In her old age," he explained, "she had one good ear and one bad. When she'd come to my gigs, there were some people in my bands that she liked and some she didn't. So she would turn her good ear to those she liked and her deaf ear to those she didn't."

Another of her physical impairments proved more problematic. Since meeting Joel Forrester in the late 1970s, Nica had also become a friend of his wife, Mary, a dancer and choreographer who often gave performances in the couple's large, if bare-boned, Bowery loft. Early in the couple's relationship, Joel had provided the musical accompaniment for most of his wife's dance pieces; by the time Nica came along, however, Mary had begun using classical music by twentieth-century masters like Stravinsky and Alban Berg. "Nica was not unlettered in classical music," Forrester pointed out. "She knew everything that Mary danced to, and she loved to come up to our loft and watch these concerts. But past a certain point," beginning in the mid-1980s, "she couldn't walk up the stairs."

Ironically, the Baroness's health took an abrupt turn for the worse just a few weeks after her cinematic surrogate had been shown tending to the ailing Charlie Parker in Clint Eastwood's new Bird biopic. When Nica entered the hospital to undergo triple bypass heart surgery, access to her room was limited to members of the immediate family. Joel Forrester managed to charm his way past the nurses, but Nica also took pleasure in pointing out that he hadn't been the only one who had made a special effort on her behalf, showing him an enormous vase of flowers courtesy of Eastwood.

Toot recalls that initially the doctors had deemed the operation a success, but a few days later, on November 30, 1988, two weeks shy of her seventy-fifth birthday, Nica suddenly died of heart failure at Columbia Presbyterian Medical Center. Later, her children recalled their mother telling them that the night before her surgery, she had sensed the powerful spectral presence of both Thelonious and her sister Liberty, who had recently passed away at Ashton Wold.

Over the next few days, newspapers in both the United States and England printed substantial obituaries of the Baroness, highlighting her

Rothschild heritage, her wartime service, and her legendary devotion to generations of jazz greats as well as the scandals that followed Bird's death and her arrest in Delaware a quarter century earlier. Barry Harris, who for almost three decades had been one of her closest friends, described Nica to *Newsday* as "a true lover of jazz" who had unfailingly supported the music and the people who made it. He also offered the tribute that would surely have meant the most to her. "Jazz," he announced, "lost one of its own. We will miss her."

A few of the obituaries noted that on the day the Baroness died, the saxophonist Charlie Rouse, Monk's bandmate for over a decade (and Nica's good friend for even longer), had also passed away, of lung cancer, at the age of sixty-four. In the next issue of *DownBeat*, Peter Keepnews honed in on this "eerie coincidence" to celebrate "the very distinctive contributions of these very distinctive individuals." While underscoring the huge disparities in the lives of Rouse and the Baroness, he observed that "the biggest lesson to be drawn from both" is that "a lot gets left out if you apply the great man theory of history to jazz." In the career of Monk's loyal sideman, for example, Keepnews saw "eloquent proof that not every musician who makes a major contribution to jazz is a bandleader"; while Nica's story "offered equally eloquent proof that not every person who makes a major contribution to jazz is a musician."

On December 11, a memorial service for the Baroness was held at St. Peter's Church. As he had done for Thelonious six years earlier in the same venue, Barry Harris organized a musical tribute to Nica featuring some of her earliest jazz cohorts, a chorus of his young vocal students, and a troupe of tap dancers. The spare, modern sanctuary was once again filled with hundreds of musicians, jazz-world insiders, and assorted Nicaphiles, along with the Baroness's five children. Naturally the mourners also included members of Thelonious's extended family, led by Nellie and Toot, who offered a moving eulogy to the woman he had known virtually his whole life.

Although Clint Eastwood wasn't able to attend the service, Bruce Ricker read a short statement from the Hollywood megastar expressing his affection and esteem. "I only knew Nica a relatively short time," it began, "but I found her to be a remarkable woman. And as a patron of that art—jazz—the Baroness will always be remembered as one whose life was inseparably joined with this music and the greats who performed it." After acknowledging the assistance Nica had provided for his recent film about Charlie Parker, Eastwood professed his gratitude for the brief time he had spent with her. "She was a truly grand lady."

Months earlier, Bruce Ricker had asked the Baroness to imagine how her life would have been different if she had never met Thelonious Monk. "I can tell you, I would have decided to take up residence in this country, in New York or in the immediate neighborhood anyway," she declared, "because I wanted to be where the jazz was." In a final tribute to the Monk melody that enticed her to settle in the city the pianist had called home, Nica instructed her children to scatter her ashes in the Hudson River "around midnight."

Although jazz may no longer be at the center of New York's cultural life, as it was when Nica began her reign as the Jazz Baroness a half-century ago, the city remains the center of the jazz world, and decades after Nica's death, aspiring musicians from around the globe still make the pilgrimage to be "where the jazz is" and to play the music they love on the ever-shrinking margins of the cultural landscape.

AS WITH OTHER FIGURES from the music's golden age who ascended to that great celestial jam session, Nica's death assured her permanent place in jazz mythology. Ironically, the earliest sign of her induction into this musical pantheon was her belated return to the elegant Fifth Avenue hotel from which she had been evicted not long after her arrival in New York.

Four decades had passed since the tabloid scandal over Bird's death had forced Nica out of her Stanhope suite, but a few years after her death, the Baroness was symbolically welcomed back when André Balazs took over the hotel's first-floor restaurant and christened it "Nica's at the Stanhope," in honor of the once-notorious former resident. Although the venue would eventually go through a couple of other incarnations before disappearing completely when the building was transformed into a luxury condominium, for a growing coterie of Nicaphiles, the short-lived homecoming represented both a posthumous vindication of the Baroness and a confirmation of her legendary status.

In the late 1990s, Thomas DeFrantz, a dancer, choreographer, and associate professor in MIT's Department of Music and Theater, debuted a new experimental work, *Monk's Mood: A Performance Meditation on the Life and Music of Thelonious Monk*. DeFrantz has described the piece, which included puppetry, high-tech video, and his own innovative synthesis of tap and modern dance vocabulary, as "an emotional narrative taking place in his [Monk's] head." But in addition to exploring the composer's creative life, the work also set out to explore the pianist's relationship with his wife, Nellie, and the Baroness.

While DeFrantz used the term "seduction" to characterize the nature of Nica's role in Monk's life, he explained that rather than embodying the temptation of sexuality, the Baroness represented "the enticement of another way to be," suggesting that such affirmation from a representative of the Old World cultural elite "may have been especially enticing to Monk." He believes that for Nica, the jazz life provided "a way for her to do her own thing, and ultimately be an artist herself," and that by committing herself unreservedly to Monk, Parker, and the other black jazz musicians she befriended—"because she was willing to take things to the end," as DeFrantz puts it, "Nica was able to gain entrée to their world."

By gaining membership in the insular and hermetic jazz fraternity, Nica achieved the ultimate fantasy of every true jazz fan. Perhaps this is the primary reason that almost a quarter of a century after her death, the Baroness remains a symbol for the music's true believers, not just in America but around the world. Currently, for example, nightclubs named "Pannonica" keep her name alive in France, Japan, and the Netherlands; the compositions that bear her name remain staples of the jazz repertoire; and she continues to be the subject of fervid speculation on jazz blogs and other on-line venues.

For succeeding generations of jazz musicians, Nica remains a venerated figure—a link not only to a golden age in the music's history but to a time when the phrase "jazz community" could be invoked without a trace of irony. It's not all that surprising, therefore, that exactly two decades after her death, when the critically acclaimed forty-year-old pianist Andy Milne completed his latest CD—a high-tech surround-sound, multitracked, electronically enhanced collection of duo piano works with his French contemporary, Benoît Delbecq—Milne's thoughts turned to the Baroness.

Having developed and recorded their costly and complex project with funding from the Canadian Council for the Arts, Chamber Music America, and the Banff Centre, Milne and Delbecq found themselves reflecting on the crucial role foundations, arts organizations, and other public institutions have come to play in the marginalized jazz scene. As the pianists waxed nostalgic about the days when the music still maintained a foothold in the popular culture and patronage was more personal, Milne posed the rueful question that would become the title of their 2009 CD: *Where Is Pannonica?*

EARLY IN THE NEW MILLENNIUM, when he learned that the Baroness had established a long-running jazz salon in a modernist house on the Jersey Palisades, Jim Walrod, a New Jersey native who doesn't just wear his love for his home state on his sleeve but has a four-inch outline of it tattooed on his left shoulder, became a man on a mission. It took a while for him to put the pieces together (a passing reference in Josef von Sternberg's memoir, along with some brief shots of the house in *Thelonious Monk: Straight, No Chaser*), but eventually Walrod made the crucial turn onto Weehawken's Kingswood Road, and there it was. Although the structure showed signs of serious deterioration, as soon as he saw it Walrod knew he was standing in front of a Bauhaus masterpiece and "one of the best pieces of architecture on the East Coast."

Lean, soft-spoken, and refreshingly unpretentious, the forty-something Walrod has acquired an enviable reputation in the world of cutting-edge tastemakers. Having developed an obsession with all things modern while still a teenager, he quickly amassed a collection of classic works of midcentury design. In the early 1980s, he opened his first vintage furniture store in lower Manhattan, and a decade later he moved to SoHo as co-owner (with Fred Schneider from the New Wave band the B-52s) of Form & Function, an upscale emporium of modernist gems.

Before long, Walrod went from tracking down rare items for wealthy collectors to designing high-profile restaurants and boutique hotels. And each step of the way, he also collected an eclectic assortment of business partners, friends, and clients, including the Beastie Boys' Mike D (who referred to Walrod as his "furniture pimp" in *Rolling Stone*). But it was another of his celebrity cohorts, the early hip-hop entrepreneur Fred Braithwaite (a.k.a. Fab 5 Freddy), who first turned him on to the music of Thelonious Monk, which spoke to Walrod's modernist soul, and told him the remarkable story of the Jazz Baroness.

One summer afternoon, when Walrod was making one of his periodic visits to the Baroness's house—taking note of such modernist elements as its extensive use of glass block, the cork tile flooring, and the wall of floor-to-ceiling windows—he was spotted by a woman sitting inside. It turned out to be Nica's daughter Berit, who, along with her siblings, had inherited the house. Although she expressed little interest in the structure's architectural significance, Berit was taken with Walrod's irrepressible enthusiasm, and she offered to send him a copy of the original 1958 real estate ad for the property, which she remembered seeing among her mother's papers.

The ad not only offered confirmation of the building's von Sternberg provenance, but it also provided the name of its architect, Ralph Pomerance, an important figure in the history of midcentury American modernism. Since Pomerance (best known for his collaboration with Sven Markelius on the celebrated Swedish Pavilion for the 1939 New York World's Fair) was a practitioner of the Bauhaus-based international style, with its flat roofs, open floor plans, and expansive plate-glass windows, the attribution made sense. But as Walrod studied the house on Kingswood Road, his discerning eye also picked out a number of what he described as "classic Neutra moves," which he believes von Sternberg picked up from the West Coast architect who had designed the director's visionary house in the San Fernando Valley back in the mid-1930s.

Aware of the Baroness's prescient embrace of the bebop-era avant-garde, Walrod is convinced that in Nica, the modernist structure on the Hudson had its ideal occupant. "There are a million houses in the state of New Jersey . . . six million . . . ten million—but there's *one* modern house. How did that history—of modern jazz—wind up in that one modern house? There had to be something about that house that appealed to her," Walrod proposed. "There had to be a modernist way of thinking at work—something aesthetically pleasing, besides the view!"

Walrod's recognition of the home's unique status—a combination of the von Sternberg provenance, great architecture, a legendary Rothschild baroness, and three decades of jazz history—makes the structure's present precarious state especially painful. "As a lineage the music is there, but that house isn't going to be. Imagine what it would be like," he analogizes, "to have every piece of Monk's music disappear." As he talks about the deterioration of the house—"It's almost a knockdown now," Walrod declares, with some hyperbole—his frustration builds. Though he expresses dismay at America's lack of appreciation for its cultural heritage, he also links the building's neglect to the ambivalence Nica's children still harbor about their mother. "If they can't buy into a celebration of what their mother did, how are you going to get past their blindness about what that house is?"

NICA'S FIVE CHILDREN are still scattered across the globe, but they remain firmly united in one respect: their refusal to cooperate with any project related to their mother's life. For example, after their cousin Hannah Rothschild began work on her documentary about the Baroness, the family immediately circled the wagons and sought to thwart her at every turn. Of course, Hannah knew firsthand of the Rothschilds' long history of obsessive secrecy; she was familiar with the family's unwritten code that one's name should appear in the newspaper only twice—when you're born and when you die—and she was aware that for generations, prominent members of the family had instructed that their personal papers be burned upon their death, a tradition that was adhered to by

Nica's father, her Uncle Walter, and her brother, Victor. Now, it seemed, Rothschild syndrome had been passed down to yet another generation.

With the door to the family archive closed and Nica's unpublished memoir securely locked away (along with her treasure trove of Cathouse tapes), Hannah's film briskly charted the major episodes in her great-aunt's event-filled life. In the process of debunking some of the enduring misconceptions about the Baroness, she discovered that even the story of Nica's exotic name had been obscured by the mists of legend.

"Her father gave her that name after a butterfly that he tried to catch," Monk had announced in the introduction to the original record-ing of his composition "Pannonica." But when Hannah visited the reposi-tory of Rothschild specimens housed at the Natural History Museum in London, she discovered that the tiny winged creature pinned to the display case "was not a butterfly at all—but a moth." Although Hannah expressed some chagrin at having exposed yet another romantic myth, the dusky moth Nica's father had captured the very year she was born seems a fitting symbol for the Pannonica who transformed herself into a shadowy creature of the night.

Nadine de Koenigswarter fared considerably better when she approached Nica's children with the idea of publishing their mother's scrapbook of Polaroid photos and the secret wishes of three hundred of the greatest musicians in jazz history. Nadine was given permission to take the manuscript to Paris, and in 2006 the book—which Nica had sought to publish decades earlier—was issued in France under the title *Les Musiciens de Jazz et Leurs Trois Voeux*. After it received the Academie du Jazz award for Book of the Year, the original prints of her photos were featured at Les Rencontre d'Arles, one of Europe's most prestigious pho-tography exhibitions. An American edition of the book, *Three Wishes: An Intimate Look at Jazz Greats*, was released two years later.

Like so many other performers whose lives the Baroness touched, the soprano saxophonist Steve Lacy (who was a little-known twenty-six-year-old sideman when Nica encouraged Monk to hire him in the late 1950s) continued to sing the praises of Monk and the Baroness until his death, in 2004. In an interview that appeared on a French jazz blog late in his life, Lacy defended Monk against the old canard about his lack of technique while lobbing an affectionate jibe at Nica: "He invented all sorts of techniques . . . He invented sounds that were like diamonds, pearls, emeralds and rubies. There was a brilliance in his sound that no one else could get. That's why Baroness Nica de Koenigswarter was so appreciative. She knew pianists, and jewelry."

Recently, musicians from Nica's innermost circle have also begun speaking publicly about their relationship with her. "I try not to do interviews about people I knew," Sonny Rollins declared in a *New York Times* article about the publication of the American edition of Nica's *Three Wishes*. "But I wanted to say something about the Baroness." Rollins went on to describe the courage Nica had shown in challenging the racism of the 1950s. "By being with the Baroness, we could go places and feel like real human beings," he recalled. "It certainly made us feel good. I loved the Baroness. She really wanted to help jazz musicians. I think she was a heroic woman."

While she remains virtually unknown to the wider public, the latest outpouring of reminiscences, documentaries, and publications has only enhanced the Baroness's eminence in the annals of jazz. But in their collective opposition to sharing their mother's story, Nica's five children remain as adamant as ever. In declining a recent request for an interview, Nica's youngest daughter explained that she and her siblings are merely honoring their mother's longstanding policy. "The reason that so few know about her contributions to jazz," Kari wrote from her home in Scotland, "is that she had a firm view about any publicity . . . She valued her privacy and that of her family." Yet their unwavering intractability seems to go beyond both Nica's personal predilections and the weighty demands of Rothschild tradition. Nica's children lost their mother once when she escaped the suffocating constraints of her marriage to embrace a new identity—and a surrogate family—in the jazz world. By asserting control over her legacy, they seem determined to stave off the prospect of losing her again.

However, Joel Forrester tells a story that calls into question the fundamental premise of Nica's veiled private life. He suggests that at some point, the Baroness's Garboesque persona had become a self-conscious strategy to cultivate the aura of a mystery that becomes a legend most. The pianist recalls how in a conversation with his wife, Mary, Nica confessed that rather than acquiesce to the increasingly avid entreaties of the media, she had come to prefer "all manner of things imagined about me."

Having known her better, and thought about her more deeply, than most, Forrester may also have come closest to answering the question that has always been at the heart of the story of the Jazz Baroness: what was it that really motivated her to abandon a world of wealth and privilege in order to immerse herself in the marginalized and precarious lives of a couple of generations of black jazz musicians?

"It's not a vexed question, I don't think," Forrester explained. "Simply put, she followed her heart." As he continued, Forrester spontaneously elevated Nica into the pantheon of jazz immortals with whom she had felt such a special connection. "True self-belief is rare. She would have heard it in Bird's tone, in Monk's generous translations of his temporal moods. These were her masters and her peers; how else honor them unless she could match them in self-belief? Could she expect to be reviled? To arouse hatred and suspicion? To appear absurd? Worse, to lose much otherwise dear to her? Oh, without doubt. But a Nica without her resolve would have long ago departed from memory; while the Nica who really was as weird as all that . . . lives on and will while *that beat* stirs human hearts."

SELECTED DISCOGRAPHY ——————————

Among the score of compositions dedicated to the Baroness, two have become jazz classics, with on-line music purveyors offering approximately 150 different versions of each. Others have also been recorded by an array of jazz artists. What follows, therefore, is a highly selective discography of "Nica tunes."

"PANNONICA" (THELONIOUS MONK)

Artist	Album
Thelonious Monk	*Brilliant Corners* (Riverside)
Chick Corea	*Now He Sings, Now He Sobs* (Solid State/Blue Note)
Joe Lovano	*Joyous Encounter* (Blue Note)
Peter Bernstein	*Monk* (Xanadu)
Steve Lacy	*5 × Monk × Lacy* (Silkheart)
Fred Hersch	*Thelonious* (Nonesuch)
McCoy Tyner	*4×4* (Milestone)
Tito Puente	*Salsa Meets Jazz* (Concord)
Johnny Griffin / Horace Parlan	*Close Your Eyes* (Minor)

"NICA'S DREAM" (HORACE SILVER)

Artist	Album
The Jazz Messengers	*The Jazz Messengers* (Columbia)
Horace Silver	*Retrospective* (Blue Note)
Stan Getz	*Cool Velvet* (Sony)
Blue Mitchell	*Blue Soul* (Riverside)
Phineas Newborn, Jr.	*Solo Piano* (Collectable Jazz Classics)
Kenny Burrell	*Introducing Kenny Burrell* (Blue Note)
Oscar Peterson	*Will to Swing* (Universal)
Wycliffe Gordon	*Boss Bones* (Criss Cross)

"LITTLE BUTTERFLY" (T. MONK, J. HENDRICKS)

Artist	Album
Carmen McRae	*Carmen Sings Monk* (Novus)
Esther Miller	*A Place in the Sunlight* (Tristan)
Kevin Mahogany	*Double Rainbow* (Enja)
Cheryl Bentyne	*Talk of the Town* (Telarc)
Whitney Marchelle	*Me, Marsalis & Monk* (Etoile)

OTHER NICA TUNES

Composition	Album
"Nica" (Sonny Clark)	*Sonny Clark Trio* (Century)
"Tonica" (Kenny Dorham)	*Jazz Contemporary* (Time)
"Thelonica" (Tommy Flanagan)	*Thelonica* (Enja)
"Blues for Nica" (Kenny Drew)	*Kenny Drew Trio* (Concord)
"Nica's Tempo" (Gigi Gryce)	*Nica's Tempo* (Savoy)
"Nica Steps Out" (Freddie Redd)	*San Francisco Suite* (OJC Records)
"Theme for Nica" (Eddie Thompson)	*Eddie Thompson Trio* (Tempo)
"Inca" (Barry Harris)	*Barry Harris Plays Barry Harris* (Xanadu)
"Nica's Day" (Wayne Horvitz)	*First Program in Standard Time* (NWR)
"Weehawken Mad Pad" (Art Blakey)	*Les Liaisons Dangereuses* (Universal)

The following compositions, dedicated to Nica, have either never been recorded or are no longer available:

"A Waltz for the Baroness" (Ray Draper)
"Here's Nica" (Matthew Gee)
"Pannonica's Nocturne" (Samir Safwat)
"Nica's Gift" (Joel Forrester)
"The Name is Nica" (Joel Forrester)
"My Nica, the Girl I Love" (Bliss Bowman)

ACKNOWLEDGMENTS ————————————

In its article about the death of Charlie Parker, the *New York Daily Mirror* startled readers with the news that the notorious "Bop King" had spent his final days in the hotel suite of a Rothschild heiress who identified herself as an "avid music lover and jazzophile." While Nica's quaint colloquialism may have fallen by the wayside over the intervening half-century, she has emerged as a patron saint for a couple of generations of "jazzophiles"; it is the reminiscences and recollections, insights and anecdotes of this hard-pressed, if resilient, community that have made this book possible.

I owe an enormous debt of gratitude to Professor Robin D. G. Kelley, author of the definitive biography of Thelonious Monk, whose authoritative analysis and heroic research are only matched by his unstinting generosity. Over the past two years Bruce Ricker, the documentary filmmaker and chronicler of America's musical heritage, has provided encouragement, wise counsel, and unreserved access to his private archives. The pianist and composer Joel Forrester, whose affection for the Baroness is undimmed by the decades, shared memories of his long friendship with Nica, along with his incisive observations about her role in the New York jazz scene. T. S. Monk spoke with candor and eloquence about Nica's lifelong devotion to his father, his family, and the entire jazz *mishbocho*.

As my project evolved, I received crucial support from the following: Professor Garth Alper, who published my 2006 article "Nica's Story: The Life and Legend of the Jazz Baroness" in the journal *Popular Music and Society*; Daphne Carr and Robert Christgau, who selected the article for inclusion in the 2007 edition of Da Capo's *Best Music Writing* series; my agent, Paul Bresnick, who recognized the potential for a book about Nica's amazing life and times, and who placed it into the hands of the consummate professionals at W. W. Norton; my editor, Tom Mayer, who shepherded the book from proposal to publication with a rare combination of rigor and sensitivity; copyeditor Liz Duvall, for her deft oversight of the manuscript; Assistant Editor Denise Scarfi, for her able assistance; and Eleen Cheung, whose book jacket captures the essence of the Jazz Baroness.

I also extend my deep appreciation to the following great musicians, jazz-world insiders, and Nicaphiles for sharing the stories of their own close encounters with the Baroness: David Amram, Harry Colomby, Robert Kraft, Jon Hendricks, Dan Morgenstern, Gale Monks, Phoebe Jacobs, Horace Silver, Phil Schaap, Frank Richardson, Barry Harris, Gary Giddins, Jackie Smith Bonneau, Elisa Bonneau, Ran Blake, Bob George, Hal Willner, Annie Ross, Paul Jeffrey, Hannah Rothschild, Buell Niedlinger, Jim Walrod, Maureen Stickler, Don Sickler, Dr. Michael Hittman, Don Schlitten, Charles Mingus III, Klara Polatai, Chris Albertson, Andy Milne, Nadine de Koenigswarter, Charles Turyn, Iggy Termini, Jean Bach, Freddie Redd, Larry Ridley, Roni Ben-Hur, Peter Duchin, Sarah Jane Freymann, Giacomo Gates, Fred Ho, Peter Sharrad, Hettie Jones, Steven Rea, Nica Stapel, Mary Barnet, Bob Lemkowitz, Toni Behm, Larry Finn, Annie Kuebler, Tad Hershorn, Mario Escalera, and Ariel Warner.

OVERTURE / Bird in the Baroness's Boudoir

3   "You know, Bird": Ross Russell, *Bird Lives! The High Life and Times of Charlie (Yardbird) Parker* (New York: Da Capo, 1996), p. 347.

4   "Bop King Dies in Heiress's Flat": Richard Kenny and Dan Mahoney, *New York Daily Mirror*, March 15, 1955, p. 3.

4   "Mr. Parker was ranked": "Charlie Parker, Jazz Musician Dies," *New York Times*, March 15, 1955, p. 17.

5   "We colyumed about": "Walter Winchell of New York," *New York Daily Mirror*, March 17, 1955, p. 10.

5   "fowl play": Robert Reisner, ed., *Bird: The Legend of Charlie Parker* (New York: Da Capo, 1975, reprint of Citadel edition, 1962), p. 132.

5   "Blinded and bedazzled": Ibid., p. 132.

6   "the most fabled figure": Nat Hentoff, "The Jazz Baroness," *Esquire*, October 1960, p. 98.

6   "He had Bird's name": Reisner, *Bird*, p. 132.

8   "I suppose you would call Nica": Hampton Hawes with Don Asher, *Rise Up Off Me: A Portrait of Hampton Hawes* (New York: Thunder's Mouth, 1972), p. 85.

8   "It was named": *Thelonious Monk, Straight, No Chaser: Original Motion Picture Soundtrack*, Columbia CK45358.

9   "Delicate things": Jon Hendricks/Thelonious Monk, "Little Butterfly" (Boobar, 1958).

CHAPTER ONE / A Weird Mishbocho

11   "Maybe I do come": Max Gordon, *Live at the Village Vanguard* (New York: Da Capo, 1980), p. 121.

12   "The royal family": Charlotte Zwerin and Bruce Ricker, *Thelonious Monk: Straight, No Chaser,* Warner Home Video 11896.

13   "That's my music": Frederic Morton. *The Rothschilds: Portrait of a Dynasty* (New York: Kodansha America, 1998), p. 67.

13   "The Medicis were never": Ibid., p. 153.

14   "Fate had, in fact": Miriam Rothschild, *Dear Lord Rothschild: Birds, Butterflies and History* (Glenside, Calif.: Balaban, 1983), p. 87.

18   "We had twenty-two camels": Kenneth Rose, *Elusive Rothschild: The Life of Victor, Third Baron* (London: Weidenfield & Nicolson, 2003), p. 24.

18   "Do you think": Rothschild, *Dear Lord Rothschild*, p. 96.

19   "the rich, heavy": Ibid., p. 95.

19   "the wedding of the Hon.": London *Times*, February 7, 1907, p. 7.

19   "There was not room": Rose, *Elusive Rothschild*, p. 23.

20   "I am so glad": Rothschild, *Dear Lord Rothschild*, p. 95.

20   "all boxed up together": Derek A. Wilson, *Rothschilds: A Story of Wealth and Power* (London: Andre Deutsch, 1986), p. 95.

21   "Your mother was": Rothschild, *Dear Lord Rothschild*, p. 247.

21   "She was altogether remarkable": Nat Hentoff, "The Jazz Baroness," *Esquire*, October 1960, p. 99.

22   "and make me a good little girl": Hannah Rothschild, *The Jazz Baroness* (New York: Storyville, 2009).

22   "were not classical": Hentoff, "The Jazz Baroness," p. 99.

23   "ferocious buggery": Rose, *Elusive Rothschild*, p. 30.

25   "If you should ask me": Gordon, *Live at the Village Vanguard*, p. 118.

25   "Afterward he'd play for me": Ibid.

25   "for another lesson": Hentoff, "The Jazz Baroness," p. 99.

25   "all wore wigs": Ibid.

27   "love at first sight": Robin D. G. Kelley, *Thelonious Monk: The Life and Times of an American Original* (New York: Free Press, 2009), p. 175.

28   "the Baron and Baroness": *New York Times*, October 16, 1935, p. 20.

29   "to be Lord Rothschild in name only," Rose, *Elusive Rothschild*, p. 6.

29   "mildly left-wing": Kenneth Rose, "Rothschild (Nathaniel Mayer) Victor, third Baron Rothschild (1910–1990)," rev., *Oxford Dictionary of National Biography* (Oxford University Press, 2004).

30   "state publicly": Rose, *Elusive Rothschild*, p. 280.

30   "I got a lot more fun": Wilson, *Rothschilds*, p. 425.

31   "Wordlessly, her sister Liberty": Kennedy Fraser, "Fritillaries and Hairy Violets," *The New Yorker*, October 19, 1987, p. 77.

32   "He left my mother a map": Jessica Zafra, "The Baroness of Jazz," *The National*, May 29, 2008.

32   "I'm not a crier": Nica interview for the film *Thelonious Monk: Straight, No Chaser*.

CHAPTER TWO / *Battlefield Dispatches:*
From the Front Lines and the Home Front

33   "But has the last word": London *Times*, June 19, 1940, p. 6.

34   "his hair had thinned": John Chilton, *Song of the Hawk: The Life and Record-ings of Coleman Hawkins* (Ann Arbor: University of Michigan Press, 1990), p. 156.

36   "He is as great a giant": Ibid., p. 375.

36   "a child who is accustomed": Robert F. Keeler, *Newsday: A Candid History of the Respectable Tabloid* (New York: Arbor House, 1990), p. 99.

37   "waiters and patrons": "Troubled Exiles," *Time*, March 10, 1941.

37   "stunned local society": Nancy Ellen Lawler, *Soldiers, Airmen, Spies and Whisperers: The Gold Coast in WWII* (Athens: Ohio University Press, 2002), p. 106.

38   "casually told his friends": Kenneth Rose, *Elusive Rothschild: The Life of Victor, Third Baron* (London: Weidenfeld & Nicolson), p. 64.

38   "Who else combined": Virginia Cowles, *The Rothschilds: A Family of Fortune* (London: Weidenfeld and Nicolson, 1979), p. 240.

39   "When one takes a fuse": Rose, *Elusive Rothschild*, p. 67.

39   "Quick to give": Ibid., p. 72.

39   "appallingly rude": Derek A. Wilson, *Rothschilds: A Story of Wealth and Power* (London: Andre Deutsch, 1986), p. 383.

39   "I spent two years": Naomi Gryn, "Dame Miriam Rothschild," *Jewish Quarterly*, Spring 2004, p. 54.

41   "Negro [band]leaders": Geoffrey Ward and Ken Burns, *Jazz: A History of America's Music* (New York: Knopf, 241), p. 281.

41   "As before, of course": Nathan A. Pearson, Jr., *Goin' to Kansas City* (Urbana: Illini Books, 1994), p. 193.

41   "Should I Sacrifice": *The Pittsburgh Courier During World War II: An Advocate for Freedom*, www.yurako.net/vv/courier.html (accessed April 16, 2009).

43   "Boy, I never did run": Pearson, *Goin' to Kansas City*, p. 192.

43   "much-publicized and long-term stint": Douglas Henry Daniels, *Lester Leaps In: The Life and Times of Lester "Pres" Young* (Boston: Beacon, 2003), p. 252.

44   "cool enough to hold": Al Young, "Lester Leaps In," in *Moment's Notice: Jazz in Poetry and Prose*, Art Lange and Nathaniel Mackey, eds. (Minneapolis: Coffee House, 1993), p. 254.

44   "violation of the 96th Article": Daniels, *Lester Leaps In*, p. 257.

44   "Young's refusal to lie": Ibid., p. 261.

45   "guards would get drunk": Ibid., p. 263.

45   "Liner Here Safely": *New York Times*, January 24, 1942, p. 3.

47 "we heard a knock": Frank Richardson, personal interview, April 28, 2008.

49 "For the first time": Nat Hentoff, "The Jazz Baroness," *Esquire*, October 1960, p. 101.

CHAPTER THREE / *New World Order:*
The Rise of Midcentury Modernism

52 "I would go to his pad": Nica interview for the film *Thelonious Monk: Straight, No Chaser*.

52 "a 'way back' figure": liner notes, *Black, Brown and Beige: A Duke Ellington Tone Parallel to the American Negro*, RCA Victor DC 39, 1944.

53 "I heard that": Frank Richardson, personal interview, April 28, 2008.

54 "the blues form": Geoffrey Ward and Ken Burns, *Jazz: A History of America's Music* (New York: Knopf, 254), p. 312.

54 "We felt like we were liberated people": Scott DeVeaux, *The Birth of Bebop: A Musical and Social History* (Berkeley: University of California Press, 1997), p. 167.

55 "opening at the Onyx Club": John Birks Gillespie, *To Be or Not to Bop* (Minneapolis: University of Minnesota Press, 2009), p. 202.

55 "I never got paid": DeVeaux, *The Birth of Bebop*, p. 219.

56 "Sometimes you couldn't": Nat Shapiro and Nat Hentoff, *Hear Me Talkin' to Ya: The Story of Jazz by the Men Who Made It* (New York: Dover, 1955), p. 291.

56 "On afternoons before a session": Ibid., p. 337.

56 "I'd been getting bored": Ibid., p. 354.

57 "I could play": Shapiro and Hentoff, *Hear Me Talkin' to Ya*, p. 354.

57 "We all stood there": Ibid., p. 305.

57 "the other half": Leonard Feather, "A Bird's-Ear View of Music," *Metronome*, August 1948, p. 14.

58 "all art constantly aspires": Walter Pater, *The Renaissance: Studies in Art and Poetry* (London: Macmillan, 1919), p. 135.

59 "real jazz": Dennis McNally, *Desolate Angel: Jack Kerouac, The Beat Generation, and America* (New York: Da Capo Press, 2003), p. 38.

60 "*blowing* (as per jazz musician)": Ann Charters, ed., *The Portable Jack Kerouac* (New York: Penguin, 1995), p. 484.

60 "Lester Young, actually": Mark Robinson, ed., *Ginsberg's Improvised Poetics* (Anonym, 1971).

61 "spontaneous bop prosody": Allen Ginsberg, *Howl and Other Poems* (San Francisco: City Lights, 1956), dedication (unpaged).

61   "the goof of life": Charters, *Portable Jack Kerouac*, p. 556.

61   "an intellectual": Ira Gitler, *Swing to Bop: An Oral History of the Transition in Jazz in the 1940s* (New York: Oxford University Press, 1985), p. 225.

61   "For some reason": Ibid.

62   "the most extensive experiment": Douglas Malcolm, " 'Jazz America': Jazz and African American Culture in Jack Kerouac's *On the Road*," *Contemporary Literature* 40, no. 1 (Spring 1999): 85.

62   "Technic is the result": Dennis McNally, *Desolate Angel*, p. 148.

62   "He would get into grooves": B. H. Friedman, *Jackson Pollack: Energy Made Visible* (New York: McGraw Hill, 1972), p. 88.

63   "culture of spontaneity": Daniel Belgrad, *The Culture of Spontaneity: Improvisation and the Arts in Postwar America* (Chicago and London: University of Chicago Press, 1998).

64   "What do we need": Lewis MacAdams, *Birth of the Cool: Beat, Bebop, and the American Avant-Garde* (New York: Free Press, 2001), p. 88.

64   "At a certain moment": Harold Rosenberg, "The American Action Painters," in *The Tradition of the New* (New York: Horizon, 1959), p. 25.

64   "the revelation contained in the act": Ibid., p. 26.

65   "I had never even heard": Nica interview for the film *Thelonious Monk: Straight, No Chaser*.

65   "My father was a very": Jessica Zafra, "The Baroness of Jazz," *The National*, May 29, 2008.

65   "the kind with drums": Nat Hentoff, "The Jazz Baroness," *Esquire*, October 1960, p. 102.

65   "Jazz didn't do my marriage": Max Gordon, *Live at the Village Vanguard* (New York: Da Capo, 1980), p. 117.

66   "There are only two": Frederic Morton, *The Rothschilds: Portrait of a Dynasty* (New York: Kodansha America, 1998), p. 57.

66   "It's everything that": Nat Hentoff, "The Jazz Baroness," *Esquire*, October 1960, p. 102.

CHAPTER FOUR / Nica's Dream: The Birth of the Jazz Baroness

69   "You could tell by her pearls": Jean Bach, personal interview, June 10, 2008.

69   "Nica had long black hair": Leslie Gourse, *Straight, No Chaser: The Life and Genius of Thelonious Monk* (New York: Schirmer, 1997), p. 128.

70   "I didn't particularly care": Phoebe Jacobs, personal interview, January 10, 2009.

71   "Monk is the guy": Marc Crawford, "The Long March of Thelonious Monk

(1917–1982), www. theloniousrecords.com/Profiles_interviews/Crawford1. htm (accessed March 3, 2004).

71   "I used to get it": John Chilton, *Song of the Hawk: The Life and Recordings of Coleman Hawkins* (Ann Arbor: University of Michigan Press, 1990), p. 217.

72   "He can't play, lady": Lorraine Gordon with Barry Singer, *Alive at the Village Vanguard* (Milwaukee, WI: Hal Leonard, 2006), p. 66.

72   "Every day I would plead": Nat Hentoff, *The Jazz Life* (New York: Da Capo, 1975), p. 198.

73   "In my city": *The Godfather*, Paramount Pictures, 1972.

73   "Black musicians were prime targets": Harry Shapiro, *Waiting for the Man: The Story of Drugs and Popular Music* (London: Helter Skelter, 1999), p. 67.

74   "Heroin was our badge": Ibid., p. 38.

74   "Don't forget": Jacobs, personal interview, January 7, 2009.

74   "I wouldn't say": Nat Hentoff, "The Jazz Baroness," *Esquire*, October 1960, p. 98.

75   "I'm sure as can be": Julio Cortázar, trans. Paul Blackburn, "The Pursuer," in *End of the Game and Other Stories* (New York: Pantheon, 1967), p. 217.

75   "I used to think": Hentoff, "The Jazz Baroness," p. 102.

75   "a number you could call": Hampton Hawes with Don Asher, *Raise Up Off Me: A Portrait of Hampton Hawes* (New York: Thunder's Mouth, 1972), p. 86.

76   "The only important truth": Ibid., p. 85.

76   "She had a huge record collection": Horace Silver, *Let's Get to the Nitty Gritty: The Autobiography of Horace Silver* (Berkeley: University of California Press, 2006), p. 83.

76   "We didn't dig": Hentoff, "The Jazz Baroness," p. 102.

76   "hang-out buddies": Freddie Redd, personal interview, April 14, 2009.

77   "She loved the music": Horace Silver, personal interview, January 29, 2004.

77   "the greatest traditions of old money": Andrew Alpern, *The New York Apartment Houses of Rosario Candela and James Carpenter* (New York: Acanthus, 2002), p. 23.

77   "A lot of paintings": Hawes, *Raise Up Off Me*, p. 85.

78   "She always drove": Jessica Zafra, "The Baroness of Jazz," *The National*, May 26, 2008.

78   "it was only when she settled": Jacobs interview.

79   "I saw it at its best": Teddy Wilson, *Teddy Wilson Talks Jazz* (New York: Cassell, 1996), p. 89.

79   "a last-minute addition": Robin D. G. Kelley, *Thelonious Monk: The Life and Times of an American Original* (New York: Free Press, 2009), p. 170.

79   "His chords were shockingly dissonant": Ibid., p. 172.

80   "played too modern": Nica interview for the film *Thelonious Monk: Straight, No Chaser*.

80   "They're not really listening": Kelley, *Thelonious Monk*, p. 173.

80   "attitude toward Monk," Ibid., p. 174.

80   "I went backstage afterwards": Nica interview for the film *Thelonious Monk: Straight, No Chaser*.

81   "the most significant relationship": Kelley, *Thelonious Monk*, p. 174.

81   "hit it off": Nica interview for the film *Thelonious Monk: Straight, No Chaser*.

81   "a low rumbling sound": Hawes, *Raise Up Off Me*, p. 103.

82   "I don't think": Kelley, *Thelonious Monk*, p. 26.

83   "She preached": Nat Hentoff, "Just Call Him Thelonious," *DownBeat*, July 25, 1956, p. 15.

83   "He was playing the same": Linda Dahl, *Morning Glory: A Biography of Mary Lou Williams* (Berkeley: University of California Press, 1999), p. 190.

84   "I always used to be": Nat Shapiro and Nat Hentoff, *Hear Me Talkin' to Ya: The Story of Jazz by the Men Who Made It* (New York: Dover, 1955), p. 341.

84   "Monk seemed more like the guy": Ibid., p. 342.

84   "I was about twelve": Kelley, *Thelonious Monk*, p. 34.

85   "Monk's room": Lorraine Gordon, *Alive at the Village Vanguard*, p. 63.

85   "Contrary to popular mythology": T. S. Monk, personal interview, March 5, 2004.

85   "this 'special person' ": Jackie Smith Bonneau, personal interview, April 9, 2008.

86   "Nica's story is so integral": T. S. Monk interview.

87   "I have known four": Nica Letter to Teo Macero, April 2, 1963, NYC Library for Performing Arts, Teo Macero Collection, Box 39, File 21.

87   "I needed an interpreter": Nica interview for the film *Thelonious Monk: Straight, No Chaser*.

87   "smudge of mad genius": Kenneth Rose, *Elusive Rothschild: The Life of Victor, Third Baron* (London: Weidenfeld & Nicolson, 2003), p. 51.

87   "Charlie Parker died": T. S. Monk interview.

88   "the rich white bitch killed him": Ibid.

88   "There are no plots": Nica's drawing, Rutgers Institute of Jazz Studies, Mary Lou Williams Collection, Box 4.

88   "I'm sick of this": Robert Reisner, ed., *Bird: The Legend of Charlie Parker* (New York: Da Capo, 1975; reprint of Citadel edition, 1962), p. 132.

89   "His thirst was incredible": Ibid., p. 133.

90   "One can imagine": Hentoff, "The Jazz Baroness," p. 101.

90   "We'd talk about everything": Reisner, *Bird*, p. 134.

92   "I thought that would help": Max Gordon, *Live at the Village Vanguard* (New York: Da Capo, 1980), p. 119.

92   "She wired us": Horace Silver, *Let's Get to the Nitty Gritty*, p. 87.

93   "I had lots of bread," Hentoff, "The Jazz Baroness," p. 101.

93   "My mother was comfortable": Zafra, "The Baroness of Jazz."

94   "I never heard": Colomby interview for the film *Thelonious Monk: Straight, No Chaser.*

95   "Do you want to be": liner notes, *Misterioso*, Riverside OJCCCD–206–2, 1958.

95   "I don't know how rich": Gourse, *Straight, No Chaser*, p. 106.

95   "I had no idea": Colomby interview for the film *Thelonious Monk: Straight, No Chaser.*

95   "There was this regality": Gourse, *Straight, No Chaser,* p. 105.

96   "I am convinced": Harry Colomby, personal interview, October 16, 2003.

96   "he thought it was cool": Colomby interview for the film *Thelonious Monk: Straight, No Chaser.*

97   "It's a prize-winning model!": Kelley, *Thelonious Monk*, p. 201.

97   "I think when Nica": Colomby interview for the film *Thelonious Monk: Straight, No Chaser.*

97   "She was drinking too much": Colomby, personal interview, June 10, 2003.

98   "The truth is, I use". Hentoff, "The Jazz Baroness," p. 100.

98   "spent the next year": Zafra, "The Baroness of Jazz"

98   "[Monk] would be up there": Nica interview for the film *Thelonious Monk: Straight, No Chaser.*

99   "wealthy East Side dowagers": Colomby, personal interview, October 16, 2003.

100   "not illegal": "Two Doctors Here Known to Users as Sources of Amphetamines," *New York Times*, March 25, 1973, p. 48.

100   "We'd hear people say": Steve Turner, *Hard Day's Write: The Stories Behind Every Beatles Song* (New York: HarperPerennial), p. 14.

101   "Sonny Rollins": Nica interview for the film *Thelonious Monk: Straight, No Chaser.*

101   "Her apartment was too full": Orrin Keepnews, e-mail to author, June 30, 2008.

101   "hearing this fantastic music": Nica interview for the film *Thelonious Monk: Straight, No Chaser.*

102   "Well, if you have nerve": Colomby, interview, June 10, 2003.

CHAPTER FIVE / Monk and the Baroness Each Find a Home

104   "the greatest inside look": T. S. Monk, personal interview, March 5, 2004. List of tapes from the "Pannonica Collection," accessed from thelonious records.com on September 19, 2006.

104   "He had to always bail me out": Nica interview for the film *Thelonious Monk: Straight, No Chaser.*

104   "utter fucking crap": Hannah Rothschild, personal interview, April 12, 2008.

104   "He may have spied": Nica interview for the film *Thelonious Monk: Straight, No Chaser.*

105   "If you ever": Hannah Rothschild, interview.

106   "He was just going crazy": Harry Colomby interview for the film *Thelonious Monk: Straight, No Chaser.*

107   "They started sending": Nica interview for the film *Thelonious Monk: Straight, No Chaser.*

107   "any room, place or space": Maxwell T. Cohen, *The Police Card Discord* (New Brunswick, NJ: Scarecrow Press, 1993), p. 17.

108   "It was thought that": Paul Chevigny, *Gigs: Jazz and the Cabaret Laws in New York City* (New York: Routledge, 2004), p. 58.

108   "responded in the only way": Cohen, *The Police Card Discord*, p. 55.

108   "My right to pursue": Brian Priestly, *Chasin' the Bird: The Life and Legacy of Charlie Parker* (New York: Oxford University Press, 2005), p. 93.

109   "it worked": Robin D. G. Kelley, *Thelonious Monk: The Life and Times of an American Original* (New York: Free Press, 2009), p. 225.

109   "She would have been an obstacle": Leslie Gourse, *Straight, No Chaser: The Life and Genius of Thelonious Monk* (New York: Schirmer, 1997), p. 132.

109   "I have no idea, really," Nica interview for the film *Thelonious Monk: Straight, No Chaser.*

110   "the artists were the ones": Iggy Termini, personal interview, March 15, 2008.

111   "In the beginning": Joe Termini interview with Phil Schaap, WKCR, October 10, 1989, author's collection.

112   "In a way": David Amram, *Vibrations: The Adventures and Musical Times of David Amram* (New York: Thunder's Mouth, 2001), p. 228.

112   "the cream of Washington's hip underground": "Interview: David Amram (Part 2)," www.jazzwax.com/2007/10david amram-p-1.html (accessed September 10, 2009).

112   "was able to get into the groove": Amram, *Vibrations*, p. 228.

112   "We would sit around": Ibid., p. 224.

113   "She was lovely": David Amram, personal interview, January 22, 2008.

113 "Sometimes, in fact": Hentoff, "The Jazz Baroness," *Esquire*, October 1960, p. 99.

114 "I swear that I am": Ibid.

114 "The love was so strong . . . to play music": Amram, interview.

115 "The struggle painters had": Dan Wakefield, *New York in the Fifties* (New York: St. Martin's/Griffin, 1992), p. 308.

115 "The painters taught me": Amram, *Vibrations*, p. 262.

116 "most of them were abstract": John S. Wilson, " 'Village' Becomes Focal Center for Modern Jazz," *New York Times*, October 27, 1960, p. 43.

116 "The painters not only made": Amram, *Vibrations*, p. 263.

117 "In a corner": "New York's Spreading Upper Bohemia," *Esquire*, July 1957, p. 50.

117 "I was looking": Colomby interview for the film *Thelonious Monk: Straight, No Chaser*.

117 "I'd heard of him": Termini interview with Schaap.

117 "Monk-idiomatic": Nat Hentoff, *Downbeat*, June 13, 1957, p. 29.

118 "I was exhilarated": Colomby interview for the film *Thelonious Monk: Straight, No Chaser*.

119 "calling through the window": Hampton Hawes with Don Asher, *Raise Up Off Me: A Portrait of Hampton Hawes* (New York: Thunder's Mouth, 1972), p. 87.

120 "The Five Spot was different": Wakefield, *New York in the Fifties*, p. 307.

120 "there'd never been": Nica interview for the film *Thelonious Monk: Straight, No Chaser*.

121 "I went from being": "Buell Neidlinger: From Taylor to Zappa to the Carpenters," http://www.allaboutjazz.com/php/article.php?id=910 (accessed November 21, 2010).

121 "With all these pawn-shop freaks": Buell Neidlinger, personal interview, February 1, 2008.

122 "Oh, Georges Braque": Charles Turyn, personal interview, January 23, 2008.

122 "Good evening, everybody": *Thelonious Monk: Live in New York, Vol.1*, Explore Records, EXPR 0030.

123 "We'd drop him off": T. S. Monk, interview.

123 "To me, she was a real patroness": Dan Morgenstern, personal interview, June 25, 2008.

124 "She understood what culture is": Jon Hendricks, personal interview, June 20, 2008.

125 "a big half-eaten sandwich": Bob Dylan, *Chronicles, Volume One* (New York: Simon & Schuster, 2004), p. 94.

125 "As a man": Nica de Koenigswarter, "A Remembrance of Monk," *The Daily Challenge*, December 22, 1986, p. 17.

126 "The place was incredibly small": Wakefield, *New York in the Fifties*, p. 310.

126 "American existentialist": Norman Mailer, "The White Negro: Superficial Reflections on the Hipster," in *Advertisements for Myself* (Cambridge, MA: Harvard University Press, 1992), pp. 337–58.

126 "in order to 'honk' ": Carl Rollyson, *The Lives of Norman Mailer* (New York: Paragon House, 1992), p. 110.

127 "Angelheaded hipsters": Allen Ginsberg, "Howl," in *Howl and Other Poems* (San Francisco: City Lights, 1956), p. 9.

127 "It makes sense": Barry Miles, *Ginsberg: A Biography* (New York: Simon & Schuster, 1989), p. 253.

127 "Thelonious Monk, 1960?": The Ginsberg Library, Item No. 0061.

128 "He loved it": Nica interview for the film *Thelonious Monk: Straight, No Chaser*.

129 "Another ivory tower": Josef von Sternberg, *Fun in a Chinese Laundry* (San Francisco: Mercury House, 1965), unpaged.

130 "Nica furnished her new home": Kelley, *Thelonious Monk*, p. 240.

131 "She had so many expenses": Jessica Zafra, "The Baroness of Jazz," *The National*, May 26, 2008.

CHAPTER SIX / Beyond the Five Spot:
Midcentury Modernism Goes Mainstream

134 "The moon": Stanley Dance, "Three Score: A Quiz for Jazz Musicians," *Metronome*, April 1961, p. 48.

134 "New York, man": Lewis Lapham, "Monk: High Priest of Jazz," *Saturday Evening Post*, April 11, 1964, p. 73.

134 "When he does get in trouble": Nat Hentoff, *The Jazz Life* (New York: Da Capo, 1975), p. 188.

134 "My biggest fear": Colomby interview for the film *Thelonious Monk: Straight, No Chaser*.

135 "When ten minutes passed": Max Gordon, *Live at the Village Vanguard* (New York: Da Capo, 1980), p. 120.

135 "found Monk staring at her": "Baroness, Jazz Pianist in Jam—with Cops," *New York Post*, October 16, 1959, p. 5.

135 "I guess we did look": Gordon, *Live at the Village Vanguard*, p. 120.

135 "Monk refused to get out": Superior Court of Delaware, New Castle County,

The STATE *of Delaware v. Nica* DE KOENIGSWARTER, *also known as Kathleen de Koenigswarter*, January 19, 1962, 177 A.2d 344 (Del. Super. 1962).

135   "One cop was beating": Gordon, *Live at the Village Vanguard*, p. 120.

136   "I feared they would": Marc Crawford, "The Long March of Thelonious Sphere Monk," *Time Capsule*, Summer/Fall 1983, p. 31.

136   "devotee of the 'cool' sound": "Baroness, Jazz Pianist in Jam—with Cops."

136   "enough for one stick": Gordon, *Live at the Village Vanguard*, p. 120.

136   "Everything kind of caved in": Colomby interview for the film *Thelonious Monk: Straight, No Chaser*.

137   "spiraling into a deep depression": Robin D. G. Kelley, *Thelonious Monk: The Life and Times of an American Original* (New York: Free Press, 2009), p. 254.

137   "taken to Long Island City Hospital": "Monk Collapses on Way to Court," *Amsterdam News*, October 25, 1958, p. 1.

137   "German Baroness": Irma Lawson, "Stormy Hearing for Pianist Monk," *Baltimore Afro-American*, November 1, 1958, p. 1.

138   "This column believes": Baker E. Morten, "Monk's Mysterious Arrest in Delaware," *Baltimore Afro-American*, October 25, 1958.

138   "Didn't one of those people": Hentoff, *The Jazz Life*, p. 189.

138   "Thelonious abhorred liars": Nica interview for the film *Thelonious Monk: Straight, No Chaser*.

138   "sentenced to three years": "Baroness Sentenced," *New York Times*, April 22, 1960.

139   "Well, I'm not going": Nica interview for the film *Thelonious Monk: Straight, No Chaser*.

139   "Today is the day": Nica journal entry, March 23, 1960, Rutgers Institute of Jazz Studies, Mary Lou Williams Collection, Box 4.

139   "without due process": Superior Court of Delaware, *Delaware v.* DE KOENIGSWARTER, January 19, 1962.

140   "Darling, I never dreamed": Gordon, *Live at the Village Vanguard*, p. 120.

140   "INTERESTED IN THELONIOUS MONK MUSIC": Kelley, *Thelonious Monk*, p. 247.

141   "a forty-pound monkey": David Meeker, *Jazz in the Movies* (New York: Da Capo, 1981).

142   "began shooting": Marshall Fine, *Accidental Genius: How John Cassavetes Invented American Independent Film* (New York: Hyperion, 2006), p. 95.

142   "The jazz musician": John Cassavetes and Raymond Carney, *Cassavetes on Cassavetes* (New York: Faber and Faber Inc., 2001), p. 79.

142   "No, man—can't do it!": Ibid., p. 81.

143   "a guy who worked": David Amram, *Vibrations: The Adventures and Musical Times of David Amram* (New York: Thunder's Mouth, 2001), p. 291.

144 "Everything will be improvised": Ibid., p. 311.

144 "The day we began filming": Ibid., p. 312.

144 "His words were like": Ibid., p. 75.

144 "I never sounded": David Amram, *Offbeat: Collaborating with Kerouac* (New York: Thunder's Mouth, 2002), p. 80.

145 "heart was still on the bandstand": "The Naked Truth," Episode One, *Johnny Staccato*, September 10, 1959.

145 "The Five Spot: Home of Thelonious Monk": Amiri Baraka, *The Autobiography of LeRoi Jones* (Chicago: Lawrence Hill, 1995), p. 235.

146 "it wouldn't be a problem": Larry Finn, personal interview, June 12, 2008.

146 "It was very close": Brad Gooch, *City Poet: The Life and Times of Frank O'Hara* (New York: Knopf, 1993), p. 328.

147 "The audience en masse": Paul Bley and David Lee, *Stopping Time: Paul Bley and the Transformation of Jazz* (Montreal: Vehicule, 1999), p. 63.

147 "Every night the club": A. B. Spellman, *Four Lives in the Bebop Business* (New York: Limelight Editions, 2004), p. 125.

147 "I think he's jiving": David Lee, *The Battle of the Five Spot: Ornette Coleman and the New York Jazz Field* (Toronto: Mercury Press, 2006), p. 66.

147 "followed Coleman": Ibid., p. 67.

148 "Coleman may be": Ibid., p. 63.

148 "the greatest thing": Jack Chambers, *Milestones II: The Music and Times of Miles Davis Since 1960* (Toronto: Toronto University Press, 1985), p. 19.

148 "Hell, I did that": Kelley, *Thelonious Monk*, p. 280.

148 "The Baroness was uneasy": Hentoff, *The Jazz Life*, p. 187.

149 "an aging child": Nat Hentoff, "The Jazz Baroness," *Esquire*, October 1960, p. 98.

149 "wildly slanderous": Pannonica de Koenigswarter, *Three Wishes: An Intimate Look at Jazz Greats* (New York: Abrams Image, 2008), p. 10.

149 "courage [she had] demonstrated": Hentoff, "The Jazz Baroness," p. 102.

149 "her first charges": Ibid.

150 "the drummer could have anything": Bruce Wright, *Black Justice in a White World* (New York: Barricade Books, 1996), p. 120.

150 "many rumors and gossip": Ibid., p. 120.

150 "Nica was Blakey's girlfriend": T. S. Monk, personal interview, March 5, 2004.

150 "I don't know anything about that": Jon Hendricks, personal interview, June 20, 2008.

151 "That *you* loved me": de Koenigswarter, *Three Wishes*, p. 57.

151 "sat around a few": Hentoff, "The Jazz Baroness," p. 102.

151 "She knew the music": Robin Kelley, personal interview, April 23, 2009.

151 "She was very nice": Chris Albertson, personal interview, May 26, 2008.

152 "She used to go": Nica interview for the film *Thelonious Monk: Straight, No Chaser*.

153 "It was great": Jackie Smith Bonneau, personal interview, June 10, 2009.

154 "Shorty with his grandson": Malcolm "Shorty" Jarvis with Paul D. Nichols, *The Other Malcolm—"Shorty" Jarvis: His Memoir* (London: McFarland, 1998), p. 136.

154 "After the baby": Bonneau, interview.

154 "My father and mother": Lord Rothschild, *Meditations of a Broomstick* (London: Collins, 1977), p. 13.

155 "She is fanatical": Nica interview for the film *Thelonious Monk: Straight, No Chaser*.

155 "It was as if": Kelley, *Thelonious Monk*, p. 291.

156 "Norman Mailer came in": Spellman, *Four Lives in the Bebop Business*, p. 11.

156 "become friendly": Hentoff, *The Jazz Life*, p. 245.

157 "Thelonious was a great admirer": Nica interview for the film *Thelonious Monk: Straight, No Chaser*.

158 "I'm really keen": Nica letter to Teo Macero, April 2, 1963, Lincoln Center for the Performing Arts, Teo Macero Collection, Box 39, File 21.

CHAPTER SEVEN / The Sixties:
The Best of Times, the Worst of Times

162 "America is deeply rooted": Sonny Rollins, liner notes, *The Freedom Suite*, Riverside Records, 258, 1958.

163 "My music is not": Frank London Brown, "More than Myth, Monk Has Emerged from the Shadows," *DownBeat*, October 30, 1958, p. 45.

163 "A lot of guys": Harry Colomby, personal interview, October 16, 2003.

163 "I remember sitting": Colomby interview for the film *Thelonious Monk: Straight, No Chaser*.

165 "mystical utterances": Barry Farrell, "The Loneliest Monk," *Time*, February 28, 1964, p. 86.

165 "mascot": Ibid, p. 88.

165 "Behind the façade": Theodore H. Pontifelt, "The American Way," *Liberator*, June 1964, p. 9.

166 "Baroness Nica de Rothschild": Charles McHarry, "On the Town," *New York Daily News*, December 13, 1963.

167 "There'd be a whole bunch": Robin D. G. Kelley, *Thelonious Monk: The Life and Times of an American Original* (New York: Free Press, 2009), p. 311.

169   "No, muthafucka": Jon Hendricks, personal interview, June 20, 2008.

170   "in French, with a charming": Francis Paudras, *Dance of the Infidels* (New York: Da Capo Press, 1998), p. 266.

171   "Hey Erroll": Ibid., p. 283.

172   "smoke-filled bar": Ibid., p. 1.

172   "Stop that, man!": Ibid., p. 2.

173   "Ornette suggested": Ibid., p. 320.

177   "tries to help": Nat Hentoff, "The Jazz Baroness," *Esquire*, October 1960, p. 98.

179   "tolerated rock and roll": Kelley, *Thelonious Monk*, p. 402.

179   "One afternoon": Paudras, *Dance of the Infidels*, p. 328.

180   "He had delusions": Kelley, *Thelonious Monk*, p. 383.

180   "Monk had more poems": Sascha Feinstein, "Epistrophies: Poems Celebrating Thelonious Monk and his Music," *African-American Review* 31, no.1 (Spring 1997).

181   "She really unloaded": Dan Morgenstern, personal interview, June 25, 2008.

182   "the story was picked up": John Chilton, *Song of the Hawk: The Life and Recordings of Coleman Hawkins* (Ann Arbor: University of Michigan Press, 1990), p. 374.

182   "a prime example": Dan Morgenstern, "Personally Speaking: Mr Hawkins and Mr. Gleason," *DownBeat*, 1967, p. 14.

183   "didn't sleep": Kelley, *Thelonious Monk*, p. 405.

184   "Coleman Hawkins was an epileptic": Max Gordon, *Live at the Village Vanguard* (New York: Da Capo, 1980), p. 121.

184   "benign leprechaun": Seymour Krim, "All That Jazz," *Village Voice*, January 28, 1981, p. 39.

184   "MAGNIFICENT": Nica letter to Seymour Krim, February 10, 1981, Collection of Unversity of Iowa Libraries.

184   "Bean (whom I never referred to as 'the Hawk')": Chilton, *Song of the Hawk*, p. 382.

185   "Often I was suspicious": Mary Lou Williams letter to Nica, December 26, 1965, Rutgers Institute of Jazz Studies, Mary Lou Williams Collection, Box 4.

185   "A lot of people": Morgenstern, interview.

186   "Not all members": Barry Singer, "The Baroness of Jazz," *New York Times*, October 19, 2008, p. 37.

187   "Happy, happy, *HAPPY*": Nica letter to Mary Lou Williams, January 2, 1968, Rutgers Institute of Jazz Studies, Mary Lou Williams Collection, Box 4.

187   "All the family was here": Nica letter to Mary Lou Williams, February 15, 1979, Rutgers Institute of Jazz Studies, Mary Lou Williams Collection, Box 4.

187 "You know, they have been playing": Nica interview for the film *Thelonious Monk: Straight, No Chaser.*

188 "One night he saw me": Kelley, *Thelonious Monk*, p. 403.

CHAPTER EIGHT / *Chez Nica: The Cathouse Years*

189 "I am really seriously ill": Nica interview for the film *Thelonious Monk: Straight, No Chaser.*

190 "No one knew": Robin D. G. Kelley, *Thelonious Monk: The Life and Times of an American Original* (New York: Free Press, 2009), p. 418.

190 "I have been in more nuthouses": Nica interview for the film *Thelonious Monk: Straight, No Chaser.*

191 "Nellie made preparations": Mario Escalera, personal interview, October 16, 2008.

192 "had Monk in the best hospital": Paul Jeffrey, personal interview, May 14, 2009.

192 "Monk had become": Kelley, *Thelonious Monk*, p. 439.

193 "living out in New Jersey": T. S. Monk interview for the film *Thelonious Monk: Straight, No Chaser.*

193 "He used to lie": Nica interview for the film *Thelonious Monk: Straight, No Chaser.*

193 "a fine tremor": Kelley, *Thelonious Monk*, p. 436.

193 "He was just very uncomfortable": T. S. Monk interview for the film *Thelonious Monk: Straight, No Chaser.*

193 "When he stopped playing": Nica interview for the film *Thelonious Monk: Straight, No Chaser.*

194 "I have a line": Nica letter to Mary Lou Williams, November 3, 1977, Rutgers Institute of Jazz Studies Collection, Mary Lou Williams Collection, Box 4.

194 "Where did you get the energy?": Nica interview for the film *Thelonious Monk: Straight, No Chaser.*

194 "When I see Nellie": Nica letter to Mary Lou Williams, February 15, 1979, Rutgers Institute of Jazz Studies, Mary Lou Williams Collection, Box 4.

194 "Things changed drastically": Jackie Smith Bonneau, personal interview, April 9, 2008.

195 "My mother loved him": Elisa Bonneau, personal interview, December 14, 2008.

196 "tug of war": Linda Dahl, *Morning Glory: A Biography of Mary Lou Williams* (Berkeley and Los Angeles: University of California Press, 1999), p. 335.

196   "Though it may make you angry": Nica letter to Mary Lou Williams, April
        18, 1977, Rutgers Institute of Jazz Studies, Mary Lou Williams Collection,
        Box 4.

197   "Since I had": Doug Ramsey, *Rifftides: An Artsjournal*, "The Bebop Bent-
        ley," www.artsjournal.com/rifftides/archives/2006/12/the_bebop_bentl.hmtl
        (accessed July 14, 2009).

198   "Barry was out on stage": Kelley, *Thelonious Monk*, p. 441.

198   "I got paid": Gourse, *Straight, No Chaser*, p. 287.

198   "It was like he wasn't here": Nica interview for the film *Thelonious Monk:
        Straight, No Chaser*.

198   "Monk was more or less": Paul Jeffrey, personal interview, May 14, 2009.

199   "Did you hear about": Nica letter to Mary Lou Williams, Rutgers Institute of
        Jazz Studies, Mary Lou Williams Collection, Box 4.

199   "the first major composer": Hentoff, *The Jazz Life* (New York: Da Capo,
        1975), p. 186.

199   "the greatest living": Kelley, *Thelonious Monk*, p. 442.

199   "I knew who she was": Joel Forrester, personal interview, November 8, 2009.

200   "In a sense": Gourse, *Straight, No Chaser*, p. 292.

200   "The things he couldn't tolerate": Joel Forrester, personal interview, March 7,
        2004.

201   "What we're talking about": Joel Forrester, personal interview, November 8,
        2009.

203   "I'm not a crier": Nica interview for the film *Thelonious Monk: Straight, No
        Chaser*.

203   "If there was anything": T. S. Monk interview for the film *Thelonious Monk:
        Straight, No Chaser*.

204   "I didn't cry": Nica interview for the film *Thelonious Monk: Straight, No Chaser*.

204   "I once came across": Marc Crawford, "The Long March of Thelonious
        Sphere Monk, *Time Capsule*, Summer/Fall 1983, p. 31.

204   "There is a race": Ibid., p. 31.

205   "Considering the prospects": Kelley, *Thelonious Monk*, p. 449.

206   "What happened": Charlie Rouse interview for the film *Thelonious Monk:
        Straight, No Chaser*.

208   "I knew about her legend": Hal Willner, personal interview, September 9,
        2009.

208   "I received a letter": Robert Kraft, personal interview, December 3, 2003.

209   "You certainly ARE": Nica letter to Robert Kraft, November 8, 1985, Collec-
        tion of Robert Kraft.

209   "Here a hand reached down": Robert Kraft, personal interview, December 3,
        2003.

210 "We present the 52nd Street sound": Gary Giddins, "The Beat Goes On: Hot Jazz Clubs," *New York*, March 10, 1980, p. 47.

211 "She was genuinely": Phil Schaap, personal interview, January 20, 2004.

212 "I think I've been a teacher": "Jazz Pianist a Teacher for Next Generation," *New York Times*, August 21, 1983, p. 56.

212 "Right away, Barry made": Roni Ben-Hur, personal interview, April 2, 2009.

213 "I used to hang around": Ariel Warner, e-mail to author, October 14, 2009.

213 "Hi, I'm your great-niece": Hannah Rothschild, personal interview, April 12, 2008.

214 "Shush": Hannah Rothschild, *The Jazz Baroness* (BBC Storyville and HBO), 2009.

215 "had a gift for life": Nadine de Koenigswarter, personal interview, November 5, 2009.

215 "As soon as the musicians": Nadine de Koenigswarter, introduction to *Three Wishes: An Intimate Look at Jazz Greats* (New York, Abrams Image, 2008), p. 14.

216 "just sitting there": Larry Loewinger, "Get Real: Charlotte Zwerin's Documentary Directions," *The Independent*, July 1990.

217 "Clint Eastwood seems to be": Nica letter to Victor Mitz, May 24, 1988, Rutgers Institute of Jazz Studies, Mary Lou Williams Collection, Box 4.

218 "Well, I started a book": Nica interview for the film *Thelonious Monk: Straight, No Chaser*.

218 "the Thelonious film": Nica letter to Victor Mitz, May 24, 1988.

CODA / The Legend Lives On

219 "It was like those early attempts": Joel Forrester, personal interview, November 8, 2009.

221 "a true lover": Obituaries, *Newsday*, December 2, 1988.

221 "eerie coincidence": Peter Keepnews, "Rouse & Nica," *DownBeat*, November 30, 1988, p. 54.

221 "I only knew Nica": Clint Eastwood eulogy, Pannonica de Koenigswarter Memorial, Saint Peter's Church, December 11, 1988. Courtesy Bruce Ricker.

222 "I can tell you": Nica interview for the film *Thelonious Monk: Straight, No Chaser*.

223 "an emotional narrative": Thomas DeFrantz, personal interview, September 18, 2003.

224   "one of the best pieces": Jim Walrod, personal interview, April 27, 2009.

227   "was not a butterfly": Rosie Boycott, "The Secret Life of the Jazz Baroness," London *Sunday Times*, April 11, 2009.

228   "He invented": *The Tireless*, http://blog.allumesdujazz.com (accessed March 12, 2010).

228   "I try not to do interviews": Barry Singer, "The Baroness of Jazz," *New York Times*, October 19, 2008, p. AR23.

228   "The reason that so few": Kari de Koenigswarter, letter to author, April 24, 2004.

229   "all manner of things": Joel Forrester, personal interview, November 3, 2003.

229   "It's not a vexed question": Joel Forrester, letter to author, November 6, 2003.

INDEX

ABOUT THE AUTHOR

DAVID KASTIN is the author of *I Hear America Singing: An Introduction to Popular Music*. His work has appeared in *DownBeat*, the *Village Voice*, and the Da Capo *Best Music Writing* series. From 1993 to 2003, he taught a course in American literature and popular music at Stuyvesant High School in New York City. He lives in Brooklyn.